'As a feat of scholarship, angling, and creative empathy, this book is an extraordinary achievement' Seán Lysaght, *Dublin Review of Books*

'What a marvellous book *The Catch* is: a time-slipping, genre-shifting exploration of lives and landscapes, in which poetry, memoir and biography swirl and braid most beautifully together. Obsessive, passionate and deep-pooled, Wormald's pursuit of Hughes becomes, over its course, unexpectedly and movingly personal: a journey inwards in spirit as well as backwards in time, moving against the flow. *The Catch* leaves both its writer and its reader – to borrow a phrase from the book itself – wonderfully "lost in water".' Robert Macfarlane

'An absolute gem ... Mark Wormald's love of angling and of Ted Hughes's poetry come together beautifully. I was delightfully lost by the river throughout' Paul Whitehouse

'I'm perhaps more fish than fisher, but like Ted Hughes's *River*, this book tugs at an atavistic, aquatic consciousness at the base of my brain. Wormald's quest has me swimming in the same brilliant flows, settled in the same rooty riverside nooks, vividly drowsy, deeply awake. I loved it' Amy-Jane Beer

'A torrent of a book, its swirling deeps and dark backwaters lit with hard-won insight' Luke Jennings

'Engaging and enlightening, a new and convincing key to Hughes's extraordinary poetic gifts' Richard Beard

'A brilliant book. Complex, kaleidoscopic, brilliant in its originality, *The Catch* is a love song to a lifelong obsession' Katharine Norbury

'A rare piece of work – modest, brilliant, moving. Quietly profound' Ian Sansom

'Mark Wormald takes what is, on the face of it, a meaningless act – the pursuit of exact, often remote places where a famed poet and fisherman has stood, floated, angled – and makes of it a parable of what angling and poetry share. The act of stalking, the stalking of fish by man, but also the stalking by man of his true self in poetry, the moment of the catch, at the instant of self-forgetfulness' Harry Clifton

'Here is a book and a writer and a sense of the world and of language which are all as marvellous as the subject deserves' Adam Nicolson

MARK WORMALD has been fishing since the age of four. He is an award-winning poet, winning the Newdigate Prize at Oxford in 1988 and an E. C. Gregory Award from the Society of Authors in 1995.

Mark has been a Fellow in English at Pembroke College, Cambridge, since 1992. His first office was once the bedsitting room in which Ted Hughes dreamed of a burned fox. Mark edited Charles Dickens's *The Pickwick Papers* for Penguin Classics and more recently co-edited two collections of essays: *Ted Hughes: From Cambridge to Collected* (2013) and *Ted Hughes, Nature and Culture* (2018).

The Catch

Fishing For Ted Hughes

MARK WORMALD

BLOOMSBURY PUBLISHING
LONDON · OXFORD · NEW YORK · NEW DELHI · SYDNEY

BLOOMSBURY PUBLISHING
Bloomsbury Publishing Plc
50 Bedford Square, London, WC1B 3DP, UK
29 Earlsfort Terrace, Dublin 2, Ireland

BLOOMSBURY, BLOOMSBURY PUBLISHING and the Diana logo are
trademarks of Bloomsbury Publishing Plc

First published in Great Britain 2022
This edition published 2023

Copyright © Mark Wormald, 2022

Mark Wormald has asserted his right under the Copyright, Designs and Patents Act,
1988, to be identified as Author of this work

[For legal purposes the Acknowledgements on p. 321
constitute an extension of this copyright page]

The Catch draws heavily on the work of Ted Hughes, published and unpublished. Of the
unpublished material, wide-ranging use has been made of Hughes's fishing diaries, which
are held in the British Library, Add MS 88918/122–5, as well as unpublished material
in the Manuscripts and Rare Books Library of Emory University and of letters held in
the Barrie Cooke Archive, Pembroke College, Cambridge. The author is grateful to the
Estate of Ted Hughes and to his publishers, Faber and Faber Ltd, for permission to use
material from published and unpublished works, and acknowledges the tremendous
debt due in the use of unpublished material – which, in the diaries, includes reference
to particular words and phrases and an imaginative vision that belongs uniquely to Ted
Hughes – in the text at hand.

Bloomsbury Publishing Plc does not have any control over, or responsibility for, any
third-party websites referred to or in this book. All internet addresses given in this
book were correct at the time of going to press. The author and publisher regret any
inconvenience caused if addresses have changed or sites have ceased to exist, but can
accept no responsibility for any such changes

A catalogue record for this book is available from the British Library

ISBN: HB: 978-1-5266-4424-4; PB: 978-1-5266-4421-3;
EBOOK: 978-1-5266-4423-7; EPDF: 978-1-5266-4420-6

2 4 6 8 10 9 7 5 3 1

Typeset by Newgen KnowledgeWorks Pvt. Ltd., Chennai, India
Printed and bound in Great Britain by CPI Group (UK) Ltd, Croydon CR0 4YY

MIX
Paper | Supporting
responsible forestry
FSC® C171272

To find out more about our authors and books visit www.bloomsbury.com
and sig up for our newsletters

Contents

For my family, and the fish

I

Contact

Sunday 29 May 1983. Very first thing.

He was up at 4.30, to be back at the Torridge by ten past five. He's parked on the grass verge beneath the Celtic cross just before the tarmac on the lane runs out, then ignored the path he tells friends to walk, up the short tunnel of trees to the field gate across the sky, then over the brow of the hill, down across the meadow to the crossing point. This morning he follows the bed of the unmade lane as it twists down to the river at the top of the beat. At the gate he's turned upstream, followed the field edge past the monument to the drowned fisherman. And then he's at Okement junction, the pool he strictly doesn't have the rights to fish, but who's to stop him now? He's shouldered through the overgrowth on the high bank – cow parsley, Himalayan balsam, dull green still in the grey before sunrise – then picked his way down to the water's edge. Now he stands on the gravel beach below the high bank that masks his bulk – he's a giant of a man but with a heron's eye – and is in place, where the Okement's clearer water, Dartmoor runoff, meets the stained Torridge as it turns north, a mile before the hills crowd in around it and its gorge begins.

The dull morning simmers: with birdsong and expectation. He has unfinished business.

Last evening he'd made the longer drive round, and approached from Meeth, on the west bank. Then he'd had a longer walk than this morning. From the farmyard he'd trudged up and over the high top of that bulging little hill that guards the river, then let himself down, once more, 'in the green Devon evening light, among the marvellous female curves of the coombes, into the cleave of the river'. It was his first visit back since the party to launch *West Country Fly Fishing* at the Arundell Arms the previous Saturday. He's got an essay in it, 'Taw and Torridge'; those lines are his. Paradise, he called it. Now he's more interested in what to do when he got in there. Recent rain had left the height and colour of the water in perfect shape. The sea-trout must have made it this far upriver by now; he'd had two on the Friday morning down on the tidal water at Beam, in the weir pool he'd been fishing for three years now. And later that day Peter Norton-Smith had caught two bigger fish, one a salmon, one they couldn't decide whether a sea-trout or salmon, five miles upriver at Little Warham.

He'd worked his way down to a pool he'd decided not to mention in the essay. He knows it too well, has too much invested in it. Sometimes he calls it Concrete, sometimes by the name it had thirty years ago, Island Run. And yesterday it was Concrete Ramp.

Now as last night he has his trusted team of lures. A big silver-bodied yellow-winged fly on a heavy hook – yellow's a colour that works on the Torridge – hanging a few inches off a short branch line or 'dropper' of nylon knotted onto the main leader, and adding weight to sink swiftly, reach the fish; and then a yard below, on the point of his nylon leader, a smaller black and silver body, the Stoat's Tail, named for the source of the black fibres that made its wing. This fly has a small deadly addition: a tiny trident under those fibres, a treble hook the smallest he can buy, a size 16. And it's a mixed blessing: twice this year already, since the season began in mid-March, it's got him into the best kind of trouble, when salmon attracted by the bigger lure turned away, took this smaller one instead. Twice he'd held them too hard; they'd straightened the fine forged steel, got away.

Last evening, as the current swum those flies round and he began to lift his rod for another cast, the line stuck for a moment, jolted, then came free – as though it had brushed a snag on the bottom. The depth of the water there, eighteen inches, made that unlikely. So it could have been a small trout. And then a couple of casts later he noticed something stuck on the point fly: inspection revealed that one of those tiny trebles had acquired a large solitary scale. Could it have been another of the pool's residents, a dace? They sometimes go for the Stoat's Tail. But he also knew better: a salmon or a big sea-trout had lunged at the big yellow fly, or just turned to inquire of it, then brushed against the tail fly.

That single scale is why he's back, now.

To give the river the benefit of the doubt. Not to stay long, just to cast over whatever came at him last night.

He begins. As he casts out into mid-river, where the clear water of the Okement meets the Torridge, a touch: a trout? But then a big fish, salmon or sea-trout, slash-crashes nearby in mid-river, whether to burn off the rest of the energy that made it go for the fly in the first place or just to have a look, as he's heard killer whales do. But he knows enough about the lens in a fish's eye and the relative refractive indices of water and air to make him doubt that. And remembers Irish wisdom: a jumping fish is a pricked fish.

He fishes on downriver. Clambering over the fence at the top of Sprackmann's Pit sends a duck wallowing her way down the hundred yards of the pool, all exaggerated broken-wing theatrics drawing the eye and danger from her brood of ducklings, who sprint upstream, a clot of toffee-coloured chitter. And then the bullocks get in on the act. They stand, knees to the wire that keeps them a yard away from the bank edge, stretching their noses at him. He tries rapping them with the tip of his rod, and a few half-hearted casts. It's the god that protects fish, he thinks.

But then a cormorant goes upriver: so the sea-trout *have* made it.

And finally – it must be six o'clock, and the sun hasn't yet cleared the hills to the east – he can do what he came for. Start in on Island Run, fish whatever it was that came at him last night, then head home early.

It's his seventh consecutive day fishing. Until last evening, they'd been full days: fishing by eight most mornings, and ten-hour, twelve-hour days. Four Devon rivers – Dart, Taw, Dart again, Exe, then Torridge, Torridge, Torridge. Not to mention the hours in the car there and back. Three hundred and thirty miles in the week.

Something – Peter Norton-Smith's example, maybe: those two salmon on Friday came to huge, long, glittering lures, more like the Alaskan bucktails he's thought of doctoring himself than the small Torridge patterns he's tended to trust, with an eye to the smaller sea-trout – makes him exchange his small point fly for a bigger version, heavier: a 1½-inch tube, its brass body designed to get it down. Maybe it's his sense of the lie of the water, the flow of the current, from this bank, a bank he's rarely fished it from – when the water permits, he's usually waded the river at the tail of Sprackmann's Pit, crossed to the west bank to fish on down. He sees how much better the pool fishes from here, the match of water and current. It lets you hang over the flow where it's deepest, over the line where he supposes the fish are lying.

And at once it pays off. A firm take: a trout of a pound, the biggest he's seen in years, since the ones Nicky caught as a teenager, on a jigged loach. This one connected as the fly comes over the line of stones the Ward brothers put in opposite the cut-away bay below the concrete ramp; they'd filled that bay, too, with wire, saplings, brush, against further erosion, loss of their flood-plain meadow. As he releases the trout – he no longer kills browns – it occurs to him that a bigger fish would be a handful.

And then, a few casts later, it happens.

A really deep and solid take in mid-river, about a foot down; everything stops dead. And he knows he is into something quite big. And everything in him revives.

It is, he will reflect that evening, the single most enthralling moment of all his Torridge fishing.

The fish doesn't bolt. And for the moment he holds him. He tries to guess the weight from the wrenching thuds, but knows it's a salmon, for all that he can't see him yet. And soon he's into the logistics of the problem that trout didn't force him to solve: how to keep the salmon from seeking the shelter and line-abrading underhang of the concrete ramp, the tangle of infill on the banks of the bay beyond, ten yards below the fish surging upstream now, then down. At first it's all about side-strain: lowering the rod, guiding the fish, a negotiation. A finger on the rim of the reel stops the salmon running as it would on the free check. He holds him a while. Him.

Then the fisherman does the dangerous thing, follows him down below that ramp, into that bay; thinks, from a tottering position on the bank, nearly sheer, that the single back eddy behind the ramp near the bank might be the water he can guide him into, land him if he can only keep his footing, before the salmon surges down into the pool below, and the Froth Pot on the bend below that. He's known fish go that far. He can see the yellow fly on the dropper, clear of the water. But no sign of the salmon yet.

But as he's concentrating on all this, and not losing his balance, everything comes away slack.

There's time, then, and later, for the aftermath. He appraised himself, sickened as usual. The worrying, now it was too late, of course: at the wrong choice of knot – why had he used a surgeon's? In future double blood must be the rule. At the wrong strength of line, at the carelessness and sheer lack of thought that cost him a fish, at the failure to check the nylon for dents, weaknesses, after a snag or a strain. Why hadn't he found a better response to the salmon's thought – if he had thought of that – of using the concrete ramp for refuge? Why hadn't he worked out before that, rather than holding him too hard – the third he'd held too hard, and lost, this season – he could have thrown him more line, trusted to the hook barb in the gristle of the jaw, kept in contact, while he took a step back, retreated upstream, waded across at the usual place, then played and landed him from the shallower, easier bank on the west of Island Run?

Meanwhile, he is thinking, feeling, about the fish: about how big he is down there. Felt like a smallish salmon.

After that he did wade across, forgot his thought of packing in early, fished on, for three hours. The river seemed empty. But the mayflies were up; he should have tried a nymph. Sea-trout would have taken one fished deep.

*

I come up for air, and the sounds of this winter afternoon: the murmur of issue desk inquiries, a pencil being sharpened. The occasional cough. Beyond that, the rumble of the city's thunder: buses, lorries, taxis on the Euston Road.

Then I look down. I'm shaking. I can't believe my luck.

It's January 2012.

The leather-bound Victorian ledger lies open on the desk. It's my first visit, and I'd started with something that I thought would give me my bearings. Two hours ago it had seemed like a false start: an odd third of a page: notes of trips to still waters, half-hearted fishing, in company. His partner, Roy, too amazed to strike when a trout rose to the woolly worm he was dragging over the surface. A broken rod, that must have got damaged on Nicky's trip to Ireland. Thick water. And fishing in company prevents him from the patient searching of it with a sunk line he could have done alone.

But then I'd turned the page and here seemed proof. What I'd come for. The fishing diary I'd heard of, and heard an authority I had no real reason to have doubted dismiss as a curiosity, nothing more, eighteen months before; the only one, in the library catalogue's description, that seemed obviously about the Devon rivers I knew he fished. And the first full page of closely written looped prose, in ink, following the faintly printed horizontal lines of the ledger, ignoring the bookkeeper's columns. Still, though, precise. He's dated it May 1983, and again, 28th May 1983. The Saturday night. 'Begin here', he's written.

So I began. Struggling with some of the names, marvelling at the richness of observations. Tight snakehead fists of ferns unfurled on the steep banks of the Dart beside the carcass of a sheep, her lamb still distraught beside her: she'd lost her footing, got stuck, couldn't roll back up the slope and dared not roll down: that dark clear water. Her fear killed her, then. Words unfurl too across the page from the hand that held the pen; they trail off, sometimes I'm not quite sure how. Was that burn-off of energy at the Okement junction close to the operatic, or to the operation? Either seemed perfect. I began taking notes. Not having a pencil, and noting the Reading Room's ban on ink, I opened my laptop at the moment when, eight pages in, he'd written his way back through the season to date to his starting point, the discovery of that big scale on the treble hook on the evening of the 28th.

And since then I haven't let up, looked nowhere but the pages of the book and my laptop screen. The pages of the ledger seemed to turn themselves. This is why I learned to touch-type as a teenager. That battle with the salmon has held me hard.

So when I do look down, rest my hands, turn them up, in wonder, see exactly where I've been taken, it must be minutes too late.

There's a darkness on the pad of my left index finger.

An inky fingerprint.

Gingerly I retrace my steps. He's holding his finger to the reel, to stop the salmon surging on the free check. And a matching smudge there across it, where – I see it now – I'd licked my finger, flipped the page.

I can't believe my guilt.

And then through the recrimination I think: the last time that ink was wet was when it flowed from his nib, at his desk, in his writing shed, in the garden just above the Taw, on the day this happened.

And I have unfinished business of my own.

2

River

Two teeming months pass. I teach, and term leaves time only for a couple more dashes to the station, the hour's train journey south, and delicious silent afternoons in the Reading Room. (My reader's ticket still gets me in: I've not confessed to that crime, if that's what it is.) But those are enough to whet the appetite, and the hook that's already buried in me. I browse, discover so much more: not just in that leather-bound ledger, but in paper-clipped sheaves of small pages torn from reporter's notepads, in school exercise books. Some are in verse. Some have sketches, detailed illustrations. They're in some kind of order, but it's not obvious. And they're from all over the place. Iceland. Scotland. Only that ledger is devoted to Devon. I discover whole seventy-page accounts from Alaska, many more shorter tales of trips to Ireland. I reckon there are a thousand pages in total, and they span the last twenty-one years of his life. Sometimes the paper's blotchy – rain, I guess, not tears. But there are other smudges, and sometimes to the point, unlike that one single smudge I've left over the reel rim, where you can't quite be sure what he was saying.

Or: writing.

These same months I've been fishing in print, too. Selections of his letters have been published, and I discover, in one he wrote to a friend in June 1980, just before the first of his Alaskan trips, and then in an interview he gave to a Canadian fishing magazine more than a decade after that morning by the Torridge, but published, like that letter, only after his death in October 1998, two versions of the same wondering truth. When he'd been fishing alone, as he had been that morning, he lost the power of forming words completely, sometimes for hours. Concentrated silence by the river left him physically unable to speak at all. He knew this was unusual – he'd heard or read nothing about this phenomenon anywhere else, he told that friend. But it intrigued him; in Iceland, he said, he'd even tried alternating, between that wordlessness and the most immediate record of it he could find.

So: the fishing diaries were where the words came back.

And both the wordlessness and their return mattered more, and was a matter of much more substantial mystery, than for most of us who fish, whether or not we have noticed the same thing in ourselves. (I've never met anyone who has.) We might justify an afternoon or evening by the river as a hobby, a break, from our lives: from family, work, stress. The fishermen I've come to call my friends since that afternoon in the British Library know it's much more than that. But even if it is more – a plunge back into our childhood, or into the hunter in us, a way of staring at and into the water in the hope of seeing things our day jobs have no time for; even a religion: 'Let's go church', one West Country sea-trout specialist used to tell his friend on Sunday mornings, meaning the river. He told me this as we sat beside the Taw, where he'd just shown me lampreys at their writhing work in a shallow run above Umberleigh – even if the break has been an act of worship in disguise, even if we keep fishing diaries of our own, and look at them from time to time, to remind ourselves of the odd great moment, or to arm ourselves with inspiration or the excuse to buy that new bit of kit in advance of the next trip, the moment of re-entry can be managed in the meantime. We slip more or less easily back into our usual routines, our work clothes, meetings, desks. Who cares if we mumble a bit that first morning back? Plead indulgence. Blame any lingering incoherence on the long drive home the night before.

But for this fisherman, the stakes were higher. Words were at least his living, even his life, and if they didn't come to him as he sat at the desk where he wrote, in a raised wooden hut in his big garden he climbed three steps to reach, he could hardly blame the commute. This stretch of the Torridge was only twenty minutes away, and her sister river the Taw flowed no more than five minutes' walk below the house. Or perhaps that was the problem. He knew the seductive dangers of this position: never write anywhere near fishing, he'd tell a (non-fishing) writer.

But he never left that house in the village above the river, and the words did come. And those he dealt in weren't just those of the fishing hack. He was a poet, too, a poet first. Even in the essay he'd published, just the week before that morning on the Torridge, on the country of the two rivers, and their waters, and their fish, you can sense it. 'A Taw flood can look like blood.' And again: 'The most enthralling thing about Torridge and Taw sea trout night fishing is that the least touch can be anything from half a pound to seven or eight – which is like the difference between a swallow and a tiger. There is a weird kind of anticipatory terror about this, and it leaks an especially high-quality adrenalin into the blood – which is no doubt the drug we are hooked on.'

If you don't fish, if you're not one of us, you may think this looks like a deranged form of exaggeration. In fact, it's both understatement and afterthought. And something else, too: prose afterglow of searing poetry. Four years before, the author of these words had written a poem on a similar theme: the moment when, fishing one summer night for these wild creatures, he became aware they'd entered a pool on the river on their journey back up their native rivers from the sea. It's called 'Night Arrival of Sea-Trout', and now that moment of dangerous excitement doesn't just affect the 'something' that leaps clear of the water, 'an upside-down, buried heaven' released into the world of air. Flowers become the creatures their names have always held: the dogrose, the foxglove, rediscover their bellies, their touch; even the honeysuckle has fangs. The lobworms couple; the stars in this strange summer night bite at the neck's nape. Earth itself begins to sing. And out in the cornfield by the river, something still more ancient, wilder:

a horned god
Running and leaping
With a bat in his drum.

This wild energy was one he wanted to share. The poet had got his son Nicholas, then seventeen, to print it, on an old offset press they kept in one of the outbuildings, named for an Irish goddess not quite as old as Pan. They printed it, sold it; the poet sent at least two proof copies as gifts to new fishing friends, one of them also a poet.

And now, four years on, 'Night Arrival of Sea-Trout' was about to appear again, in a collection of poems I remember admiring sometime that year, 1983. I was seventeen in 1983. Of course I knew nothing about printing presses or fishing diaries then. But I did fish, and already loved rivers, more strongly and clearly than I then loved poetry. Which is why I admired that book. Its no-nonsense title: *River*. I remember handling it. It didn't resemble your usual collection of poems. And it was much more expensive. A glossy coffee-table volume, full of big landscape colour photographs, one facing each page of text. The photographs were by Peter Keen, the poems by Ted Hughes. I'd vaguely heard of him. I certainly didn't buy it at the time: much too expensive. But that one poem, 'Night Arrival of Sea-Trout', caught my eye, and more than my eye.

That summer we'd holidayed in Devon, staying in a self-catering annexe of a posh fishing hotel, the Arundell Arms, where my parents had paid for me to go on a fly-fishing course. It was there that, in the early afternoons when I wasn't fishing, I acquired the other skill that had got me into such trouble in the British Library that afternoon, and taught myself to touch-type. But, of course, my main business was learning the real form of casting. I'd fished for years, but had only the vaguest notion of how to cast a fly. And though I'd had my share of tiddlers, it had been years since I'd connected with the one amazing solid trout of my life, as the mist swirled over a lake two hours after sunset high in the Cardiganshire hills: 'the blind trout', my elder brothers had joked. This course in Devon was Dad taking me seriously, I thought.

As well as teaching me the real rhythm of a cast by day, the instructors Roy and David took us sea-trout fishing, at night. Sea-trout, genetically identical to resident river brown trout who for some reason have gone out to sea in the coastal waters around the river mouths to feed, grow strong and fast, return to their native rivers from late spring. They're notoriously shy fish, and you need to cast gently indeed to trick one into taking a fly by day. But by night their wildness shines. As I discovered one unforgettable night that week. From a long, still pool under trees above a weir on the Lyd, a tributary of the Tamar, I didn't just touch one of these snarling careering creatures (in truth, much more of a swallow than a tiger), which had truly given me the fright of my life when it snatched the fly I'd somehow flicked into the darkness, and moved me beyond words as, two long minutes later, I brought that pale glimmer over my net; I also heard sea-trout leap, sometimes apparently in concert, for no reason I could think of then except for the wild ancient joy of the night, up and down that pool. I heard the fins whirr in the blackness, and sometimes, through the leaf canopy, even saw them in their leaping catch and release the moonlight. I'd seen that upside-down buried heaven, felt it.

So *River* is the book I return to now, almost thirty years later, in the first months of 2012. In the weeks before and after that first afternoon in the British Library I dip into it, to test so far as I can the strength of the contact, between the poet, and the encounters I'm beginning to see he'd drawn those words from, on rivers I realise I may have fished myself. I read its poems, not in any particular order, and they take me back to the feel of that week as a teenager on the Tamar and its tributaries; moments I thought I'd forgotten. Shading your eyes and peering, at afternoon, deep into pools, and convincing yourself that when Roy pointed out a grey shape you saw the fish in it, too. And not just that week, but in the days fishing I'd managed to eke from family holidays in the intervening decades. Once, when we had sons of our own, my wife and I rented a cottage for one August week by the West Lyn above Watersmeet on Exmoor, the northernmost of Devon's two wildernesses. The river bordered the garden, and under sunken tree roots right below my feet I showed them something I dared not really believe I saw: a vast grey shape that really was a salmon. Wherever it had come from, it had certainly somehow leapt the falls and rapids further down the valley. It deserved the rest it may have been taking down below us. But it was sunk, too, that fish, in something that looked, as I watched, like contemplation, so deep, three feet below the surface, that it made our own peering feel like an impertinence, even a violation. But here, in *River*, is just such a salmon, 'in the upside-down cage of a tree'. And it – he – isn't just contemplating. If the sun's at the correct angle, and if you catch the right mid-morning moment,

> You can see the floor of his chapel.
> There he sways at the altar –
> A soul
> Hovering in the incantation and the incense.

It was reading these poems, and feeling their rightness, not just for me but for the fish and their pools, sensing that somehow these poems were doing them justice with a wondering precision that the photographs facing them now, when I looked at them, rarely did: it was revisiting *River* that made me begin, idly at first, to wonder where these pools lay, and the fish in them, and the insects that rose from them, and when the poet saw what he so evidently, precisely, did. And that didn't seem so difficult. Some titles helped. 'The Morning Before Christmas', 'Stump Pool in April'. 'Four March Watercolours'. 'August Evening', 'An August Salmon', 'September Salmon', 'October Salmon'. Others shared intimacies for which details like months didn't seem necessary: 'Last Night', 'That Morning'. Some named rivers I'd heard of: 'Dee', 'Torridge', others I hadn't heard of, adding a spice of mystery or age or something I couldn't yet altogether place: was 'River Barrow' a name or a tomb? And what, and where and when on earth, was 'Milesian Encounter on the Sligachan'? Well, even that one seemed exactly placed: '"Up in the pools," they'd said, and "Two miles upstream"', and even more exactly timed: 'early August, in a hot lateness (only three hours before my boat)'. I may not know which boat, but I could guess it was one he needed to catch almost as much as a fish, and I could recognise the upside-downness of that kind of dilemma, in the worst (warmest) kind of fishing weather, if you've been given a tip you can't afford not to follow on the one day you have. I knew – I thought – how he felt.

I wanted to find out more. The poems made me want to. They felt, some of them, like diaries.

I fished in print, then. But also in the archive. The British Library holds the letters between Ted Hughes and Peter Keen, the first dated seven long years before the publication of *River*. Poet and photographer were, it seemed from the letters, fishing friends; or at least became friends and collaborators through a shared passion for fishing. On 4 June 1976, early in that terrible drought summer, Hughes tells him about another early start on the Torridge the week before, hoping to benefit from rare recent rain by getting up himself at six, and being there on the one day he had free 'to be present at every possibility until about 2.30'. But the river was like cocoa and had risen only an inch, and the water temperature remained high. That July, he turned to business, said how fascinating he found Keen's idea of a river-book, something he'd had a notion of doing himself (he already had quite a few pieces). He wondered how many fishermen would have the aesthetic interests needed for the book, so promised to try to write evocative poems that might fit any river, and respond to Keen's photographs. But an early confession: 'I'm bedeviled by a need to supply evidence, in writing, of what I'm writing about: a concrete presentation of the setting + characters involved.' ('Concrete', I noticed: was that, even then, a nod to the pool he'd come to call Concrete Ramp?) There was a sign of the vulnerability of that setting to human intervention: the Torridge, he said, was not just the most polluted but among the most poached of the rivers of the West Country. In April 1979, a sign of more than progress on the book, he sent Keen a proof copy of 'Night Arrival of Sea-Trout', in his son's printing, along with a note about a recent 6½-pounder ('but it wasn't a sea-trout'), and two other treasures: a letter and a cluster of maps drawn in blue ink, one to a stretch of the Taw, two for the Torridge, with directions, different instructions and access points according to the height of the river. He gave him Charlie Weeks's number, as bailiff. 'Explain to him, I've arranged with Mike Morpurgo for you to fish on the Nethercott water.'

In 1981, he's telling Keen about the chapter he's writing, which he proposes to do by interviewing the riparian owners; Peter might join him, camera in hand, for a bit of extended research ... But then one later 'Wednesday', I guessed in 1982, the mood has changed. The business of the book, its production costs, the demands of the publisher, took hold. A long letter, in clenched type, between sadness and anger, lays out the work on the poems he'd done: the redrafts, the long reworkings, taking forty pages or more, in one case 150, over nine months. Just so Keen knew how much he had invested, of himself, in *River*.

There was the odd letter to other friends about the project, too, which expressed a different, earlier version of the same frustration. In April 1980, the poet told the critic who was closest to him that he thought he'd 'finished more or less a text for a book of Peter Keen's photographs of rivers & their associates'. I liked those 'associates'. But that made it sound like Keen's book, not his. He worried about 'the subtle limits' that 'writing for accompaniment set', and even murmured a kind of rebellion, nonsensical, I thought, for a poet who made his living by writing. What he really wanted to do, while he was still 'in the material', was to 'write a whole other book of pieces not intended for readers'. Could the diaries be that book, I wondered? Or at least, that material? By that same September, still three whole years before *River* finally appeared, this same friend got another, bleaker version of the same grumble. It wasn't even going to be a coffee-table book, but the kind of gift ambassadors or at least fisheries officers would receive. And because 'the verse text is simply text – nobody, who is going to buy the book, is going to read my verses'. Or understand them. The original plan, for Keen's photographs to do the descriptive work and his own poems to be evocative, now meant that they were only 'decorative – with a respectable aura'. Even if the subsidiary plan his publishers were now mooting came off – an ordinary poetry book with just a few photographs – he worried about the number of poems that he could, if he were being 'conscientious', put in such a book. He thought eight or nine. One of them might be about the mating ritual of a damsel fly, and the role its male played in an archaic insect drama. 'But who'll know what I'm talking about?' 'Do you know Agrion Splendens?' I didn't, not then.

There was at least one person who knew. At least one reader. Not an ambassador, not a fisheries officer. (Though he'd soon become one.) And that Christmas the poet gave him the book with those pieces in it. A beautiful gift, leather-bound, marbled endpapers. *Animal Poems*. It was second-hand, almost, and complicated. A local Devon firm had printed it in 1967, and it had received its binding and slipcase in London. Later he'd got as far as signing it, as if to give or sell to someone else, but had got no further. 'Ted Hughes, 25 September 1971'.

A strange book, then, certainly not in the 'ordinary poetry book format'. But an answer to his own worries about what *River* was going to be. When you open this book, only one of each of the pair of pages that face you is printed. The other is left blank. Now Ted proved why, for the first two of the book's dozen poems: 'An Otter' and 'Pike' adding careful manuscript copies of the verses on the facing page. Poems, both, from his own early years as a published poet, before the one intended reader of this book was born. And then he added a new inscription: 'To Nicholas, Xmas 1980 / love / from / Dad'. And then wrote out, across the endpapers of this rare book, in fair copy manuscript seven more poems, none of them then published, though two would be shortly: Nicholas would print them, with Dad's illustrations, that spring. They're about a caddis fly, an eel. One's about the salmon and bears with whom father and son had shared 'One Morning' that July in Alaska, and stood, in such company, elect, transformed: 'alive in the river of light / Among the creatures of light, creatures of light.' One's about peering down into running water and wondering whether that was a trout you saw. Rivers and their associates, then. But three more are about pike, in dark, still waters, two of them about reservoirs. And one of those at least I'd never seen in print. But I'd eventually see it again, and only then understand the settings and characters involved, the arc that bound them over, and beyond, a lifetime.

*

The last week of March 2012 was a week of petrol shortages and blazing sunshine. I'd already found enough, I thought, to write about *River*, if not about the smudge on my finger that had really started it. And friends offered me their cottage above the Tamar. So I risked a full tank and headed south-west, taking the miles of the A30, Devon's spinal cord, at speed, then turning south at Launceston, not even taking the detour that memory prompted me to and drive past that fishing hotel, the Arundell Arms at Lifton. Rose Cottage was a haven and a suntrap. Here to work on my essay, and remembering Hughes's warning, I didn't take a rod. Instead, I read *River* again, and walked the banks of the river. One morning, I spotted what I thought were otter prints in the grey sand, and went back to read 'Visitation', found again 'these pad-clusters on mud-margins'.

On the Wednesday afternoon, encouraged by such evidence, I headed north and east. I went, first, to North Tawton, then north up the by-road to the bridge at Bondleigh, the first of the maps Hughes had drawn for Keen. Then, after a rapt half-hour of watching a Taw brownie twitch and glide and rise and hold position in the current under the bushes from a high daffodil-crowded bank, I drove west through bright lanes, towards a church spire rising from between green oaks: Iddesleigh, and the second of those maps. Here was the road out of the village, here the crossroads, here Nethercott House, here the two farm lanes, and there, beyond a green verge, was the stone Celtic cross where he'd told Keen to park. I did the same, nosing the car into thick grass, trusting to instructions thirty-three years old. Getting out, I unfolded, into a deep rural peace. But also one that seemed to keep its secrets, river-wise, more closely to itself than the Taw. There was the track between trees on the map I'd transcribed; but it led up, steeply, to the imminent brow of a hill, not down. What lay beyond? The lane did twist down to where the tarmac gave way, but however hard I listened, there was no sound of water. So I was deep but not close.

And I was being watched, and not just by the cows and sheep in the fields beyond the hedges, alert to a stranger. On the brow of a knoll between me and the nearest farm, a knot of children stood around an adult, who detached himself from the group, approached, in friendly wariness. We chatted briefly over the farm gate, exchanged names, mobile numbers, as the children watched on.

That was as far as I got that sunny afternoon. It took two days for what, even then, I realised were border checks, frontier clearances, to be completed. David Ward – even as I typed his surname into my phone a silent bell rang in my head – had farmed these fields for thirty-plus years. His brother, Geoff, over the lane at Parsonage Farm likewise. But this portion of deepest Devon wasn't just theirs. There were others at stake. Yes, he said, cautiously, he knew Ted, yes, he parked there – but, even once I told him how I knew, showed him my clumsy copy of Ted's map for Peter Keen, he said he would need to check before … I'd understand, of course? Of course. Before he let me in. This was a peculiar kind of private property. And that caution gave me pause. I didn't want to trespass, of course, either a farmer's land or what it meant. And I had some idea, too, not just what, but who, David might be guarding. These must be city children he'd been showing his farm. Nethercott House was still home to Farms for City Children, the charity which Iddesleigh's most famous literary residents, Michael and Clare Morpurgo, still run. Already back at the Duke of York in the village, there were posters of *War Horse*; the Spielberg movie of Michael's novel had been released just the year before. And the urgent conversation that had inspired the book, which its author had overheard between one young visitor, previously assumed to have nothing to say, and the farm's horses, may for all I knew have taken place in David's farm buildings, just behind him. How did he know I wasn't just another city grown-up, pushing his nose in?

But if I was here after Ted Hughes, well … Deeper waters still. He wasn't just a poet who fished. He had been, is still, for many readers, Her Husband. With reason. His first wife, the American poet Sylvia Plath, and the mother of their two children, Frieda and Nicholas, killed herself in February 1963, gassing herself in the oven kitchen of her London flat while her children slept next door, nine months after Ted had started an affair with another poet's wife, Assia Wevill. In March 1969, Assia, too, herself took her own life, copying Sylvia's method; and took Shura, their three-year-old daughter, with her. Ever since, there have been those who blamed Ted for all this. Others, particularly in Devon, protected him and his family with a fierceness to match the outrage. I reminded myself that, for all David Ward knew, I might be a mischief-maker. I might even be the tenth he'd had to fend off this year.

But once I'd made a phone call to North Tawton – I had met Carol Hughes, Ted's second wife for the last twenty-eight years of his life; after her own initial caution she sounded intrigued, genuinely interested; and yes, would contact David – he texted back. He'd be happy to take me. By the time I pulled into his yard I had another reason to reassure me. On the Friday en route north from Rose Cottage I left myself an extra hour. I wanted to call in at the Arundell Arms, for old times' sake, mostly. I flicked through the copies of *The Field*, *Country Life*, *Trout and Salmon* you'd find in any fishing hotel, and then the books in the grand lounge. Found *West Country Fly Fishing*, as, of course, I knew I would: it was edited by Anne Voss Bark, the woman who as its proprietor for decades had made the hotel's reputation, placed the ads in *Trout and Salmon* my father had acted on back in 1983. I read Ted's essay, there and then, in place: told myself, if he was promoting this water, and in particular the stretch where the Torridge enters its gorge below Okement junction, I was just following his guide. At reception I wondered whether by any chance Roy Buckingham or David Pilkington, the instructors who'd taught me in 1983, were still around. Ten minutes later David appeared. Of course he didn't remember me, but he was at once unforgettably himself. Once I'd stopped being a teenager, he was interested, too. Oh yes, he said, he knew Ted. Had given him some salmon casting lessons, down on the Lyd, early eighties, must have been? And then the current proprietor, Adam Fox-Edwards, Anne's stepson, emerged from his office, with another unexpected souvenir: a framed manuscript of a poem by Ted, a gift to Anne and Conrad, her second husband (had I met him? Yes, of course: the old gentleman who'd given us a fly-tying

demonstration in the bar one evening on that course). Christmas
1983. Why didn't he put it, frame and all, through the Xerox?
Would I like a copy? I still have it above my desk: 'The Mayfly'.

Doors were opening.

That afternoon David Ward took me on a quad bike down the
rough track below Town End farm. At once he dispelled one of
my doubts. Yes, he said, they get quite a few people wanting to
see War Horse Valley, and Morpurgo admirers often have a drink
at the Duke of York, but no one had ever asked about Ted before.
He showed me his field at the junction of the Okement and
the Torridge, and the monument to the drowned man in it. Ted
would fish this, yes, he said; and early, yes. His car would often
be parked under the cross when David got up for milking. And
Ted wasn't really one to bother too much about beat boundaries,
either: David owned the rights to this pool; his brother Geoff
to the pool immediately downstream; Michael's stretch began –
well, why didn't he show me? We passed a fishing hut, which
looked ancient, but still hadn't been there so long – David showed
me where it used to stand, in the next field. It occurred to me to
ask then: did he happen to know of a Charlie Weeks? Ted had
given Peter his name, too, in that letter introducing the fishing,
and there's a 'Charlie' in one of Ted's poems. Oh yes, David said;
Charlie wasn't at all well, now, but he still lived in the village.
And, I asked, remembering a line in the same poem, 'Peter the
corn farmer'? That would be Peter Banbury, David said at once.
Used to farm West Park; nodding downstream. But then we came
to a long, straight pool, and there, at its tail, the start of streamy
water; there, forty yards down, a bay, cut away. Yes, David said,
looking a bit surprised, we did do a bit of infilling there, around
the concrete of the collapsed bridge.

He left me to it then, roared up the hedge-side track on his quad
bike to the brow of the hill I'd walk myself in half an hour: the
track Ted had indicated in his map for Peter Keen, the map beyond
the brow of the hill that lay beyond the farm gate, the gate that
opened onto the Paradise he'd described in the essay I'd read that
morning. But first I wanted to relish the feeling of being in it.
I walked back to the tail of that long pool, and wondered: could

that be Sprackmann's Pit? Then looked down to what may just be Island Run, stood on the high bank of that cut-away bay, got as far downstream as a ditch and a barbed-wire fence and a stream would let me, looked upriver, imagined where Ted Hughes would have stood, playing that salmon. And, because my iPhone held the transcript of the diary entry that had hooked me, I read it back to the pool as the March sun lit the river.

And for the moment, for the rest of that week indeed, that was almost enough.

*

But two questions nagged at me as the days passed, and I left Rose Cottage with a long rough draft of my essay about *River*, and which I'd promised to show Carol Hughes. The first was a practical doubt, which I dared not mention in that draft of my essay, but which deepened the more I thought about it, and read. That letter of Ted's about the practicalities and cost of a book that featured colour photographs as well as poems mentioned a publisher, James of Exeter. But Faber and Faber, Ted's publishers, ended up publishing it, if with sponsorship from British Gas. It appeared, I knew, in September 1983, three months after that morning on the river. If that moment when the salmon took really was 'the most enthralling' of all Ted's years of fishing on the Torridge, it came too late to make it into *River*. The book must already have been in press months before then.

What's more, for all its poems' loving presentation of a year in the life of a river, and their dedication of the months of the year to the pursuit of different fish, salmon and sea-trout and trout and bream and the eel among them, there was none so far as I could see devoted to salmon in May. There was one poem, 'Four March Watercolours', that I now saw is set on and in 'the pool by the concrete buttress'; its fourth section dwelt on a snow-melt flood, and concluded that 'If there are salmon / Under it all, they are in coma'. The poet had to work as they did to imagine them; neither could see for sure. Down he looked into melted chocolate. Up they looked 'At a guttering lamp / Through a sand-storm boil of silt / That scratches their lidless eyes'. Even if I had looked down onto the same pool – and could I be really sure that this was the only pool by a concrete buttress, given all I already knew, from Ted's diary of that one long week's fishing, on the Exe, the Dart, the Taw as well as the Torridge? – I certainly wasn't looking at it in the same mood. And was it even the same river?

It would take me four years and thousands of miles to find the answer to this question. Two more years to act on it.

So why wasn't I deflated by those doubts? Because of the second question that occurred to me that bright March afternoon beside the Torridge. This one was more easily answered, and though I couldn't know it then, gave me the strength to answer the first, and to cope with all the knocks and setbacks and diversions and checks and cautions – the catch – in the journey I barely knew I was starting on. As I stood there, alone, implausibly, reading Ted Hughes's diary entry of an entirely wordless encounter with a fish he never saw on this same stretch of river self-consciously to myself in the shallows at the tail of Concrete Ramp, and loving it, I realised something else about this presumptuous act of standing in his footsteps and imagining, hoping, adding words and physical sensation to a picture. It was something I'd missed, or taken for granted somehow, in the excitement of that afternoon at the British Library.

What made that moment 'the most enthralling' – enthralling, the same word he'd used in his own essay on fishing these rivers for sea-trout – of all his Torridge fishing, wasn't just the moment of contact with that fish, that deep, strong take, mid-stream. It was that he was standing in someone's footsteps, too, when it happened. Someone he admired. That morning, trying to put himself in exactly the position to add the fish to the mysterious scale snagged in his flying treble hook, he'd fished for the first time in his life from where, he recalled, someone in a photograph in *Torridge Fishery* was standing. To have imagined casting from that same place, and now to be doing it, and now to have that imagined moment 'so marvellously realised', by a real contact with a real fish … that was what did it. Ted Hughes may have been a poet, but as a fisherman he also read fishing books, fishing magazines, before he wrote for them. Just like me. Reading his essay in the Arundell Arms that morning, I'd seen it. *Torridge Fishery*, by 'Lemon Grey', or L. R. N. Gray. Gray had favoured using yellow in the flies. Hughes credited Gray with it.

Back at Rose Cottage that evening, I checked the online catalogue of the contents of Ted Hughes's library, now in an American university. There it was; he owned a copy. I checked my own University Library's catalogue. There *Torridge Fishery* was. The day after my return home, I became the first reader ever to borrow it. And there, in a black and white photograph, 'the author' was, too, casting from Island Run, just upstream of the rope footbridge he'd built across the river for his guests when he ran the Torridge Fishery of the title.

There was more. Some weeks later, another trip to the British Library produced another catch – I noticed that early drafts of 'Strangers', his poem about sea-trout, happened to be written on the back of a printed version of the hand-drawn map he'd given to Peter Keen. Why would he have had this printed? And then, on a whim, thinking as a fisherman of the very few times when I'd paid for fishing, been given directions, I went back to the University Library and flicked through copies of *Trout and Salmon* for the early 1980s. And there it was, in three successive numbers, March, April and May 1982: a box advertisement, offering salmon and sea-trout fishing on a mile of the Torridge, '(part of Lemon Gray's Old Fishery) [sic]'. Accommodation was offered, too, in a farm cottage, also to let. Throughout the season, March to September. Contact details supplied: address, and number. 'Apply Hughes', the advertisement told you: 'after 6 pm.'

Ted Hughes was by the early 1980s reckoned by the critics I knew to be a shy, haunted giant of a man, a poet who sometimes shunned readings, who felt a dread of anticipation of heckling, barracking abuse. Yet here he was publishing his address and telephone number, advertising the fishing he was, in the months that box appeared, himself writing about. Why? Because this poet was also a fisherman, who believed in the community of fishermen. He wanted them to apply Hughes.

And when they didn't, he kept on trying. The book he'd spent seven years on, refining, discarding everything that wasn't first intensity, wasn't, he discovered, finished with its publication. It was admired, yes, but not recognised for all he'd given it, of himself. And he knew it was incomplete. Within a year he told one non-fishing artist friend that it still lacked its central poem. It had its golden eggs, sure, but not the goose that laid them. He added angry poems, about the pollution of the rivers he knew and loved best, the Torridge and the Taw: that poem with Charlie and Peter the corn-farmer was called '1984 on the Tarka Trail', and he was aiming for the dark Orwellian tones. Other fishing poems followed, from other trips, further afield, and found homes elsewhere. But when the chance came a decade after it had first appeared to republish it along with two other books that had began as collaborations with artists or photographers, he'd made it his own. The poems now spanned thirty years, the notes he added many more. But they also made the salmon its hero.

A fine poet I know, Clive Wilmer, knew Ted Hughes. Clive visited him at Court Green ten years after these advertisements appeared, and during a break in their conversation when Hughes was called out of the room he glanced at proofs of two of the poems that had first appeared in *River* and were now to appear in a new selection of his verse. Returning to the room, Hughes saw this, and asked, with a gruff, eager urgency: 'Are you a fisherman?' He was, Clive told me, visibly deflated at the reply.

'Fishing is my way of breathing,' Ted once told a girl I have come to know well in writing this book. She's about my age. She spent dusks and dawns with him and Nicholas and her own father, their close friend, in Ireland and in England. She knows. He needed to fish. It sustained him. It took him into the natural world and reminded him of who he was, who he had been. It was his longest love affair. When the waters he loved were under threat, and as a farmer and countryman he knew better than most how vulnerable the Torridge was, he was ready to speak, publicly, on oath, in their defence. But he wanted, needed, others to share it, too. And had been trying for years before he came to *River*, years before he had even thought of catching a salmon or sea-trout, years before he moved to Devon.

3

Stealing Trout

They both knew it. It was Sylvia who wrote to a friend who knew them and their poetry well enough to understand her barely coded message, 'Ted's main dream come true. The River Taw is thick with fish.'

This was at the end of August 1961, on the eve of their move to Devon, barely six weeks after they'd left their baby daughter Frieda with her mother, visiting from the States, and spent two days touring possible properties in the West Country. And though it had broken a rule they'd set themselves – no thatch – Court Green charmed them both at once. London-bound since their own return from the States, flat-dwellers, and with Frieda almost a toddler, the ancient house, its walls castle-thick in places, had what they needed: nine rooms, two and a half acres of land, including what Ted described to another American friend as a prehistoric tumulus or barrow, and – not bad for an old farm, eleventh century in parts – the little market town that had grown up around its walls. North Tawton had a church, just over the garden wall, banks, post office; even, they discovered, after months of hiss and crackle, a shop with a VHF radio and a man to fit the aerial up on the roof which brought the Third Programme crisp and clear into their front room. The children's playground had stunning views to Dartmoor, seven miles south. Best of all, perhaps, for a literary couple who'd just turned their back on commitments, the railway line from Okehampton to Exeter had a halt only a mile away. London was four hours by express train; this became a mantra in Sylvia's letters to metropolitan friends and journalists they really hadn't turned their back on. And the BBC work Ted was doing – a commission, that February, to write and record talks about writing for eleven- to thirteen-year-olds, to be broadcast on Friday mornings as part of a long-going series – made that commute essential. It was lucrative work, gained on the back of the success of his second book of poems – his BBC producer Moira Doolan had loved the directness of the way he drew on real experiences, real animal energies, and wanted him to share that with her young audience. It worked; he worked. It had already bought them their first car, the Morris Traveller in which they'd driven down, found the place. He set Sylvia up with a desk he'd made for her of elm planks in one of the six first-floor bedrooms, and took to writing in his own study in the attic, right under the thatch with its 'billion birds', as Sylvia liked to say. Her study was as airy, in the mornings when she wrote, as his was dark and secret, in the afternoons and evenings; they juggled Frieda, settled into a routine that balanced renovations to the old house, planting and harvesting vegetables in the garden. But the darkness and the secrecy worked, meant he could do what he did at the microphone: speak directly to those youngsters listening, without any of the complications of classroom crowd control.

But all this business came at a price. Months, the worst two-thirds of a year, in fact, passed before he could at last step into the stuff, the real element, of his dream. Writing and domestic commitments, finding their feet and the realities of a draughty house in a small town in the wettest and longest winter in seventy years, and Sylvia's advancing pregnancy, saw to that. Literary celebrity brought its own pressure: invitations he needed to decline. No, he wouldn't do a programme showing the growth of a poem from start to finish.

Meanwhile, the country and village and weather conspired around them. Rain fell; clouds gathered; bullocks standing up to their knees in quaggy fields beyond gates in fields that shrank below huddled rainy hills; sometimes, too, the locals in the town could feel part of Cow Country, the way they stared.

All this meant that the closest he got, for months, to his dreamland, the country of the two rivers he'd held in his head ever since he'd been a boy, in industrial South Yorkshire, twenty years before, when he'd borrowed Henry Williamson's great violent story of the 1920s *Tarka the Otter* from the school library and kept it out for eighteen months, committing it to heart, every word of it to memory, doing all he could to imagine the Devon where, for nine months before the war, his elder brother Gerald had been an estate gamekeeper; the closest he got to all this was the trickle of water off the leaking thatch and down, searching for the river and sea as he couldn't. The house felt like an old coffin, and concerns about his own heart, which he kept to himself throughout those months, rather than worry an anxious expectant mother, hounded and pounded at and within him.

And then the year, and his spirits, turned. On 17 January, just before midnight, Nicholas entered their lives after a long and painful labour for Sylvia; suddenly he was there, in a wall of water, a gush that soaked them all in the room: midwife, doctor, Ted, little Frieda. Ted, soaked by life, decided he wasn't going to die, and a spate of life followed. First snowdrops, then primroses, then, despite the continuing rain, the daffodils Court Green was famous for began to bloom. And the new trout season arrived: the last had ended in September before he'd had a chance to fish. Even then he had to wait weeks for it, weeks of continuing rain. Right into April, and through it. Only on Easter Sunday, late that year, did the world relent. But when it did, Ted was ready for it. On his very first visit to the Taw, in late April just below the town, a sign: he met an otter, running along a ditch towards him from the Taw. He was in Tarka country after all.

On Wednesday 9 May 1962, Ted returned from fishing to find a letter from Gerald, by then much better established in his own new world, with a young family in Australia. Ted sat down to a breakfast of the trout he'd come back with in his haversack and told his brother what he was missing. Twice a week he'd begun getting up at five, and could be down at the river in ten minutes. The Taw, just below the village, was as wide as Hebden Water, the river Gerald would have remembered at Hardcastle Crags, in Calderdale, from the idyllic years before their own first move south to Mexborough. But the Taw was sunk ten feet deep, and its banks, these spring mornings, were all primroses and aconites and its own wild daffodils. Why so deep? Well, the great spongy heights of Dartmoor lay only seven miles south, and the river rushed off there, cut deep through the fields: the wet winter and recent rains had kept it roaring. Birds loved the river, and came out to inspect him: pheasants crowing, kingfishers bolting past.

And Sylvia had been right: the Taw was indeed thick with trout. This morning he'd caught four, beautiful, red-spotted creatures, which he dispatched with the handle of the knife Gerald had made in North Africa during the war, brought home as a souvenir. It was tricky, he told his brother: he had to wade upstream, casting up against the swift current, and the fish would grab his worm as it came back towards him. Upstream worming requires finesse, not just in avoiding overhanging branches as you cast. You need feel, an instinct for the depth your bait is fishing, trundling or rushing back downstream towards you; you need to keep the line taut, too, so you can react quickly, stop the fish spitting out the hook or, worse, swallowing it too deep, risking a gored throat. You're always on the move. But Ted could do all this. Loved it. Got results. Two of the four trout he kept were half-pounders, and very strong, one only nine inches, all decent breakfast fish; he'd returned another good one, lost one of about the same size and had pricked and lost several others, 'just a tug & a thump or two'. His fourth fish bore on its spotted flanks the scars of an encounter with something altogether more serious, teeth marks. Either an otter had mauled it – he mentioned that recent encounter, only the week before – or a predator, cannibal trout. He'd yet to connect with those much bigger fish, he said, in the quiet pools and deep places, nor had he yet 'devised tactics to'.

Whatever else Devon's famous for, fishermen know it for its minnows: nineteenth-century artificials invented by an enterprising tackle-shop keeper in Totnes, they have angled fins set like propeller blades into the shaft of the hollow body which whirrs around a wire shaft threaded through it, with treble hooks behind the tail to snare a trout that lunges at them. That morning, writing to Gerald, Ted thought the swiftness of the river would make that a problem. The currents that brought his worm trundling at its pace back downstream would make controlling that little whirring fish, bringing it downstream at a dash even faster, to keep the line taut, really tricky, a challenge he hadn't yet worked out how to solve.

Not that it seemed to bother him at the moment. He knew there was more fishing within reach – sea fishing to the north (Gerald had once taken him to Tenby in South Wales), and free fishing on the tidal lower stretches of the Taw. He'd yet to buy tackle for that, but of course that wasn't a problem. And for now, his little seven-foot split cane rod, and the fixed spool reel he'd bought in America, served him well. What mattered most was being out with the dawn, enjoying the complete solitude of those mornings.

At which point Sylvia wanted to add her own note, from the desk in her study Ted had made for her. Yes, she said, she was half aware of him rising at 4.30, a shadow in the gloom; and was about to eat at least one of those beautiful trout for her breakfast. She was looking forward to her mother visiting; then, she wrote, with a determined brightness that more or less deliberately missed Ted's point, she could join him on one of those trips, indulge the perpetual beginner's luck she had, thinking of the success they'd had fishing for flounders on Cape Cod in 1957, in the first weeks of their American years. She meant it: a few days later she was writing to her mother asking her to be sure to wrap and bring their rods over with her when she came to visit the following month. Especially, she said, her 'spry' little rod.

But well before Mrs Plath arrived – it must have been sometime between writing that letter to Gerald on 9 May and a weekend visit they were to be paid by the couple to whom, on moving to Devon, they'd sublet their London flat for the remaining three years of their lease – Ted rose to the challenges he set himself. Or plunged into them. He went further. Deeper. Wilder. Bigger. Found more excitement, and more danger, than he could ever have dreamed, much closer to home. He went stealing trout on a May morning, and then, almost immediately, wrote a poem about it, as swift and urgent and as wild a celebration of his manhood in this place, this rushing river, as the experience he'd just had. It's been called 'the best ever evocation of what it's really like to go fishing', and that, I guess, is one reason why, when Ted came as close to making *River* his own as he could, in 1993, he made sure he added 'Stealing Trout on a May Morning', the first great poem of Nicholas's life. But that's only half the story, as he himself came to discover.

*

'Stealing Trout' is no romantic transport of delight. It's a guilt trip, and the family's Morris Traveller is not just what takes him there, that May morning. It's 5.00 a.m., and parked half in the ditch, the car's his weapon and accomplice. He sits there, aware of the engine fumes, the 'long gash' he's just torn in the lacy veil of the dawn; he needs that hot ticking engine to be cold steel, and now; he needs to be 'secreted three fields away'; he needs the occupants of those fields and nearby farms to drift back to sleep after the disturbance they've just felt.

Easier said than done. Still in the car, the tension wires him. He's aware of how far this intimate hill country of farms and managed gardens is from empty wilderness; even the leaves on the trees are well connected, plushly on the watch for the invader he is. And he knows, and fears they know, in the returning hush of this lacy light: the 'delicate business' he's told himself he's here on is something else. 'Something improper is going to happen.' And every sheep knows, too, for miles around. They're staring at him, like priests, from their high ground.

But then he's out, and the world's suddenly made new. The air has no memory; the tracery of sunlit dew on the blades and stems of grasses is a brilliant new surface, to which the earth, for a moment like a mysterious fish in its darkness, still has to rise. He crosses the field, as calm as it is still; those primroses, those sheep, accept him, as he makes his way to the river, feeling the edges of this morning. And the river, when he gets to it, looks down on it from the field edge, and the sun clears the brow of the hill and floods the water with light, is 'amazed with itself', too. Even before he sees the fish, 'rising / And sinking for the sheer novelty', their gills charged with that brand new liquid light, you know that this is what Ted meant in that letter to Gerald. Whatever else he's here for, he's catching himself, catching the whole morning.

And now he follows the fish, becomes one: 'My mind sinks, rising and sinking', as he plunges into the tunnel of trees, mostly hazels, exchanges the sky's embrace for something suddenly savage. The stuff beneath his boot is wild, plunging, and at first he can't name it: it's 'a thing black and sudden'. He needs to stand in it, square, confront its force, before 'it is river again'. He's getting his bearings: stones, gravels, weeds, fish, and, under the hazel roots, gaping open like mouths above the flow, the stain which the runoff from the latest rain has 'bled in' to the water from lanes and ploughed fields. The Taw in flood can be the colour of blood, I remember from his essay, still twenty years in the future. That red soil leaves its fingerprint.

It fascinates him, this water, its effects. And though he claims he 'can hardly look at it' – because of that 'delicate business' he's here on, because he's here to poach on a beat he hasn't paid to fish? No, just because of the rushing complex marvel of it – he immediately sees a world sliding past. In this light under the trees, the wide pool tail is as smooth as a table on the move; where it breaks into a fast run over the lip of a weir, it makes him think of corrugated-iron sheets on shanty-town roofs. Then every one of those corrugations becomes a twist, a braid, boiling up, the tiniest suggestion of an explosion as spray leaps from a boulder. It's a dazzle of blacks and whites, a mirror-slither, with always the hint of danger as he feels his way, wading. One false step and he could be dragged down into 'drowning skirts' of white water and whatever's beneath. But that danger's all part of it, the glamour: anything, any temptation, the water throws at him, roping round his knees, even 'A drowned woman loving each ankle', he's heavy enough, man enough to resist. Or at least, to 'wade with them upstream' as, now, at last, he starts to fish. He's fishing the river, loving the play of light and risk and deception, tackling, realising all the challenges he'd only been wondering about the week before to his brother:

Flashing my blue minnow
Up the open throats of water
And across through the side of the rush

This is speed fishing: reading those lines, speaking them, you feel him casting them. He feels his way through the body of water, and parts of other bodies: beards of debris from spate hang from hazel roots. Even the moss or waterweed he presses over as his boots slide nervously, a high-wire act in knee-deep water, is 'wild nape hair'. You feel the hairs on the back of your own neck stiffen at all this.

And then he's really in it. It? The river, of course, but other depths, too. 'Soon I deepen.' Seven miles off the moor, how long has this water taken to get here? And what's it brought with it into this first light? He hears voices in this moorland river, and the pressure mounts, becomes 'panic' at all it holds, all it tells him. But there's no escaping this: he presses on, into it. Had there been another storm that night, up on the moor? Is he out of his depth? Fishermen take stupid risks wading – twice I've teetered, wobbled, in fast water, chest-height, thought: is this it? then drawn back – but this is something more than that. Somewhere upstream, in the Taw's headwaters or his, a battle has been fought, and lost – 'this headlong river is a rout' of all kinds of battlefield debris from another, older time: gun carriages, tumbrils, metal, rags. Is this even his dream or his father's? Willie Hughes was a quiet man, a shell-shocked Gallipoli veteran, who would, Ted's sister Olwyn told me, only open up to his children about his war first thing in the morning, when she and Ted would slip into his bed and listen. Or was it something else? All of Dartmoor's water, all the river's bedrock granite, trail past him now, 'its frights, its eyes / With what they have seen and still see'. And they unman that heavy man flashing upstream with his blade of a rod and minnow, undo any pretence of skill he'd had, any aspirations to raise his own one-man company standard:

They drag the flag off my head, a dark insistence
Tearing the spirits from my mind's edge and from under …

From under what? He can't or chooses not to say, even now, even back in his dark, secret study under the attic, when all these words have come back to him.

The fish saves him, pulls him savagely clear, back, up, into reality. It was there, somewhere, all along, in that headlong rout of a river, this jumble of dreams and words and letters: it had been there for four years, he reckons. What made the river – dew, lightning, granite – went into it. 'A trout, a foot long, / Lifting its head in a shawl of water.' It's his biggest yet, of course. And for just a moment you can convince yourself that its shawled head is lifted in greeting. But at the end of the fight, the battle, as the strength of this fish, all its fins strained taut against the line, his split cane rod, that American reel, and the little treble hooks in his Devon minnow in its mouth, it stares him down as the sheep had done, pricks his conscience, goes deeper again, 'getting / A long look at me. So much for the horror / It has changed places.' The catch. He doesn't need to say: the kill.

And then the scene changes one last time, as the morning comes. The sun has its way with the frost, and pear-blossoms unstiffen. Like barmaids in a country pub, 'brassy wood-pigeons' add their voices to the river's. And over the mantelpiece of that pub, just under an old mangy fox head, there's a painting, from the first years of the century, before Henry Williamson had gone to war, or returned to write *Tarka*. And it's Ted. He has entered his dreamland, taken his place.

*

If this is what stealing trout is, how could I not want to try all this for myself?

It's Friday 19 May 2017.

Back at home I've done my homework, of course. I have a rod of the right length, if not weight, a diminutive carbon-fibre wand I was given in Japan, and a matching reel. I've never used either. I already have reasons to be in Devon in May, so I go online, order both a blue Devon minnow and a green. They are plastic, unweighted – but that's a judgement about the water flow I can expect – and mass-produced, squeezed from some template, not thoroughly made. But their trebles prick the polythene slips they sit in. I'm armed.

I've also returned to the poem and consulted the largest-scale maps I can. The Ordnance Survey Explorer, 1:25,000, for Okehampton shows field boundaries. I start looking for spots, 'below the village', which Ted could reach within ten minutes, and where the road is three fields away from the river.

And the day before, I do my reconnaissance: I drive off Dartmoor through North Tawton, through Bondleigh, and double back. Bondleigh Wood – a farm there. Will the farmer wake, first thing? I try what the map tells me is a road parallel to the river. It turns into a track, unmetalled, beside a house, which looks uninhabited. There is a likely looking ditch, and a gate onto a sheep-filled field that drops riverwards. One ewe stares me down.

Sleep that night is fitful: adrenaline and owls. Through my open window at the Half Moon in Sheepwash I hear them in the small hours, their calls and, better still, their claws on the roof above my room.

And then it's 4.20, and I'm awake, and on the road by 4.30. This time the sky's grey, and lightening: the difference a week makes. I drive in my waders, to save time; I've also put up my rod, tied on my minnow. I'll start with the green, because I'm a novice at this; when, as I'm sure is bound to happen, I lose that, on some deep-sunk rock, or by wrapping it round some irretrievable high branch, I'll graduate to blue. At 4.50 I'm within range, but lose three agonising minutes waiting for a herd of cows to make it into the parlour for the first milking. What will the farmer make of this strange car in the lane? Will he take my number?

And now I'm inching past that farm, window down, ear agog for barking dogs, and nosing along the track, and am here. Not quite half in the ditch – what if I can't get out? How could I ask a farmer for a pull with his tractor? How could I possibly explain, without making things worse? A friend, with whom I've risked the barest outline of this plan, at once saw how absurd this was: offered to bring me a file in a pike.

It's not just trespassing, not just poaching. Since Ted's day, spinning has been prohibited on the Taw. It is too easy. But I'm a fly fisher. I always have been. This doesn't feel easy to me. I've been practising lobbing the minnow across our garden lawn. Even on that flat expanse, it is a hit-and-miss affair. Earnest, relentlessly optimistic North American wilderness YouTube tutorials have hardly reassured me. This is North Devon, not Colorado. So I remind myself, as I cross the third field, scattering ewes and their lambs, checking for *River* as well as spare line and blue minnow expectant in my wader pocket: this is a pilgrimage. This will be a ritual cast. I am here for the place, for the experience. I am, I realise, doing the best to let myself off my treble hooks even before I'm at the river.

But then I, too, have to turn my back on the sky, confront the river sunk ten feet below me under the dark canopy of hazels. Ted could hardly look at it in its ferocity. Knowing this heightens my curiosity for what I'm about to enter. Even as I'm scrambling as quietly as I can manage down over roots, mouths, limbs, and letting my first boot in, I know it's not the snarling water it was, whether fifty-five years or a day ago, after Wednesday's heavy rain. That will already have passed through. But still I wade, still I deepen. I manage to flick, not flash, that green minnow upstream; remarkably, it comes back, sometimes it's true after a brush with weed. It runs beside those hazel roots, those mouths, open still. I even forget why I'm here. Light is strengthening, too. The sun hasn't yet emerged over the ridge to the east, but already, in two or three quiet pools I come to, easing quietly upstream, fish are rising and falling, and, yes, rising to flies, snouts bulging the surface for some insect about to break through the meniscus. They look serious, those rise-forms, determined. Hunger keeps you keen.

I find boulders mid-river at the head of a pool, and remember, below their braids, to turn and watch the water round my ankles. Drowned women? Maybe not. But then I'm not Ted Hughes; his solitude, and the life he leaves to find it, is not mine.

I am a fisherman, though. And now I've rounded another corner, and I'm beside a run. I decide to go with the flow. Full of admiration for Ted, in a river that was once twice this strength, I want to try casting as convention says I should. If nothing else,

I want to feel the spinner alive against the current, feel the thrum of those whirring pectorals. The minnow goes out, fully fifteen yards, into the water at the far bank. I start to retrieve, bringing it up through the widening, slackening water towards my casting position at the head of the run, then cast again, this time searching the water on the near side of the current's full force, then once more, as close as I can to mid-river, right into the flow.

And then it happens. The rod bucks, and jags, and I have one. A real member. A red-spotted trout. The energy is extraordinary. I lift it, after thirty thrilling seconds, and I want to shout! Instead, I lift it through the shawl of water, and discover – only a little trout. A Taw reckling. Only twice as long as the minnow itself. But a dorsal fin like a schooner's mainsail and a spirit to die for. Or – no – to live for. I dampen my hand, slip the hook free of where the fish had grabbed it, through the cartilage of its lower jaw, admire it, slip it back. It surges away.

I have what I came for.

4

'I fished in still water ...'

It was the next weekend, days after he'd learned to spin, stolen that trout, written it up. They were entertaining the latest in a string of visitors they needed that spring, to make up for the long, wet months of winter. This time it was the Wevills, the couple who'd taken on the lease of their flat in London when they'd made the sudden decision to move to Devon last summer. They'd got on when they met at the flat; David was a poet too, a Canadian, whose own studies at Cambridge had overlapped with Sylvia's. The new tenants had even lent the Hugheses their dining table, the flat being too small for it.

Assia worked in advertising. David was her third husband. Later, her boss recalled that before she left the office that Thursday she'd told her boss: 'I'm going to seduce Ted!'

On the Saturday morning she came into the kitchen and told Ted and Sylvia of a dream she'd just had. The old house had produced vivid dreams already. Ted's had been of Court Green waiting for them, before they moved in: not quite vacant possession. A huge golden serpent had risen up through the floorboards from the well at its heart, at just the place where a well did lie.

So why wouldn't Ted have encouraged Assia to share hers now? Her dream was of a giant fish, and not just any fish: a pike. The pike 'Had a globed, golden eye, and in that eye / A throbbing human foetus'.

According to Ted, Sylvia was 'astonished, even envious'. For as long as they'd been married she'd envied him his own dreams as much as she'd feared, denied hers. What lay under sleep.

She'd wake, relieved, afraid, to report: 'No dreams.' For his part, remembering all this years later, he 'refused to interpret'. But at once he felt it, knew something. Contact of a kind he couldn't resist. The following morning, Sunday, he and Assia were alone together in the kitchen, where she was making a salad, Sylvia with David outside. But Sylvia got up, suddenly, went through to the kitchen, did not return as she'd promised. And at lunch was silent. On the train home that afternoon, after Sylvia had driven them to the station, Assia told David that Ted had kissed her, and that Sylvia had seen it.

*

Ted knew all about dreams of pike, and other animals, and what happens when you share them.

The seven years from his late teens to his mid-twenties, National Service, between school and university, and then the years between Cambridge and London, was the one period in his life he hadn't fished. But every night he'd dreamed of fishing. Sometimes it was the canal, or a version of the canal, in Mytholmroyd, the West Yorkshire village where as a five-year-old he'd started fishing daily, with a net made from the kitchen curtains: he caught bronze bearded loaches from their crevices in the canal wall. Mostly it was Crookhill, the pond he'd discovered years after Gerald, eighteen when the family had moved south in 1938, had left their new home in Mexborough in disgust, first for that job as a gamekeeper in Devon, eventually for war. It was in 1944 or 1945, at fourteen or fifteen, that he'd befriended John Wholey, the son of a gamekeeper at Crookhill Park, once a country house, but in those days a care home and sanatorium for sufferers from tuberculosis. Ted had spent long weekends there; John's friends, like him two years older than Ted, remember the lengths Ted went to, the birds he shot and let decompose on a pile of corpses, to breed huge maggots for bait. The focused ingenious amorality of boys.

Now his Cambridge nights revisited, reclaimed, overwrote those days. In these dreams, in the years when writing had replaced fishing, he sometimes caught pike. That meant good contact with himself. The larger the pike he caught in his dreams, the better the contact. Sometimes the pond or canal was lined with concrete, and then he caught nothing: poor contact with himself.

Ted believed in dreams. So did his mother, Edith, and Olwyn, two years his elder. They'd shared them, interpreted them. A family habit.

So now, in February 1957, Ted told Gerald of all this, and of one dream in particular. That night he was back at Crookhill and fishing from the corner near the outflow when he caught 'the grandfather pike'. Johnny Wholey was there, and so was Gerald, 'pulling at its fins', and Ted was heaving it down the slope, and between them they had twenty feet of pike out, but most of it was still in the pond. And the next morning he sold his first poem and married Sylvia. They married in London on the morning of 16 June 1956. Bloom's Day, the day on which James Joyce's Leopold Bloom wandered Dublin, the day *Ulysses* unfolds. But also, in Britain, the first day of the coarse fishing season, when the fish that have spent the early spring spawning have recovered, no longer need protection from anglers and their bait.

Three things he didn't tell Gerald in that letter.

First, that he'd told Sylvia this dream, just as he had another of his Cambridge dreams. In that one, which he'd had in his second spring there, 1953, a burning fox, standing erect, man-size, had rounded the door, come down the three steps into his bedsitting room, walked across to his desk, where he'd been sitting up till two, failing to write an essay – he was studying English literature – and told him, 'Stop this. You are destroying us.' Then put a bleeding, charred paw on the page. He'd taken this dream seriously. Acted on it. Abandoned the study of literature, switched to anthropology instead.

Second, Ted didn't tell his brother what his new bride had done with these two dreams. It was in October, when they were living apart during the week, Sylvia studying in Cambridge, Ted in London. She'd poached them. Or, as she told him, 'shamelessly plagiarized them', popped them into a single paragraph of a 'terrible humorous little story' about young American newly-weds, Harold and Agnes. Even if you don't know where this story would lead, it makes you shiver.

Harold and Agnes have been married as long as Ted and Sylvia had, three months. By then, the amusement Agnes had first felt, when she discovered Harold's rich and vivid dream life on their wedding night, has become a 'strange jealousy', which has 'been growing on her like some dark, malignant cancer ever since'. Long gone are her own 'fertile childhood days', when, in her seventh year, she dreamed of 'a wishing box land above the clouds where wishing boxes grew on trees', where you could pick a box and the dream came true. Now her own infrequent nightmares are dark landscapes peopled with ominous unrecognisable figures, who fade as she wakes. How can she tell Harold this? How can she compete with the story of his own burned fox?

Harold's fox is not quite the real thing, not Ted's. Once, in the troubled times before they met and married, he'd dreamed of it running through his kitchen; now, in the more auspicious days of their marriage, it returns, miraculously healed, bringing him a bottle of permanent ink. (Her private joke: a tribute to the poem Ted had written, one snowy night in London months before he met Sylvia, inspired by his dream, and other encounters with foxes in his Yorkshire childhood. 'The Thought-Fox'.)

Harold's version of Ted's pike dream is not quite the real thing either. It – he – is too big, too old, to be true. Harold tells Agnes one sultry August morning, 'There was this pond, where my cousin Albert and I used to fish; it was chock full of pike.' Last night he'd caught 'the most enormous pike you could imagine – it must have been the great-great-grandfather of all the rest; I pulled and pulled and pulled, and still he kept coming out of the pond.' Harold's pike is two generations older, and even more male, than Ted's. But it's not just the pike that's swelled. Agnes's resentment grows too. She seeks distraction, consolation, in books, then TV, then alcohol, sleeping pills. The story does not end well.

The third thing Ted did not tell Gerald may have been what made him write that letter. Two weeks before, in January 1957, Sylvia had published her story, 'The Wishing Box'; it appeared in *Granta*, the leading Cambridge student literary magazine, five pages from David Wevill's first published poem. That month, Assia Lipsley, who had just met him on the transatlantic crossing from New York, was telling her second husband one thing while spending the weekends with David in his college room. And, whatever else they were doing, reading.

*

August 1958. An afternoon in Elm Street, Northampton, Massachusetts, where Sylvia has spent the academic year teaching literature at her alma mater, Smith College. Ted's been doing a bit, too, for another university. And his first book of poems has met with great success. But he's been here on her terms, and is far from home. He brings it back, now, brings it up, not the pond that American husband Harold fished with his cousin, not what Sylvia had done with it, but his: 'A pond I fished.' 'It was as deep as England.' And the pike, too: not chock-full, because he's seen with his own eyes how even small pike keep each other in check. He and Johnny have kept three baby pike, new that summer, in a tank, watched the three become two become one killer's grin, one sagging belly. Big pike are as bad. In the children's encyclopedia he'd read in those war years – his father's newsagency sold its monthly instalments – an entry on the pike mentions two Loch Tay six-pounders found in the 1920s, one rammed past the gullet down the jaws of another. Both dead. That goes into his poem, too. And then the ones you can't catch, 'So immense and old' that, fishing alone – 'A pond *I* fished' – he could barely cast for them. And it ends in growing darkness, the sense that he's being watched by one of these monsters; the harder he listens for owls in the darkening woods, the more he knows he can't resist the dream that 'darkness beneath night's darkness had freed'. He can only imagine the eye that moves, the eye that watches him, rising towards him.

That's the poem, the fish, the pond he catches, and keeps, in *Lupercal*, and then, in October 1961, reads in the first of his broadcasts for eleven- to thirteen-year-olds. 'Pike' was the poem that had caught Moira Doolan's eye, made her approach him. It had grown so directly from observation and experience, she said. And was simpler than the other poem she admired, 'An Otter'.

So he shared it now: the feeling he'd like to go pike fishing again, in circumstances when a real fishing trip wasn't possible; the intense summer heat, huge pike out there under the surface like logs, under the lilies. All this he opens to classroom after classroom of rapt children and their teachers that first October in Devon. And he adds the other poem of his dreams, too: 'The Thought-Fox'. Though, of course, he mentions neither dream, nor the darkness beyond night's darkness that had already freed them into an unnerving uncontrollable existence beyond him.

Even before that visit the following May, that curious fertile human pike's eye in Assia's own story of her, or Sylvia's, or his own dream, his words came back to bite him.

The broadcast went out on the first Friday in October 1961, their first Devon autumn, three days after he'd gone up to London to record it. Three weeks later, on 27 October, Sylvia's birthday, Moira Doolan reported that a teacher and his class in a Gloucestershire school had identified the pond in 'Pike'. It was in Woodchester, near Stroud. She didn't suppose it was; still, might he let her know? He didn't. Thirty-five years later, he told a friend of mine who was planning a tour of Hughes country that the location of that pond was still 'classified secret'.

*

And now it's October again, 9 October 1962, and Moira Doolan is writing to him once more. She'd like another script he's just sent her to appear in the little pamphlet for *Listening and Writing* that will accompany the programme, scheduled for the following spring. It's about 'Learning to Think'. But it's also about fishing. And 'the fishing is perfect', she tells him. But she's troubled: won't the parts about thinking, the kind that goes on all the time in everyone's heads, more or less unknown to most of us, and then the skill you have to learn, the raid, the ambush, you need to make to access that world of imagination, final reality: won't all that be too hard for his young audience? While, yes, she agrees with him that children do apprehend more than they comprehend, don't children of that age feel before they think? At any rate, she needs the final text in ten days' time.

On 9 October Ted was at Court Green. But only to pack his bags, reveal his awkwardness with the children, baby Nicholas in particular: once Ted managed not to strap him into his cot, and he'd fallen, hitting his head on the new hard concrete floor. These were dark days, after dark months, of all kinds of wounding wildness, in and beyond words. The kiss on 19 May had not, when Assia told David, troubled her husband too much; friends flirt. But by Friday 13 July, David, in London, knew he'd been jilted, and between suicidal despair and rage at what Assia told him of her new lover's behaviour set off across the city with a knife, turned back, then took an overdose; after having his stomach pumped David threatened to kill Ted if he came near his wife again. In Court Green, Sylvia knew, too: 'The virginity of [their] marriage' was over. She'd gone up into Ted's study, found a beautiful poem she knew was about Assia, and letters, too. These she burned. Wrote a poem of her own: 'Burning the Letters'. No longer would the hooks of the letters in Ted's sloping hand, written under that dark thatch, be there to catch her, and she wouldn't 'be strung just under the surface, Dumb fish / With one tin eye'. But her words give her away: the glint of that 'tin eye', the envy at her rival's giant pike, its eye golden.

*

For the moment, for weeks, months, that summer and autumn of 1962, of Assia, they had all lived with this, in the aftermath. Ted and Sylvia kept up a front, without making peace, in the weeks that followed. Ted had returned from London; they'd travelled, in early September, to stay in Connemara with a mutual friend, the poet Richard Murphy, who sailed a Galway hooker and sold fish. Their unease was plain enough to him. He'd taken them to Yeats's tower, Thoor Ballylee. Even today along better roads it's a good two hours each way; in Richard's little van on the long journey that day, Sylvia talked openly to him about marriage and divorce, while, braced in the back, Ted talked to Richard's crew, a fifteen-year-old lad called Seamus Coyne, about poaching and guns and fishing. Tensions grew. Sylvia flirted with Richard, rubbing his leg under the dining table on the Friday evening; then, on the

Saturday, returning from a morning on the boat he sailed for a living, Richard found Sylvia alone. She told him Ted had left that morning, to go fishing for salmon and trout with the painter Barrie Cooke, in Co. Clare.

Really? There are times, I guess, where to the person who doesn't fish, or the spurned wife, going fishing is code for something even more improper. Delicate business. And in letters she wrote on her return to Court Green, alone, deserted, it had become grouse shooting, and then unspecified absence. It meant, of course, they all meant, she meant: Assia.

But Ted did visit Barrie Cooke. They'd met at least once before, in London, when they'd gone to the zoo together; later, a friendship forming, they'd traded notes about their close encounters with big beasts. Barrie had seen tigers mating in Dublin Zoo; a lion had urinated on Ted. Ted wins. They didn't go grouse shooting. Instead, Barrie took him up on the extraordinary limestone plateau of the Burren, to a lake Barrie had known since he'd moved to the banks of the River Fergus, at Kilnaboy, six years before.

Fishing had taken him there; fishing and poetry. Barrie, born in Cheshire, moved to America as a teenager, and studied. At Harvard, where he'd gone to study zoology but fell in love with painting, he had come under the wing of the Irishman Jack Sweeney, who lectured in English and ran the Woodbery Poetry Room. Sweeney was a native of Co. Clare, and in 1954, when the young wandering artist had returned to his English roots and found them withered, Sweeney suggested Ireland instead. He'd given Barrie very specific instructions. He was to go to Dublin's best fishing-tackle shop, Garnett and Keegan's on Parliament Street, and ask its entomologist director J. R. Harris for advice. Where was the best trout fishing in Ireland? Harris had spread out a map on the counter and marked the Fergus below Kilnaboy. Barrie at once rode across Ireland on his motorbike, and it was the local man, Cory Kelleher, on whose floor Barrie had slept in his sleeping bag, which he'd wrapped around his rod on his journey west, who pointed him to a near-derelict cottage in a field behind the old church as somewhere he could live, if he must.

Cory Kelleher was a teacher and keen wildfowler, who introduced Barrie to this lake, Loch Gealáin. Cory and a friend became the subjects of one of Barrie's first portraits; it was following Cory's son Declan's advice that I discovered it.

Sweeney had Clare blood in him; there were family roots in Corofin, the next village. He and his wife Maire McNeill, a historian and folklorist of Celtic Ireland, bought a summer place there on Lough Inchiquin. Their friendship deepened, then opened another. In 1958, Jack recorded Ted and Sylvia's poetry – they'd first read at the Woodbery room – and sent Barrie a recording. It was Jack Sweeney to whom Sylvia wrote about their move to Devon, the Taw thick with fish.

So now Barrie inducted Ted to his own dreamland, the skills he'd learned there. They lay in slots of rock at dusk as the geese flew in to roost from their watering grounds and heard their unearthly call, yards away, from the margins of Loch Gealáin. Barrie must have told him its English meaning: the Lake of the Flesh. Those slots became folds of ancient skin.

They did more. Barrie showed him more stone flesh: one Sheela-na-gig, an old crude Celtic fertility symbol, the wizened figure of a woman, primitive fingers between splayed legs, 'pulling herself wide open', in a carving on the wall of the ruined Kilnaboy old church; they'd have seen another at Bunratty Castle en route from Barrie's new house at Quin to the Shannon and then on to the Mulcair River, on the Limerick–Tipperary border, where they did go fishing. And in between, Barrie showed him his paintings. He'd been producing his own Sheelas, exhibiting them: a shock for Catholic Dublin in the sixties.

All of this, Barrie wrote to Jack Sweeney at about the time that Moira Doolan was writing to Ted, in mid-October – all his terrain, all his own concerns, 'the Kilnaboy Venus', the fish, the Burren, his art, Ted understood 'without need for explanation'.

Not at the time, maybe. Some male friendships depend on companionable silences; many fishing friendships do. But both Ted and Barrie knew that this one went further, deeper. During the day and the night and the day of that visit, visions had been glimpsed, wild energies tapped; plans were hatching for the future. So more needed to be said, on both sides.

Ted first. He wrote to Barrie and Harriet to thank them for their hospitality. And some of it was as the guilty father, however much businesslike briskness masked it. He hoped Harriet, as a New Yorker whom marriage had landed in Ireland's rural west, might be in a position to help Sylvia, who was taking her life and her writing into her own hands. She wanted to rent a place in Connemara for the winter. Might Harriet find a young girl, to help with childcare? No question of him being there to do it himself.

But mostly he was writing for Barrie alone, and I need the fisherman in me to decode what he's saying. Whatever else he'd said, or avoided saying, about the past days and weeks, 'The only horror was that terrible crack on the Shannon'. So: he'd managed to break his friend's rod. A cack-handed cast, I'm guessing, as he wielded a fly rod for the first time: it's timing, not brute force.

And until he could lay his hands on some lengths of greenheart to replace them – Barrie was already an expert rod builder, as well as a knowledgeable fly fisherman, who for years had supplemented his income from paintings by selling articles to the angling press – here were what Ted could offer him in the meantime. Some recent poems, even if, he said, 'I feel I haven't disgorged anything of what's to be got out.' Something altogether more visceral than works in progress. (And I think: Barrie must have shown him what he did with the first fish of the day on the fly. Once the hook's out you slide a special spoon down its gullet, twist, withdraw its most recent meal, so you can match your artificial fly to what's been on the menu.) Ted wanted to show at least he was fishing in the same water. One of them's called 'Sugarloaf': he'd written it about a pure stream running off a snow-dusted Calderdale fell, but it's a perfect fit for the Burren mountain they crouched below that dusk waiting for the geese, the stream that was running off and eating through its limestone.

But Ted knows he's got much deeper to go. He knows this because he's spent time in Barrie's studio. Stared into his friend's radically unconventional paintings of water. Barrie's method, one leading Dublin reviewer has noted, is 'to wash on his paint in wide brush-strokes and to mingle green, blue and tones of grey until his paint begins to reveal another language of ideas than that first inspired by his contemplation at the side of streams ... not to create formal images, but to evoke the dream world which lies halfway between what we understand and what we yearn for.' Another of the poems Ted sent Barrie, 'Fishing at Dawn', seems to have arisen from this world. Where 'God yawns onto the black water', Ted's kind of angler – never more the fisher*man* – imagines shapes in the mist that beckon and chill: 'risen virginity / Of many a tough hag'. Could anyone dare to publish that poem now?

Perhaps that's why it's the nudes Barrie has been painting that really stay with Ted, strike deep. They have 'real mana', Ted tells him. 'A vital object – such as a fish or a woman – seems to bring quite a different painter out of you than your subtler subjects.'

Harriet was Barrie's model. Did she ever read this, know Ted's sense of her place in the world, after fish? If she did, was it anything she hadn't already come to realise from living with Barrie? And then I think of Sylvia, and the line Ted would write, in all tenderness, looking back over decades, about the revelation of his first night with Sylvia in her vulnerable nakedness: 'You were slim and lithe and smooth as a fish.'

But then I look again at what he says these paintings caught and released, for the painter they'd changed, and for him, viewing them. 'Real mana.'

Eventually that phrase eats into my limestone brain. Stirs a memory in me. I trace its source. It's in an essay Ted would write early in 1983, his first task after finishing *River*. The previous August he and Carol had just visited Mexico for a literary festival – they celebrated his fifty-second birthday there, and paid a visit to the Anthropological Museum in Mexico City. There he saw 'the colossal, horrendous Aztec mother and earth Goddess Coatlicue'. One hundred and fifty tons of stone carvings, and terrifying. But fertile, too. And at once female and rock-hard: 'She is a demonic lump of *mana* .... It is the very image of *mana*, the embodiment of pure *mana*. *Mana* as the goddess of the source of terrible life, the real substance of any art that has substance, in spite of what we'd prefer.'

Mana comes at a cost. 'It has to be paid for.' Sometimes, he added, sharing what he called, then, a 'curious circumstance', 'a technical discovery': 'deliberately self-inflicted suffering will buy mana.'

Self-inflicted suffering. Not to mention the suffering you inflict on others. I'm back in 1962. Barrie's art, Ted's response to it. That suffering's nowhere here. All that matters now is the source of the strange life Barrie's discovered, and made flow, somehow, in the Burren, in Coatlicue's wizened little stone-cold Irish cousin, the 'Kilnaboy Venus'. Now Ted wants some of it. He has 'a good mind to call my next book Shiela na gig [sic], with a huge reproduction on the cover'.

*

Barrie was electrified by Ted's visit. They had 'a lot in common', he told Jack Sweeney. Their families, of course: each had an American wife struggling to adjust to the country life of her husband's element; they each had two young children. And part of him wanted to believe that their friendship might be of the rounded sort, however unlikely that must have seemed. He told Jack that the two families might spend Christmas together.

But far more important than that was the two men's shared vision. Even though Barrie also knew where he fell short – 'there is a wide gap of sheer intellectual imagination' – he'd felt the energy in the time they'd spent together, and not just in the compliment Ted had paid him. His visit had left him excited, invigorated, confirmed. 'I quite honestly cannot imagine myself dying which sounds a very silly and childish thing to say. I hope I'll live to 90 and die playing a big salmon. Quite possibly I will. I intend to.'

Barrie Cooke was eighty-one when I first met him, in May 2012, at his cottage and studio where he lived, alone, painting, reading, above Lough Arrow in Co. Sligo. He was becoming frail. He'd given up fishing; the hope I had, from some of Ted's diaries I was still just getting to know, that we might fish together for trout on the lough – mayflies were dancing, and I'd packed my little six-piece smuggler rod, just in case – came to nothing. And he didn't remember much of this, or share it. Why would he? He barely knew me, then. But he loved Ted. And when he told me the sound those geese made as they lay silently in those slots of Burren limestone the hairs on the backs of my hands rose. He stood outside on the gravel round his house and pissed, entirely unselfconsciously, as we talked. He took me up onto the heights at Carrowkeel, across the lough, where he said he'd taken Ted and Nick – he loved Nick, too, missed them both – when they visited him, in 1992; he made sure I crawled into the passage tombs there, 5000 BC, because they had. I lasted a couple of minutes, nervous for my host, waiting down below; Ted and Nick stayed an hour, I later discovered. Ted found a rare thing there: he was 'completely happy' in that darkness. And then Barrie took me to Yeats's grave at Drumcliff, stood on it, poked his stick at the epitaph. 'Cast a cold Eye / On Life, on Death'. He let me buy, and watch him consume, two huge slices of cake in the coffee shop. I did too: delicious! And naughty. Barrie: his father had named him for the creator of Peter Pan, and he knew he was a boy who never grew up.

Was that self-indulgence or devotion, I've wondered often, since, about a man just a couple of years younger than my own father. The choices he made, about his compulsions. In the days after the birth of Julia, his second daughter, a year older than Nick, Barrie was beside himself, and not just with joy. The dilemma still speaks from another letter to Jack Sweeney. Someone, he complains, has brought him a beautiful rain-grey heron, a fresh corpse, to paint, but the routines of family and the demands they make of him are mud he has to wade through, and now the heron is beginning to smell.

Reading this makes me recast a memory of that first meeting with him. Barrie was living alone, hours north and west of his three daughters. At eighty-one, he may have swapped a salmon river for a trout lough. But he had his fishing rods, his paintings, his books, for company. There was even one of his earliest muddy three-dimensional Sheela-na-gigs on the wall at the foot of his bed. He took me into his bedroom because he wanted to show me his method of slow cooking, a trick he'd learned in Sarawak from months he spent living with a tribe in 1975: leave the pot he'd started on the stove under his duvet while we went to Carrowkeel. Barrie was glad I recognised her, that Sheela. More hag than dawn virgin, but fertile, made with river gravel. Legs rising from the canvas, too, either side of the muddy flow. But he made nothing more of it, was more interested in the pot under the duvet. When we returned from Carrowkeel he fished it out, a rice dish, perfectly done; we ate it off plates of his own design, a nude woman, legs apart. And he took me into his studio: he was still painting the pictures he wanted to paint, still faithful to decisions, or at least to inclinations, instincts, ideas, priorities and the consequences that flowed from them; he was still living that life.

What choices did Barrie make that my own dad, a family man, a family doctor, in 1962 with three young sons of his own, did not, could not? What choices was Ted making, at thirty-two, that wild summer and autumn?

Barrie's letter to Jack Sweeney about those memorable days on and in and south of the Burren, that September, answered my half-formed questions. He thanked Jack for introducing him to Ted's poetry. He made the words *do* things, be things. Some of the poems Ted had just sent him took time for their meaning to match their sound, but then, suddenly, one evening, after a few drinks, they seared into light. But he thanked him, too, for Ted Hughes the man. It wasn't just the intuition Ted showed in responding to Barrie's passions, places. It was his intensity. 'His intensity is literally frightening.' Not in some cliché of Romantic wildness.

I mean his ruthless search to expose himself. He is quite dedicated to extracting everything out of himself and that doesn't just mean ART. He's also the only person I've met yet who is as serious as myself about IT. Maybe more, to be honest – perhaps that's why he is disturbing. He is more ruthless than me by far and that I find terribly admirable.

Barrie himself would do a lot to save 'IT', he told Jack, if driven to it. But the man he'd just spent two days driving around Co.

Clare was something, somewhere else. 'Ted will make the move before being driven to the edge – and so save valuable time.'

'IT'? Sounds mysterious, opaque. Could it have been *mana*, I wonder? That terrible vital energy he felt in himself and wanted in his art and was already prepared to pay anything for? Whatever it was, Ted did what Barrie said. After leaving Barrie in the Burren, he wasted no time, made the move, seized the first opportunity he had. And it wasn't a breakthrough poem. That would take him years more. Nor was it a vision of a boy-who'd-never-grow-up old age beside a salmon river. Instead, he looked back. Opened his own childhood, in that script for Moira Doolan at the BBC and that audience of eleven- to thirteen-year-old schoolchildren. In those extraordinary rootless, ruthless, searching days of late September and early October, days when his marriage was falling apart, days of abandonment and discovery, or rediscovery, days of secrecy and exposure, that's what came to him. He wrote it swiftly out, in paragraphs that people, ever since, have mistaken for inspiring analogy. Five minutes was all it took to read aloud. But hundreds of hours had gone into the secret, from his own deep past, the lifeline connecting that past with his swirling adult present, which he was about to share. Sharing it made it his own again. He was reclaiming possession.

*

All of us think, all the time, in our own way, he told his young audience. 'Thinking is as natural as breathing; some sort of thinking in general's going on in us all the time.' But this thinking tends to be elusive. It had been for him. He'd been 'plagued', at school, by the idea that he had better ideas than he could ever get into words. When he tried to speak or write those ideas down, they'd simply vanished. A 'numb blank feeling' came instead. But an interest in these thoughts grew, these 'thoughts I could never catch'. Occasionally, in writing school essays, 'I got the tail end of one', but that wasn't enough. 'I couldn't fish them up when I wanted them.' Most people have these thoughts – a flash and they're gone. But if that's all they do, their minds themselves are out of reach. And that's a serious loss indeed, because this 'inner life of thought' is 'our world of final reality'. It's 'a world of memory, emotion, feeling, imagination, intelligence, and natural common sense', 'which goes on all the time, consciously or unconsciously, like the heart beat'. Ted knew, from his own recent heart troubles, that you couldn't rely on that. So we must find a way of breaking into this hidden inner world. That is the 'thinking process', a means of raiding, or persuading, or ambushing, or doggedly hunting whatever it is that lies within or below our surface selves; we have to surrender them to it. Or, rather, learn whatever kind of skill or trick it is that enables us to catch those elusive or shadowy thoughts. 'If we don't learn it, then our minds lie in us like fish in the pond of a man who cannot fish.'

Ted hadn't been taught it in school. He'd learned it fishing. And this is where he looked back, hard, practised the skill he was sharing with his young listeners. Was a boy again. Younger, even, than his teenage summers at the end of the war, trying to catch pike. He looked back from the roaring Taw, the rushing salmon-rich Mulcair, and recalled: 'I fished in still water, with a float.'

He didn't say where, didn't devote his lines, as he had before, to describing Crookhill, and so exposing himself to the risk that someone else would claim his pond was theirs. He just recalled the 'hundreds and hundreds of hours' he'd spent staring at a float, orange or yellow, the size of a lentil; and, in recalling it, to recreate it, share it. He opened the wonder of it. 'Everyone knows' that fishing is a very drowsy pastime. Not any more. 'Your whole being rests' upon that float, imagines what's beneath it, concentrates so completely on it that you enter, through your imagination, the world of beauty hidden below the surface, and itself suspended in complete ignorance of you, up there.

Except you are no longer up there. You have entered 'one of the orders of bliss'. And the fish, in the darkness below, have entered you. As moments pass, your imagination 'is alarming itself with the size of the thing slowly leaving the weeds and approaching your bait'. But the alarm is part of why you engage in this perfectly, ruthlessly, rigorously designed mental exercise. It leaves no room for wider horizons, for anything but a mesmerised focus, there, on that lentil of a float. Nothing else matters; you are aware of nothing else. You know nothing else. That is the point, the float, and your attention on it.

> The whole purpose of this concentrated excitement, in this arena of apprehension and unforeseeable events, is to bring up some lovely solid thing like living metal from a world where nothing exists but those inevitable facts which raise life out of nothing and return it to nothing.

Unforeseeable events. Inevitable facts. What do you do in this arena, this moment? You deepen. You must. You keep fishing. For the fish, while the water holds them somewhere in its depths; for yourself.

*

May 1963. The latest issue of *Listening and Writing* magazine has been printed, distributed to schools; Ted has recorded his script three days before the Friday morning broadcast on the Home Service. The recording survives. You can hear nothing but the rapt, concentrated calm this mental exercise demands. It is compelling. It draws you in. Of course. Nothing else matters, nothing. And he's a professional writer: this is his living. And the trout season had come round again. I've often listened to it driving down to Devon to fish.

But still. Still.

In the autumn and winter just passed, terrible things have happened. October and November see Sylvia accelerating, too, finding a new self in her new fury. She finds it not in Ireland, as she'd hoped, but in Devon and then in London. The poems she writes from these months of separation will make her name, seal her immortality, survive her. But the mental illness she's had for much longer than she's known Ted, the dreams she's wrestled with and only now named, of fathers, husbands, mothers, won't stay within the poetry. Early in the morning of 11 February, in the flat she's found for herself and the children in a house where Yeats once lived, she gasses herself.

Unforeseeable events. Inevitable facts. Ted is his children's only parent. What does he do, what can he do, but stand against the current, and then keep wading, deepening, and find a way of taking them with him?

*

Saturday 12 October 2012. A friend is indisposed, and has asked me to stand in for him at a literary festival in Mytholmroyd.

I'm happy to. Excited, even. By then I've made an odd discovery, which has converted my growing interest in Ted and his work into something like a fall.

This morning I meet Donald Crossley. A year younger than Ted, he fished with him in the Rochdale Canal when they were four and five. When Ted republished *River* in 1993, he returned to this canal, which he'd written two poems about in the 1970s, in a general note. It was, he wrote, like 'a lifeline' to him. And since it's remained Donald's, too, he's been sharing it with pilgrims. Donald shows us the canal wall where Ted caught loaches, 'five inches huge'. Then, when he hears of my interest, my visits to the Torridge – Ted had taken him, sometime in the 1980s, he thinks – asks me to read another poem, about a four-pound trout that leapt from the water under the long tunnel ceiling of the Burnley Road bridge and into Ted's memory, haunting him faithfully for forty-five years at least. Later, Donald comes to my talk.

When, twelve years after leaving Mytholmroyd for Mexborough, Ted Hughes had gone to Cambridge, he studied in the college where I now teach. It's a residential community, with some 200 rooms on the main site. When I arrived there, in 1992, I was given an office above the bar, looking out over the car park. It was a large, darkish room, and mine for five years.

I began to wonder about the other dream Sylvia confessed to having 'shamelessly plagiarized', of the burned fox. Ted spoke about it often, when he read the poem it inspired, 'The Thought-Fox'. He wrote out the story, 'as it really happened', in a letter to the critic Keith Sagar in 1979. Then wrote his own account again after he revised *River*, in 1993. I noticed two common elements in all these versions. One was what the burning fox-man told him as he placed that bleeding paw on the page: 'Stop this – you are destroying us.' The other was that the fox had come round the door and down the two or three steps into the room. My old office had those steps, too; I checked, and discovered that the room he'd told his critic friend was his, in another part of college, did not. And then I found another leather-bound volume, another book not intended for readers: the room register. He'd been laying a false trail to his critic friend, throwing him off his own scent. I couldn't help but know otherwise. His steps had become mine. Forty years apart, Ted and I had shared a room.

Donald seeks me out afterwards. Those years with Ted have sustained him. He wants me to find out more. He writes to me, sends me newspaper clippings. Ted and the fox. Keep going, he's telling me.

So I do. That afternoon the drive home takes me down the A1, within a mile or two of Mexborough, and Crookhill Park. It's a golf club now. The Wholeys' gate lodge is long gone. But I find the pond between the fairways, and am glad I hadn't brought my rod. It's unfishable. Clogged. Rushes, silt, Coke bottles, and a discarded golf buggy near the outflow.

But still I made a detour, one June evening – it was the 16th – on another journey north, to be at Crookhill pond in the failing dusk. I stood as night fell, listening in vain for owls hushing the woods over the rumble of lorries up the dual carriageway, then took two pictures. One was all blur; the other, with flash, could have been of an uncut hayfield.

One March, I went to Mexborough, too. The River Don never stood a chance in the days Ted knew it: draining the industrial belt of South Yorkshire, it was 'a river of such concentrated steaming, foaming poisons, that an accidental ducking was said to be fatal'. But there was hope on the other side of the river, once he'd caught the ferry safely over it to his hunting ground of Manor Farm. 'My lifeline there,' Ted's note in *River* goes on, 'was an old ox-bow of the Don, full of fish and waterfowl.' Then, one day '(early 1940s)' – when he was eleven or twelve, the age of his listeners: the age he'd made himself, and the method he'd remembered, in showing them how and what he saw, thought, imagined, still – he saw all those fish gasping at the surface. The first silage, stored in the farm barns he'd raked for mice, had seeped, a ruddy sharp-smelling vein, into a connecting drainage ditch. It was 'the beginning of the end, as it turned out', for that wild water, those wild fish. Ponds, streams, rivers without fish were like a home robbed of its inhabitants; they communicate 'one of the ultimate horrors'.

Horrors can pass. That oxbow is a going concern again, a commercial operation. The owners have split its half-moon in half again; both are now well-stocked match water. Ferryboat Fishery. One day I'll fish there. I know I should. But it's not what it was. It's regained its fish but lost its wildness. The essence of that place, as of choked, clogged Crookhill, survives only in Ted's words. They have caught and kept it.

5

Headwaters

He's done all he can to avoid a return to Devon – moving into Sylvia's flat with the children, Frieda delighted to have Daddy back; putting Court Green on the market, only for the sale to fall through and with it a move back to West Yorkshire and a house he'd found close to his parents, themselves now back in Heptonstall. One night that August, Ted finds an older, younger self again, beside the others he's had to play these past months. He's back at Crookhill pond, for the first time in over two and a half years. And he's 'catching big fish' again: good.

Contact with himself was possible, even in these months juggling other selves. Single father, widower, son-in-law, a son, a brother, and, yes, off and on, a lover. Assia has been to and fro, with David and then with Ted; never moving into that tiny flat, whatever time they spent together. And up and down, too. Terribly: she'd had an abortion, and then suffered a miscarriage. Even if she knows who or what's responsible, how, in all this, can they not be thinking back to last May's dream pike with its golden eye turned weird throbbing womb? Perhaps that's why he catches 'big fish', why he doesn't say: pike.

That August night, something else has changed from the old Crookhill dreams. This time he's fishing not with the old still-water methods, the maggots that didn't work, the copper spoon that did. He wakes to record 'fishing with flies that bit me'. Barrie's influence, maybe: I can imagine him teasing Ted with what he'd got wrong in his pike fishing, and I bet he showed off his own prowess as a fly fisherman during that day on the Mulcair River the previous September. Was that what made Ted try too hard, crack the greenheart? Even then Barrie was an old hand at this stuff: he'd been tying flies, those confections of feather and fur and thread that look like the real natural thing to trout, since he was nine.

You can tell Ted's not. Dreams pun: they confuse, accuse. These flies weren't yet familiars, haven't yet settled on the hook. They're still biting, wounding him. How you fish, as well as what you catch, catches you.

Late that September he and the children move back into Court Green. Olwyn comes to live with them; Frieda, looking back from adulthood years later, will remember confusing aunt with mother. But as well as looking after the children, Olwyn looks after Ted. Begins to manage his literary affairs, as Sylvia had once done; just as he is beginning to face the task of preparing for publication Sylvia's poems of her last brilliant, furious months.

He casts about. Apart from one poem about the weeks after her death, hearing wolves howl in the night from the flat across Regent's Park from the zoo, verse doesn't come. But he has to keep writing; words are his living. He casts back, steps forward, finds a way of standing in the current: sells 'Stealing Trout on a May Morning' to the *New Yorker*; it's published in March 1964. Books he reviews offer versions of himself, his selves: Pushkin, Russian poet, the deep country self cohabiting with the literary metropolitan. He meets the creator of his own deep country dream world, Henry Williamson, still living in North Devon, at Georgeham, above the Taw estuary.

He keeps casting, experimenting, indirectly, floating thought experiments like lures to himself. A book on superstitions makes him wonder: what if we had some way of catching them? 'If, by some spectacular development of sensitive recording equipment, all these refreshed but really very ancient and widely shared superstitions were proved ... to be fact, what an entertaining place the world would become again.' He writes his own versions of the old stories, for children, *How the Whale Became*, now that Frieda and Nicholas are chattering away. And he casts further, deeper, finds more inspiration for what he's seeking, or what he's already found, and needs, now, more than ever. Here's a book on shamanism by Mircea Eliade, a survey of Siberian and Arctic spirit healers. They've had their own share of spirit encounters. He tells his readers, in his review for the *Listener*, what shamanism is: 'a technique of moving in a state of ecstasy among the various spiritual realms, and for generally dealing with souls and spirits, in a practical way, in some practical crisis.' These spirits can sometimes rear in 'the freezing river, the clashing rocks'; once you've had that encounter, 'been chosen by the spirits, you must shamanize or die'. Again, 'the shamans seem to undergo, at will and with phenomenal intensity, and with practical results, one of the main regenerating dramas of the human psyche: the fundamental poetic event'.

All this makes me think of Ted at first light flashing his minnow on the Taw, the souls and spirits of the night tearing at him, him standing firm against the current, striding on, upstream, in stolen ecstasy, deepening, finding reality.

*

Another year has turned. It's June 1965. The 16th. Their ninth anniversary, it would have been. The day when game and coarse seasons align; anything's possible. Sylvia's book of poems, *Ariel*, which he's edited, has been out in the world three months. So has little Shura, Assia's daughter – their daughter, he will accept: but mother and baby are in London, and he and Olwyn and the older children are all still in Devon. Sometime this month, he and Assia will travel to Italy, leaving Shura with David. All this turbulence smoothed by the BBC schedule, buried in the announcement in *Radio Times*: 'Ted Hughes introduces and reads this poem which he has recently written.'

And then he speaks. And immediately this is more than a poetry reading. It's a manifesto. A defence. He speaks of the oldest, most vital passion, 'a very necessary passion'. A passion as old as life, and death, itself; little single-celled organisms and 'the mildest vegetarian' all feel it in some form, however disguised. 'This passion to pursue, capture, and kill and eat has created all the creatures on earth.' Civilisation, the competitiveness and other challenges of work and other pastimes might contain or frustrate the old hunting instinct, the bodily need to hunt that has been designed and refined over millions of years. But it's still there; without it, life would be impossible to live.

The activity in which it survives in purest form, this passion, this excitement, is fishing. But not just any fishing. Civilisation has freed us from the need to kill, and the danger that as hunters we might also be the hunted. We have learned to acknowledge the victim's pain, too: and that refinement dilutes the old excitement. And while it's true that it's still powerful stuff, still regenerates and re-energises the man who's been on a fishing holiday, that carefully arranged contact with the wild still falls short. No: 'to make the situation perfect' you need to restore that old element of danger, of vital challenge, 'the track, the tracking, the stalking, the attack'. Fishing needs to become poaching.

> I've done quite a bit of poaching in my time, and while we're poaching we're hunting the game, but we're being hunted by the keepers of the game. Those occasions stay with me as some of my most interesting memories. They go deep, those moments – and as with all other deeply natural moments they become immediate poetic experience. A special alertness; a listening apprehension; an ancient kind of excitement; the pursuit of something hidden – these are all phrases that define both poaching and the composition of poetry.

And then he records 'an occasion when the two, for me, became one'. That May dawn on the Taw, 'Stealing Trout'.

It has become non-negotiable. He needs this excitement, which will stay in us as long as we stay in our bodies. When he writes to Assia in late August, setting the conditions, house rules, she'll need to observe if she's to share his crowded life, and the children's, in Devon, this talk is still in his head, the one he mentions having to type in his account of a typical day. It's 'about how poetry is crime, and why theft is poetical, with poetical illustrations', he tells her. But – his point – she has to understand he needs to keep stealing. Which means: deepening, fishing, exposing himself to risk, alone.

It also means: finding a place, and a way of life, where this is possible.

He's been there before. That November he writes to Gerald in Australia. He's taking the kids to Ireland, where 'the life flows unselfconsciously in people and with lots of freedom. Also, fishing and shooting are at the dead centre of the visual field.' Who else is he thinking of, here, but Barrie? But he also needs space. Richard Murphy, his and Sylvia's host in that week in Connemara three years before, who will recognise Assia's beauty from her own earlier visit to Cleggan, has found them a house the newly enlarged family can rent on the southern coast, at Cashel. Doonreagan.

They travel out in January 1966; the month, incidentally, of my own birth. But the life has already started flowing in him with a freedom he will never forget. On the eve of their departure, Ted finds himself high on the upper Taw, on the northern flanks of Dartmoor, fifteen minutes but a world away from North Tawton. He's walking back downstream. No plotted fields here, just the huge wide bowl of Taw Marsh. He's been close to the source, up at Taw Head, just over the bleak ridge from Cranmere Pool, where the Dart rises. Just to the east of the source of the East Okement. Tarka the otter had ranged this high up one winter. Ted will never forget this place, this moorland river. And in January, too, the winter rains will have swelled its flow.

In his dream he comes to falls; the river tumbles over a cliff, which he climbs down. And then this little moorland river meets, or becomes, a much broader river, and at the foot of the cliffs it's full of huge leaping salmon. They're excited by the flow. Their whole bodies leap clear, come clear, of the water, doing their heroic impossible best to drive on up in their quest to spawn, relishing that oxygenated rush of fresh water. And as they leap they writhe, as they do up a weir, and release eggs and milt, mid-air, as they don't; Ted, watching from the bank, close by, is plastered in this thick of life. Covered, 'completely'.

Ted told two fishermen late in his life – one of them a Canadian journalist, and Nick – that that was the moment when salmon replaced pike as his totem. How, after that, could they not? How could *River* not bear the traces of this dream, be driven by it? And by something else, too, which Nick would understand as some Pacific West Coaster could not: 'Influence of Taw.' But even more than that, Ted came to understand, and told Nick now, how this dream, and the move it heralded, 'with a single stride plunged me right into the productive, fruitful thick of my best chances'.

It was seminal, wading deep in the water of life, and more than water.

*

And it worked. The dream stayed with him. The dream and the new waters he encountered in the Irish west came together, as the little Taw had joined that swift river. The life flowed. As Frieda, almost forty years on, remembered, 'Ireland had fish in it'. Not, yet, salmon, it has to be said. They arrived in January, had moved on in April, weeks too early in the year for the first of the salmon that, just twenty minutes' drive around the wrinkled coast, still enter the Owenmore, swim up past Ballynahinch Castle in good numbers from May, in fine numbers in July: he never fished it, and Ballynahinch would tantalise him for years. But Frieda does remember trout, cooked beside a woodland river, 'their pink flesh steaming'.

There's a reason why she remembers this. Ted went out of his way to expose them to it. There was something mad, wild, about how far he went to co-opt them. In their final week at Doonreagan, he drove west to one of the larger lakes across bleak miles of Connemara bogland. Fadda was a terrible, eerie, lonely place, where locals had seen a monster – 'one of the Plesiosaur type that are in Loch Ness'. The wind blew, hail fell, 'the mountains rose up & sank down', and 'there were three concentric rainbows' as he finally caught a little sea-trout of half a pound. A rainbow for each of the party: 'Took F & N', he told Gerald.

And Frieda remembered the move that followed, when that lease ran out and Richard Murphy found them a place converted from the outbuildings at Cleggan Farm, around the bay from his own house, on the westernmost edge of Connemara. It was, for Ted, a 'mild paradise', which gave him the space and light to write, coming back to his broadcasts for children and turning them into a book. Poems, too.

But he also found time to fish in still water again. And to do what even he couldn't have risked on Lough Fadda. On their very first morning in their new place he left Assia and little Shura at the farm and took Frieda and Nick to a lake two miles beyond Cleggan. The road takes you past knots of houses on the headlands looking seaward, past rocky inlets and beaches and rough grassland whose yellows and oranges and blacks and faded greens are in my head now as I write. Lough Aughrisburg lies like some shallow crater just inland from the Atlantic, and all three times I've visited its surface has been somewhere between wrinkled and torn by the wind off the ocean. But that early April morning the wind had not got up. 'The lake was like glass.' It took only an hour. Ted caught three trout, all of them bigger than that Taw beauty. These had a different symmetry: the first and last weighed a pound and a half; the middle one, at three and a half pounds, 'the biggest trout I've ever seen alive. I've let the children hold the rod each time, to arouse any dormant passion for the art they may have. Frieda thinks it's cruel', he notes: I'm guessing that she saw all three dead as well as alive. Then adds in the margins, '(but she's quite keen). Nicky is very keen.'

Nicky. He was just four. I envy him the wakening, the stirring of that dormant passion early that morning on glassy Aughrisburg. I feel that moment with him, even as I feel sharply the gap between us. I wish, for all my father's generosity, the gift, when I was seventeen, the year of *River*, of that fishing course at the Arundell Arms, that he'd been there to do for me what Ted did for his children. Dad's generosity was enabling, but at second hand, a gesture of generosity to match the sailing courses on which he'd sent all three of my elder brothers. A fair equivalent. He drove the family miles, watched as his boys found their own ways with water; but then, exhausted from the drive, slept and stood back. He was a photographer; always the wrong side of the shutter. I never remember him alongside me as I fished.

And I envy them both the fish.

On my first visit I travelled west towards Lough Aughrisburg full of ambition – which trout fisherman wouldn't, with stories of wild fish that size to lead him? But a local man told me, the afternoon I'd fished, that generations of visiting anglers, coarse fishermen from France and Germany, had wanted fish in greater numbers. They'd introduced roach, perch. Which in turn ate trout's eggs. Half a century on, I knew my chances were slim; even supposing some old lunkers had survived, turned ferox. Trout aren't plesiosaurs. I did cast a nymph from a finger of rock that afternoon with an old soft-actioned beauty of a Bruce and Walker fly rod I'd bought online, having learned, earlier that spring, that Ted had a similar model. After ten minutes there was contact, a darting run. And, fully thirty seconds later, a glittering gilded miniature jewel had taken my nymph. A roach, of course.

Frieda came to envy Nick, too. I can see why.

During that glittering spring month at Cleggan, among the visitors they hosted were Barrie and Sonja, the Dutch potter he'd left Harriet and their two girls for, Sonja told me. They'd just moved to Kilkenny, and an old Georgian mill house called The Island, on, and sometimes in, the River Nore, above Thomastown. They had a baby daughter of their own. Aoine, just two months older than I am. It's a long way from Thomastown to Cleggan, even these days of EU-funded roads: Barrie must have come prepared. And he took Ted fishing on one of the local rivers, leaving the women and children. Barrie knew Connemara's rivers, the Corrigan, the Owenmore. Was not, himself, averse to poaching. In 1984 he'd orchestrate an illicit raiding party, Ted a part of it, on the least accessible pool of the Erriff, to the north – Richard Murphy, who'd been a riverwatcher there in his twenties, gave discreet advice: Dead Man's Hole. Ted cast a worm into slack water, caught a salmon, to another of the party's astonishment. And another day at Doolough, the black lake laced by the Bundorragha River on which Delphi Lodge still sits. Delphi's now an exclusive fishing lodge, but then, in 1984, it was a squat. Barrie, Ted and Paul caught so many sea-trout that day that they considered making an offer for the place.

Back home in North Devon that summer and autumn in 1966, on home waters, Barrie's influence blended with the Taw's. That afternoon on the river in Connemara had made him resolve to become a workaday fly fisherman himself, Ted told him; the Taw's twiggy corners held its own decent trout, and he was determined to learn how to manoeuvre in them. And Frieda remembers the warm evenings before Christmas at Court Green – Assia and Shura had finally moved in – a Christmas of new alliances, new exclusions:

> watching father and son tying flies
> And mother and daughter sticking paper
> Feathers to wings for angels,
> With my gooseberry eyes.

*

At some point in the 1960s Ted does start catching – 'poaching', his word for it, looking back on this years later, to days when the Taw was full of salmon parr, fingerlings – the odd salmon. In truth, the excitement is bigger than the fish. In 'Taw and Torridge' he'd write that most salmon fishermen – how could he not feel this, too, after that dream of those huge writhing fecund fish high on the Taw? – come to salmon fishing 'with their hopes pre-set for anything over 5 lb'. He'd confess to the efforts he went to in order to convince himself that the first sea-trout he ever caught, at two and a half pounds, was a salmon, then that 'the first salmon I ever caught did weigh only 3 lbs'. Outdone, both, by that Aughrisburg trout. More needs to happen before he can meet the fish, or at least the salmon, of his dreams.

*

Christmas 1968. Gerald is over for a visit. Ted takes him north. Their parents are frail, their mother only months from the end. The Hughes family's relationship with Assia is fraught. From Heptonstall, Ted takes Gerald to Mexborough, for old times' sake, and to put some distance on all this. Nicky, almost six himself now, comes with them. He brings a rod.

They visit Crookhill. It's a wreck. The Wholeys' lodge is a ruin, the garden a forest. And the pond, once 'fifty yards across', 'as deep as England'? A twenty-feet-wide 'basin of black mud', befouled with litter and discarded cans of oil. Nicky has a few casts in the poisoned-looking water. A sudden downpour sealed the horrible depression they all felt. It was time to say farewell, for good. One last back cast. So Ted took the rod, 'and there among the rubbish I hooked a huge perch. The biggest I ever caught. It was very weird, a complete dream.'

*

It's the following April. Barrie Cooke is at work in his studio on the first floor of The Island, a house other friends remember for the way it welcomes, breathes, the Nore that splits to flow around, and sometimes through, its garden and its Georgian walls. He has his priorities; he paints at a safe height from the floodwaters that leave salmon caught in the chicken wire with which he and Sonja have lined the pathways to protect Aoine, a toddler now. He's packing up pictures he has sold. An unexpected visitor: Ted. They work in companionable, practical silence together, wrapping then lowering the paintings through the slot in the floor. It takes hours. Only when the work is done does Ted break the news: less than a month before, Assia and Shura had been found dead in the kitchen of their Clapham flat, the oven door open, gas on. Ted stays the night, and then, Barrie tells Jack Sweeney, in a letter full of anguish for his warm, generous friend – not at all ruthless, he realises now – 'We fished all day.'

*

He worked, too. Of course he was writing through all this, trying to find a place in it to respond to that dream on the high Taw. His great black mythical masterpiece *Crow* had begun to form, come to itself in the flood of Ireland. It was chopped off by Assia and Shura's death. But when he brought it out, episodes *From the Life and Songs of the Crow*, a foul-mouthed sharp-eyed trickster who lives by his wits in an argument with God, you can see it if you look hard: a moment when that casting around in the years after Sylvia's death mixes with that raw power, the abundance salmon stood for. A gleam in a waterfall.

At Crow's lowest ebb, humbled before earth's elemental truths, a strange figure sings him back into energy with a series of songs about water. This figure is an Eskimo shaman, a guide to the animal spirits. He has exposed himself to their wisdom, suffered great pain and great insight, in dreams, so he can return to the human world with a life replenished by the three aboriginal animals he encountered there, 'In the beginning of beginning'. First he kills elk for the flesh, then bear for the heart. Then this man, hunter – 'Firstman', he's called in the published poems, but Ted had begun with 'Fisherman' – sees something even more precious:

> a salmon
> Slipping through walls of water. He caught it
> Ate its heart. But spared its eggs.

*

And now it's June 1971. Ted, Frieda and Nick return to Aughrisburg, with Carol, the children's young stepmother. They camp beside the Lough. Barrie doesn't join them, but he's had a hand in things. He's been writing with advice on sea-trout rivers they might try, and, seized by his own obsession to catch a huge pike, shares it: has even made Nick a wooden pike plug, which he's tried, knows it's worked. He points out the teeth marks of the fish it's already caught. Whatever this says, or doesn't know how to say, about his own relationship with his daughters, he tells Ted he wishes he had a son to fish with. Nick might be that son.

All this maybe makes the other Island, Barrie's home territory, on the Nore, too much to deal with. Its bone-searching damp. Connemara is more brilliantly elemental; cleaner in its appeal, even if it, too, must stir memories of Assia. But Richard Murphy, still in Cleggan, has a new alternative, an adventure for them out of reach of the immediate past but in touch with the ancient: he has bought High Island, two miles off the coast, named for the steepness of its rocky rise out of the Atlantic. From its summit you look down from Brian Boru's well, named for an early Irish king, towards the beehive cells of an eighth-century monastery, a chapel the wind blows through, and a lochan where the monks kept fish. Ted and Nick fish it, Richard will tell me, forty years on; they catch only minnows. I feel even better about my roach.

But they also fish Lough Aughrisburg, of course. This time it doesn't renew the mid-morning bounty of their first visit: Richard remembers hearing Ted tell Nick, sternly, that if he was serious about catching fish from the lough he'd need to be up at 4.00 a.m. Nick is just nine. It's one of any number of early starts. Ten years later, Ted's Irish diary for the Easter holiday of 1981 has Nick waking him in their tent beside the Barrow with fish, then Ted and Barrie fishing the Keel River that flows into Lough Carra, both at 6.00 a.m.

But that June week beside Lough Aughrisburg proves once again that the catch can come in his sleep. Ted dreams he is casting across the lough, meets another fisherman. Himself.

*

Already he'd begun to work the dormant art he'd stirred in his children. That spring he'd written home to them from Paris, where he described the delights of La Maison de la Mouche, a particularly sophisticated tackle shop. It stocked all kinds of fancy unguents, and, best of all, glasses with special lenses, 'so you can look through the shine on water and see fish – quite expensive'. Were these his first pair of polaroids? But he was prepared to spend more to encourage his children to write. A shilling for a good story, sixpence for quite good work and a penny for the 'not good'; paintings, drawings and memory lists would earn at the same rate. The money, he suggested, could be put towards the purchase of an eight- to nine-foot rod.

*

Still, though, it took him years to bring this home, find and then catch real fish in his home waters. It was in the last year of his life that he wrote to Nick in Alaska to tell him why, man to man; both, he hoped, were far enough on from all this to confront the reasons. It wasn't just that Assia and Shura's deaths had brought to a sudden end that 'flow of good inspiration' that he'd found in Ireland, and kept thinking Ireland could restore; his mother

Edith died weeks later. Even after marriage to Carol had helped him 'solve how I could look after you and Frieda', helped him 'get more time in my hut', Ted faced, or found, more obstacles. He blamed 'the life I was living – concentration battered, social life etc etc'. It 'clobbered' him. Battered, clobbered. For a moment I see Ted himself as salmon. I'm looking at him through the thickened panes of glass in one of those underwater viewing stations installed with fish ladders, fish passes. He's been hurling himself upstream, body and mind bruised but by things placed by men and women in his natural path. I think of fish outlasting water, wonder what they'd look like, what they would suffer. But salmon have no words. At least, at last, Ted was finding words for them, to share with Nick, who'd suffered his own frustrations. His own sense of disconnection from the life he should be leading.

And in these years Ted's fishing suffered, too. It was, he told Nick, 'reduced to Reservoirs (I didn't really start salmon fishing till about 78) and fiddling with the trout on the Taw'.

Another sort of fishing dream catches all that. Ted was by an estuary, near a harbour. A large and brightly coloured ship, piled above the gunwales with 'a floating small mountain of giant salmon', and topped with many jaguars, laid like carpets 'as if they were asleep'. But they weren't sleeping. As the ship and its harvest of this wild flesh came towards him at the wharf it faded.

Immediately Ted was on a theatre stage; he had wandered on to it to perform a role – the poet, reading, the literary celebrity, the man people paid to see. But he was unmanned with drink, 'so drunk I had to sit in the chair'. Sitting down in it made him a parody of middle-aged, fine-living, decrepit angling: truly, hideously, the coarse fisherman, a million miles from the man he should be, on the move, searching for salmon. 'I somehow fished the whole of the scene', estuary and ship, 'with one of those wretched reservoir rods' – built for power, not finesse – and an appropriately named wet fly, a Grouse and Claret. The dream ended with him wandering away, drunken, dazed. He was in danger of becoming the man who cannot fish, incapable of responding to what those salmon represented, 'that boatload of truths, insights, wisdoms from the other side'.

*

But there were glimpses. In 1972 Ted bought a small farm, Moortown, to work with Carol's father Jack, himself a retired farmer. It nudged his centre of gravity, closer to the land, but to the water, too. Moortown lay exactly between the Taw and its sister the Torridge, only two miles from each; Ted was in the country of the two rivers. In the sixties, inspired by Barrie's example, he'd worked at the Taw's trout and occasionally met a salmon. Now, making 'Spring Nature Notes', he looked up in spring sunlight, from the yard, beyond trees still leafless, and caught the promise of what was coming as no one else could:

> from the warmed blue hills
> An exhilaration swirls upward, like a huge fish.
> As under a waterfall, in the bustling pool.

That pool, that fish, are in his headwaters. The current's running strong. Hope oxygenates them, strengthens the heart. But you take nothing for granted; the image is stronger than the fish itself. 'For the angler who lives near the river, the state of the water becomes the first thing he speaks of each day. He watches it as the doctor watches a patient's temperature chart.' Ted, introducing a broadcast recording of 'The River in March'. The patient's under the weather. She 'has lost her fish. And she shivers.' Suddenly in better health, a drift of kingcups spilling golden along her banks, he's not the only one to have a look:

> A salmon, a sow of solid silver,
> Bulges to glimpse it.

*

Barrie's remote encouragement – a tale, one April, of a brief encounter on the Nore's sister river the Barrow with a huge pike, jaws like a coal grate – and Ted's own example, his enthusiasm, his dedication, are paying off. If not, yet, with the prized catch. Fishing is hard: the fish are invisible, the water empty.

*

He tried. Found a way of combining them when he could, after the fact. Headwaters swirl. Take that dream he'd had camping beside Aughrisburg, the dream when he met himself fishing. In time it resurfaced, bursting out again a strange scene in his verse novel *Gaudete*. Lumb, his depraved central character, has outraged the fathers and husbands of women he's been bedding in the English village he is meant to be serving as its parish priest. As he dabs his latest wounds in the river that flows near his southern English village, he hears voices in the throat of strong water in the neck of a pool. Suddenly he looks up and is out west again, in a mountain-fringed lake. Disturbed in his own determined casting for a trout when his naked double emerges from the water of a glass-still lake and attacks his young lover Felicity. She's been frightened, pleading with him to row back, as a thunderstorm nears and light fades, but he ignores her, works his way out on the finger of rock, warily, 'lifts his line and puts his big evening fly down in its path / On the lake's glass / Over the pit of hanging mountains and torn, stilled cloud / And wakings and tremors of violet'. Even as she screams, having seen a naked figure coming for her out of the lake, Lumb has heart and senses set on another body in that water: 'A black thumb / Lifts out on the water, and presses the fly under. / He fastens into the fish automatically'; pulled, for almost too long, between Felicity's needs and this 'good fish', running deep. Even after a final struggle, when he tears a simian hand off his double, struggles 'to lever up the demonic fingers / Of the torn-off hand' and throws it after that body retreating to the waters, the hand has the last laugh: gripping his steering wheel days later, plunging his van into the river, condemning him to another weird dream, this time in the slurry of a cattleyard with other mud bodies, before coming to once more, an otter emerging from the river to discover his van in sunlight, beside the river.

*

And that was when, he told Nick, he turned to 'real salmon fishing. I dug out, with your help, the real rivers of big salmon'. But he also knew that he should have been pursuing the insights instead, 'should have done it internally, on my work on myself': an extraordinary indication of everything that salmon fishing had, symbolically, come to represent for him, 'as a person and a writer'. 'I should perhaps have done both, simultaneously.'

The power and fertility of those headwater salmon hadn't left him. Still, though, it took time to find a way of catching them, in writing and in the flesh.

*

The upward surge in both these moments, that wonderful pressure from the other world rising to watch what you watch, is also inescapably the promise of harvest, fresh-run free-ranged meat. But when, weeks after the end of the game fishing season is over, 'I go to find salmon' in 'December River', Ted has caught nothing, all year. The river is 'the Taw near here', as he told Peter Keen in 1976, sending him a copy of the collection. And though as he told his listeners 'the fact that they're so scarce now' makes it difficult, it's clear that, somewhere, between knowledge and belief, they are there, somewhere: in the river, in his head. 'The steady name – unfathomable.' Driving upstream, 'With love-madness for strength.' And still running. Now high up the river, spawning. Confidence of one fact gives him persistence in his quest. 'Here all year salmon have been their own secret', 'the heavy slipperiness in the green oils'. That's why

> This whole summer
> I offered all I had for a touch of their wealth –

And that's why he returns now. Having failed to catch a live fish, he can at least find a dead one, spawned and spent. He can stare into its button-white eye, envy 'That grimace / Of getting right through to the end and beyond it', admire the head, 'That helm / So marvellously engineered'. He can lift its crimson bulk, wedge it 'properly mine / While the moment still held open'.

It is as heavy as a child; its rubber length reminds him, in its blotched bruised rich red, of an elderly woman's upper leg, as if he were staring at some charred remains. And as he lifts it the shallow water lifts and splits, and, under the cover of the wave, which is all he sees coming straight at him, 'A broad bow-wave lifted and came frowning / Straight towards me', slides into the space he has just freed. All he can see is that frowning wave, the fish beneath. Will that be its final resting place? Maybe not; maybe it will survive this 'grave of steel / Which it could still buckle.'

*

Perhaps. But 'December River' didn't end Ted's salmon blank. Two more years passed without a salmon. Desperate measures were called for. Or a charm. It's called 'Earth-numb', and it's where salmon finally leapt out of dream and into *River*.

Ted seems to be back on familiar territory. Poaching territory. The upper Taw, and at dawn. The river is unmistakable if you've read 'Stealing Trout on a May Morning', or if you've walked it, as I did, staring into low water, in March. Rivers take on different colours and characters. Some, like the Torridge, suffer soil bleed from cow-hoof-crumbled fields. But just below Dartmoor, and under that hazel canopy, the Taw is pure water over granite. That rock gives it a stark, dark clarity. The sky smoulders, and heat pulses above the brim of a morning that simmers with birdsong. The sycamores are unfurling their leaves; the daffodils still there, maybe just on the turn.

But what lies below all this is much more terrifying than any keeper of the game, or even than a dream. It's a deeper, older uncertainty.

Hunting salmon. And hunted
And haunted by apparitions from tombs
Under the smoothing tons of dead element
In the river's black canyons.

Faced with this, the flash of a Devon minnow is no longer enough. The stakes are higher; they need him to go deeper. He really does offer all he has. Faith: 'The lure is a prayer'. Again he casts, putting even more into the angler's rite, hoping conditions are right for another bulge at the surface: 'A prayer, like a flower opening.' But prayer alone won't be enough. Nor will the doctor's bedside watch. Now, through that spinning sliver of metal in the clear dark water, he's performing surgery 'On an open heart'. He doesn't say whose.

And just as well. For with 'a bang!' the tables are turned, and suddenly it's the river which is reaching into him, 'trying to rip life off me' – has a surging run of line off a reel ever been so personal, so physical, so dangerous? The river itself comes to life, hauling at him – 'And I have one.'

But nothing is settled yet. It has only begun. The shock of it enthralls him. He is current. Whatever he's been hunting, whatever he's been hunted by, these years, 'something terrified and terrifying / Gleam-surges to and fro through me', confusing river and sky.

*

Wordsworth defined poetry as 'emotion recollected in tranquility'. Whatever this is, whatever it becomes, this isn't it. Some of Ted's critics, non-fishermen, confuse the end, when it comes, with cruelty. Pulled at last from the depths, 'a ghost grows solid', and then, in shallow water, finds it impossible to do what the fisherman and the poet both must: think. But cruelty's the wrong word for this. And it's not even recollection. It's imagination. A concentration, a regathering, of all the pain, life, death, dreams of those years. A realisation. A discovery at last of how to bring up into your world, and keep, convert, the energy of the other, that solid silver. A salmon charm.

When Ted read 'Earth-numb' on the radio, he told his audience that he'd set out 'to make an image like a hunter's rock painting, or those sand drawings made by bushmen and others, before the event … to compel the event to happen as I'd already created it'.

And it worked. Ted told his critic friend Keith Sagar that the day after he finished and typed 'Earth-numb', 'I caught 2 salmon, and the next day another – the first for 3 years. Hunting magic.'

*

Sunday 23 August 2012. Mid-morning. I'm at Watertown, on the Taw's largest tributary – 'the wonderful River Mole', Ted called it. John Martin has fished it for years, since well before he and his brother Michael met Ted in the early 1980s; and he's suggested that I might like to have a cast as we talk. It's one of my first mornings salmon fishing, and the first time I've ever fished with one of Ted's friends. John is watching me fish down Buckingham's pool, flicking an orange and black Cascade under the trees with the rod my father bought me thirty years before – when Ted was fishing here. And I'm self-conscious, uncertain, caught – between listening and casting.

But then the water bulges, my rod yanks down, it thumps and surges and my life is changed for ever. I can still feel the wrench in the shoulder. I have one. And soon I see it: gorgeous rivershadow, gleam surge. I want to admire it, hold it there. But I also want it, need this catch. There is business to be done. John is urgent: Get it into the shallows, less oxygen there, it will weaken sooner. He's right: 'Earth-numb' was right. And then: we don't have a net. It surges one last time, flaps, its dark purples and green becoming silver lilac as it lies there. I fall on it, hug the huge fish, all nine pounds of it, to myself, stagger up the bank, throw it on the grass while the moment holds open, claim it, kill: a stone sharp on the top of that head. And there is guilt, yes, at what I've done. The catch. But even as those eyes cloud I know I've never felt excitement like it.

*

Perhaps all I was looking and listening for that morning was some sign, even if an echo, of that influence, as I came through Belstone and saw the upper village green dipping sharply out of sight towards a rushing stream hidden in the bottom of a tree-lined valley. But I was also puzzled. Why were there no salmon poems from the 1960s? I knew from Ted's essay 'Trout on the Upper Taw' that in the early days he caught a salmon parr, a youngster a year or two old, on almost every cast. It had, he said, resembled a salmon farm. But in 1969 he'd caught his first Taw trout with the leprous fungal disease UDN, or ulcerative dermal necrosis, which became a scourge of salmonids. Lesions affect heads and flanks as salmon and sea-trout re-enter fresh water; the infection, which can kill as well as deform individual fish, spreads between species, too. Pollution and hunting led to the loss of otters; the sense of crisis was compounded by new presences: 'Mink and the cheese factory followed.' Thin glutinous strands of what he guessed was whey glistened in the water and, along with whatever else was going into the river from farms, turned the finest mile of spawning gravel in the south-west into concrete. By 1974 the trout population had collapsed, and he stopped fishing for Taw trout. So was the influence only the ghost of a dream river?

I was about to find out. My path led along a road above it, and I could see I'd be joining the river half a mile or so upstream. In a lay-by a single walker, an elderly man, laced thick ankle boots; a rucksack in his car boot looked well used. We nodded; I pressed on.

Fifty minutes later I'd made good use of my walking shoes, leaping from rock to rock up the path beside a young colt of a river in a tight cleft of valley. Gorse bushes, young question marks of unfurling fern and boulders becoming bluffs – almost small cliffs – held its wild power. The Taw here was dazzling in its beauty – wild, free, boisterous, and, given yesterday's rain, miraculously clear, but nothing like the thin stream Ted had mentioned. It seemed to have no need of that big river his dream had supplied. I hadn't yet found a cliff. I had spent too long, and taken too many pictures, beside miniature cascades, boilings and mirror slithers. I'd passed a compact stone hut, its joints and grouting surprisingly sharp and clean right above the river, but clearly not a bothy: it was windowless. And I'd found my first long, still pool right at the head of the valley's cleft; a rowan tree looked down on it, and its silent glide broke into the ripple of a rise somewhere every few seconds. Those skinny dark tiny trout seemed to be thriving; seemed, indeed, from the determined but subtle sub-surface dimples, and from the occasional glimpse of a neb breaking the surface, to have put on weight.

Then the path led up and away from the river for the first time, and I emerged into a much wider basin of moss and tussocky grass: Taw Marsh. I saw how far I had still to go. Half a mile or more ahead a peak divided two streams; I knew I'd have to follow one of them. But which? Forty yards to my right, a figure was striding purposefully along a track I hadn't noticed. We converged. That man I'd passed lacing his boots. I felt the need somehow to apologise. 'I've been dawdling,' I said, nodding back to the Taw and down to my camera. 'I love rivers.'

'So do I,' he said.

We got talking. Guardedly at first. Yes, he'd done this walk a few times, he said. Today he was heading east, he said. But then I asked him what he loved about rivers, and one sentence exposed me as an amateur. Until his retirement he'd spent thirty years monitoring river flow, first for the South West Water Authority, then for the Environment Agency. I mentioned Ted. 'Oh yes,' he said, 'I knew him a bit.' His uncle had been a neighbour in North Tawton. We exchanged names. Googling later, I found Mike Sampson's name among the officers credited for the data gathered in the first two hydrometrical surveys of the rivers of the south-west undertaken from the 1990s. Yes, he knew the stone: he pointed ahead, first to Steeperton Tor, and the gorge on its right, which I needed to follow, and then keep going, past the ford – it's longer than you think, he said; 'you'll find it easier if you gain height.'

Mike lowered his gaze and used his stick to point to something much closer, a few hundred yards away across the basin floor. 'You see those barrows?' I hadn't, of course, but now I made them out – three or four bulges from the grass, three feet high, ten in diameter. They were fenced off. Mike explained them. They were, he said, the bright idea of another North Tawton resident, Young by name: an engineer who, in 1956, convinced the North Devon Water Board he could solve the region's water needs at a stroke. The moor – this basin – caught and held in store all the rain that fell on it, far more than ever went into the Taw. More than enough. Why not tap the abundance of this hidden reservoir? Those chambers held the pumps that drove the water down the underground pipe they built in the years that followed. It all went live in 1962. That was when they removed the weir, Mike said – I'd have passed it, by that hut. Until then that was as far as salmon ever got, he said. They took out the gauge station, too, knocked it down. No need for it.

It hadn't worked. The pipeline did for the Taw, starved it of headwater. In the drought year of 1976 the upper Taw dried up completely. That did it. The pumps were decommissioned; they were, Mike said, due for removal completely. They didn't put the weir back in but they had to rebuild the gauging station. That neat stone hut by the river.

And the salmon, I asked? And the river since? I was prepared for gloom. Instead: the salmon spawn right up on the moor now – lovely gravels. And the flow? You should have been here yesterday, Mike said: more or less back to what it was before they turned on the pipe in 1962. I thought of what Ted had said about the hundred salmon he saw lying in the pool above the town bridge at North Tawton in his first autumn there, 1961; of the fifty he'd counted there in 1967; of the lone 'October salmon' that remained as his father lay dying in hospital in 1980. But I also knew that salmon are still caught, against all odds, on the Taw and its tributaries.

We parted then. I walked on across the wide valley, taking in the broad meanders of the river, flowing across dark peat and bright gravel as it turned; I turned right, following the West Taw, up Steeperton gorge's clifflets, looking back to watch Mike leap across the Taw before it divided and head up the slope east, then turned and followed the stream's tumbling path, over the ford and another long pool full of purposefully rising trout. And I found the great stone I was looking for, weathered and lichened into near illegibility in fifteen years, but part of the moor, on a bluff of mining spoil above the thinnest sliver of the young river.

But it was as nothing to what filled my head as I walked back down the river, imagining I was there in November or December 1965: the adult salmon, one or two sea-winter returners, the first generation pushing beyond their parents' old redds, or spawning gravels, and higher, higher, but in water thinner than any salmon had ever known. I had leisure to think. I met, and spoke to, not a single other person in the course of my walk. I saw, at the barrows, like disused pillboxes from a war the engineers had lost, N.D.W.B. – North Devon Water Board – stamped on plates that for all the rust they'd gathered were still more distinct than Ted's O.M. on the granite flank of his memorial stone up there at Taw Head.

I also had time, on that long trudge, to remember another autumn story. Ted told Keith Sagar of it a few months after *River* was published. Nick, aged thirteen, Ted thought, was wading right under North Tawton's town bridge. He'd spotted something, waded out. A salmon carcass. Proof of where the old redds were. Nick pulled the fish away, as Ted had that December dusk, and in the wash noticed something even more miraculous than another weary spawner surging into its place. There were orange salmon eggs appearing between the fine pebbles, welling up. He took some more gravel in his hands; salmon eggs poured away and down with the current. And he wrote a poem about this. Ted loved it, told him so. A few years later he'd go on to follow his son's example; 'Salmon Eggs' opens *River*, maybe as a tribute to Nick. Anyway, Nick showed his teacher his season song. But: 'Don't try to write about things outside your experience', he was told. It was the last poem Nick ever wrote.

6

The Catch

For almost as long as I can remember I have been driving, or been driven, long miles in search of water and fish.

The driver used to be Dad. He was a doctor, a general practitioner, in Wellington, a small Shropshire market town long since swallowed by what for years was known as Telford New Town. From 1970, whenever the duty rota permitted, which meant three weekends in every month from April to September, the family would pile into our long-wheel-based Land Rover after evening surgery on Friday and trundle west, Sprite caravan in tow, Mirror dinghy on the roof at the start of the season, the four of us plus spars and sails and rods crammed into the back. The Mirror was for my eldest brothers, Chris, then sixteen; Julian, thirteen; and Nick, eleven. I was four.

The drive into Wales was long: sixty miles, an hour and a half, sometimes two. At Atcham the road joined and then followed the Severn upstream, from Shrewsbury via Welshpool and on as the hills rose around it. It was a bumpy ride, with rituals: *Any Questions?* on Radio 4, in what I discover now was its first months in its Friday evening slot; Dad flinging his own barbed follow-ups over his shoulders about the politicians on the panel for my brothers to catch. Mum beside him in the front, quieter, watchful: 'Keep your eyes on the road, Nigel.' She must have got things ready, though of course I remember none of that. If we got to Llanidloes in time, 'a strike' – why did we call it that? – and our first fish of the weekend: battered, with chips. Before the last leg up to the caravan park, itself newly opened in a meadow on the banks of the Afon Clywedog. It was a tributary of the Severn, which it joined downstream of Llanidloes. And I loved paddling, and then in future summers, fishing, and watching my brothers fish, for the small trout, in that river.

But what mattered more than any of this, the reason Dad and the older boys were here, why I guess the caravan park was here, too, was where the little Clywedog came from, its big namesake three twisting miles up in the wild hills: a monster my age, though at the time I didn't know that either. You came across it as the road shouldered a rise: a giddying curve of concrete that had risen up the cleft of this quiet valley between 1965 and 1967 to dwarf the river from its base. At 265 feet it's still the tallest mass concrete dam in Britain. Once or twice we walked across it, in awe. Once or twice, down in the caravan, trying to get to sleep, I'd wonder: what if the dam burst? But mostly it was the vast new body of water that still lies beyond the dam wall that drew us. Llyn Clywedog.

In bringing us here Dad wasn't, I realise now, following his heart, but other men's counsel. And the example of two dentist friends of his, partners in a local practice. We knew them as Big Al and Big John, both keen sailors themselves – both ex-Royal Navy. At least one of them had had a commission. We saw more of Alan. He saw more of me: my teeth, still irregular. I remember his bow-legged seafarer's walk, too, and the way he broke into a rolling run on the way to his own dinghy, or back to the car. I remember them laughing together, backslapping. They were real men, somehow, and both the fathers of boys. Big John had even built a wall down the middle of his boys' room to stop them fighting.

Dad was somehow not in their league, and certainly never in the same boat; though he had a sharp mind and tongue, must somehow have connived at what we called them, there was never a question of Big Nigel. He only once or twice took to the water himself. But he knew it was important for us. There were signs that my brothers might be going the same way as John's boys. One infamous afternoon, one of my brothers had lobbed a dart high into the air in our back garden, and it had nestled deep in another brother's tummy, which needed a tetanus shot; the excuse given – Agincourt, archers – got marks for ingenuity, but was never believed.

So Dad followed John's and Al's advice. Get the big boys out on the water, an outlet for the hormones. Clywedog sailing club was the answer: they were looking for new members. The races and regattas would be a healthier outlet for all that teenage testosterone. Safer than darts, too. And we already had the Mirror.

While my brothers learned the ropes, I joined Richard, a year older than me, Alan and Maureen Bullock's middle son, down in the river by the caravan park that the reservoir meant never shrank in summer heat, or up at the reservoir exploring the creek along from the clubhouse. There was a track through high bracken, and then suddenly a cut-away bank where the reservoir trout went to spawn. These were big, serious fish, with dark flanks to match the hillsides, and far bigger than ever we saw in the river: Chris caught two of them one afternoon casting off a distant bank up near Staylittle, where the little Clywedog fed the vast lake. We spent whole afternoons by that creek together, leaning over the water where the still water met the side stream, watching those trout, always thinking we could tickle them, never quite managing it. Occasionally we were allowed out on the club rescue boat, in lifejackets several sizes too big for us: we peered over the gunwales, stared down into the darkness. Just this spring, fifty years on, I found photographs to prove it, pictures I'd never seen before.

But we also went further. Mammoth drives. They were Dad's specialism; we suggested, and the Bullocks followed. That same summer, our two families combined to go much further. Luce Bay in south-west Scotland. The summer before it had been Austria; in 1972, with the Mirror handed down to Nick and me, pressganged as crew, it was Switzerland, for the European Fireball championships. Then it was just us again: the Loire. Sometimes we took boats; always the fishing rods came with us, slung and tied between the handholds set into the ceiling of the back of the Land Rover. These longer holidays required more ingenious packing. Dad would fold down the back seats, take the long side bench seats out, fill the footwell between them with boxes Mum had packed, tins of baked beans and canisters of dried mashed potato, then lay sheets of plywood across the lot and airbeds and sleeping bags. Seat belts? Bah. We'd sleep, and read, and sometimes squabble, and resign ourselves to whole days in the car, leaving before first light, pulling into some caravan site sometime the next day or the one after that.

And then we'd set to. We'd find river gorges to explore, where you could impale grasshoppers on hooks and catch muscular trout from the frothy pools between the rocks, or follow the examples of the locals and dig worms and catch writhing Loire eels from sinuous stretches of the muddy river lined with high reeds. In all this, I never wondered until this last summer what other tricks of the trade Dad used to get us there. Julian did. He saw what neither Chris nor Nick, now both retired as lawyers who pride themselves on their own sharp eyes, ever did. He saw what Dad would take of a weekend, the pills – DF118s – he'd pop from the surgery, to keep him going in those odysseys. Sometimes washed down with Johnnie Walker Red Label. On those Friday evening journeys into Wales, he'd hear things, too, that the rest of us either slept through or chose to forget, from Mum in the passenger seat. 'For God's sake, Nigel, pull over, won't you?'

Was that, I asked Julian, why, when we got there, crouched on the rocks in those Alpine gorges, or stood flinging spinners across and down wide rivers from rocky shores, I have no memory of Dad fishing with us? He'd spend the first day or two of the holiday itself unconscious, recovering from his idea of the sacrifice, the dangerous denial, the heroism of getting us there.

In 1975 our weekend drives got an hour longer. Chris was at Cambridge; Julian was heading there, and wanted to be a vet. Was that the excuse, if we needed one, to buy a smallholding an hour and a dog-leg drive south over Devil's Bridge, even deeper into West Wales? It was an old house, basically habitable, in eighteen acres of thin meadows in a valley through which one of three sister streams ran down from reedier hills. The idea was that Julian would practise animal husbandry on our fifty ewes; Mum and Dad would lead the country life and restore the place, and, I guess now, themselves.

Dad was on duty the weekend we took possession of the place. Tany, we called it: actually, Tan-yr-Esgair, or Under the Ridge: if you followed the lane uphill you came to one candidate for that, a dome of sheep and hayfields and then, when the tarmac ended at a gate and the unmade bed of rough track jolted the car across a wide expanse of marsh and rushes, another gate onto the Forestry Commission land. Carry on through that, which you could reliably once someone did for the padlock, and you came at last to the other candidate, a windswept ridge with views across what felt like the whole of Wales, a lake beneath it.

Because Dad was working Mum must have driven us down – a rarity. That night there was a power cut – and a thunderstorm. I remember Mum leaving me and Nick in the strange dark house while she ventured out, resolute under her clear polythene-domed umbrella, to march down the lane to the telephone box by the bridge over the second of these streams 400 yards away, below our bottom field, to phone for advice. I remember her in the yard, lightning silvering that glistening umbrella. She was clearly enjoying herself. Her brisk 'Back soon!'

That's my last memory of her.

One Tuesday afternoon late that November, a school day, back in Wellington, she went upstairs for a snooze. Nick, then sixteen, found her on their bed when he let himself in from school. In the forty-five years since, we have never once spoken about that, or what warning signs there may have been, and were missed, or discounted, fo the heart attack. But I remember that evening. Richard's mum, Maureen, had picked us up from school, had me round for tea. When Dad came to collect me, a bit later than usual, it was dark. Auntie Maureen – always for some reason pronounced 'Marine' – kissed me hard on the forehead, pressing me to her; I remember the press of hair between her nose and upper lip. I remember sitting beside Dad in the passenger seat in the car – had he left Nick in the house? – and the orange of the streetlamps on the Whitchurch road suddenly blurring as Dad told me, but I have no memory of what Dad said. And then back home, where I do remember the words Dad chose to fill the dark house. We sat in the lounge, the three of us, and Dad played a cassette of a voice I'd never heard before. Bob Newhart, the American comic raconteur. Here he is, avuncular, bemused, interviewing Sir Walter Raleigh by phone: 'To-bacc-o. A leaf, you dry it, roll it up, and then ... then you set fire to it! Nutty Walt.' Wild laughter through the cassette player's speakers. The evening of Mum's death, 29 November 1975.

The following March, Dad drove Nick and me east. It was then a five-hour trundle to Cambridge, too long to do there and back in the day. So we overnighted in the car park at another of the new generation of reservoirs, Grafham Water: Dad snoring on the double bed, me and Nick in the bunks up in the concertina'd roof of the Volkswagen campervan which had then replaced the long-wheel-base Land Rover. We met up with Julian and Chris, and went for a walk beside the Cam, its banks thick with crocuses. As we walked along a path below King's College Chapel, Dad began dipping his hand into a white plastic Marlboro carrier bag, said, 'This is something very beautiful,' and began letting the fine grey dust trail from his stubby fingers, drift in the breeze over the lawn and out onto the river.

Mum's wishes? I think so. I had no idea until writing this, none, that she had lost her own mother in the summer before her own death, or that Dad's father had died exactly a month before Mum. Grandpa, like Grandma, who held on for another three years in the house to which they'd moved to be near their son, had stipulated that they wanted to be buried in the graveyard of the church where they had married in 1923, up in Halifax, and where they had their two children: Thelma in 1926, Nigel in January 1929.

So, I realise too late in the writing of this: he was eighteen months older than Ted. Another Calderdale boy. They were born within ten miles of each other.

We had, as boys, and still have, no idea of the discussions Nigel must have had with his posh, London-based elder sister Thelma – she taught public speaking, but neither of them specialised in the other unpaid kind. None of us even recall hearing about any of our grandparents' deaths, though Fred and Lois lived within five minutes of our home. But Mum and Dad must, in that grim autumn, before she followed them, have talked. And Mum was as proud as Dad was of their sons going to Cambridge. Even so, Marlboro? Come on, Dad.

*

That summer, the great drought of 1976, Nick, Julian and I spent weeks alone at Tany. Dad must have come at weekends, I suppose. My friend Richard certainly did. One afternoon we found an eel in the puddle that remained of the deepest pool on our stretch of stream, just within our reach, under the bank, shaded by an overhanging hawthorn, where the sheep came down to drink. We raced back up to the house, found a bucket and Julian's old net and conquered all manner of fears to squat on the exposed rocks, coax and cajole and then ram the poor eel into the bucket, then carried it into the yard, down the drive, across the lane, and down through our neighbour's two fields and down to the stream that never ran dry, fed as it was from the lake under the top ridge, to the pool where someone told us they used to dip the sheep from all the local farms. There was a rock shelf you could leap from into deep, clear water. Now we tipped the bucket on its side and watched as the eel slid out and away with never a backward glance or a word of thanks.

Nick and I graduated, that summer or next, from our side-valley streams, which came together half a mile or so below our house, to the main river, the Teifi. We knew it held big fish: trout, but salmon and sea-trout, which the Welsh call sewin, too. A theoretical knowledge, that, until we met Tommy. Tommy lived in the house across from our stream that lay within a hundred yards of the pool where we found that eel. We must have told him. He was a carpenter and joiner, a chain-smoker, even when surrounded by the sawdust in his workshop. When we called round, he'd take us into his kitchen and offer us mugs of tea and tactics. Most of it illicit: the otter board for the lake in the hills worked wonders, though you had to drop it, of course, if you heard a car on the track; and, down on the Teifi, a rare paste, made of salmon eggs – we never did see the salmon – which was, he said, deadly for eels. On condition that we were never to breathe a word, he took us, one pouring night. We sat at the river astonished with the excitement and the fear of poaching, and that he trusted us. And an eel did come – all writhe and twist around the nylon. I remember Tommy hacking at it in a fury with his knife, stuffing the rope of its body into his bag. We never tasted it.

Then it was Nick's time to go to university: Cambridge, too. I took that for granted. I started boarding. It was best, somehow, though somehow it wasn't best for Richard. In my first term – was I eleven? – I began reading *David Copperfield*. On the way home after our school carol concert that December, in the car – it wasn't a long drive, only twelve miles – Dad told me I was going to have a new mum. I thought at once of Mr Murdstone. At home there was a brightly written letter for me, which she had signed 'Mark's New Mum'. She was from Manchester. I remember thinking: how did Dad know her? She had a daughter. Did I ever meet her? At any rate, I did learn, from one of my brothers, sometime later, that Dad had discovered something about her that made them both decide it wouldn't be for the best, after all. And I never finished *David Copperfield*.

I turned twelve. That spring I started fly fishing on the Teifi. Dad bought me a Hardy Fibalite rod, eight foot six inches, from the shop where he'd bought Chris's first rods. He bought me a season ticket, too, from the village post office by the bridge. I remember him taking a picture of my standing, arm and rod stiff over the unresponsive river. I don't remember any fish, and I don't really remember any lessons, though I am guessing he must have shown me. Or did Nick? But I kept casting.

*

The following Christmas the boys – the young men – are all home. After we've opened our presents, and the sprouts and vegetables get under way, and the turkey goes in – I'm spared – Dad must have told us to lay an extra place at lunch. A friend of his is coming. Her name is Pam. She's younger than him – younger, I sense, than Mark's New Mum.

After Christmas pudding – I get the 50p! – I am allowed to get down. It isn't just on long car journeys that talk can turn to politics, discussions turn to arguments; and there is Christmas TV. I go through to the lounge. They all come through later.

In March, driving me back to their house after school, Auntie Maureen asks me how I'm looking forward to Dad and Pam's wedding. 'I didn't know they were getting married,' I said.

*

Summers after that were, whenever possible, at Tany. With my brothers if they were around; otherwise alone or with friends. I fished, too, with Tommy. One evening up at the lake under the ridge, a mist came down. ''Opeless.' So was the east wind. Still, we kept casting into the dusk. I had on a big moth pattern. A sip, a thumb, on the edge of sound and sight, and the line amazingly straightened as I lifted, and a fine trout of a pound or so was mine. 'Blind,' said Tommy, but you could tell he was tickled, as proud as I was. That blind trout entered family legend.

Until the summer of 1983, when I was seventeen, and Dad amazed me, and the family – Dad and Pam and little Peter my half-brother and I – stayed for a week at the Arundell Arms and I went sea-trout fishing at night and learned to cast and taught myself touch-typing by day, that blind lake trout was the biggest fish I had ever caught. Dad even bought me, back in Wellington, a lake fly rod, a carbon-fibre Hardy Richard Walker Farnborough, with a butt extension in case of serious fish or two-handed casting, and a matching reel. And I was thrilled, of course. But I never caught a fish with it, not then. The first serious fish it met would be that salmon on the Mole.

I can't now recall which came first – graduation from Oxford or the invitation, in a phone call, to clear my room at the home they'd moved into after their marriage. Which had, of course, until that point, been my home, too. At any rate, I did find space for my little Fibalite on a week's holiday that Sarah and I took with two friends of ours in June 1985. We'd just moved into our first flat together. I drove west, my first car, a VW Polo, crammed with their clothes; the gown Laura had just worn to our college's May

Ball! I took only shorts, to save room. But I did catch two sea-trout from the pool on the bend under the bridge of the lane fifty yards from the farmhouse we rented. The village was Coldridge, the river the Taw, five miles downstream of North Tawton.

Whenever I could, alone or with anyone I could convince, I drove west. Max, the partner of a friend of Sarah's, was a psychiatrist from Northern Ireland, and every inch the dry scientist. I taught him to cast in the University Parks, then took him to Farmoor, the concrete bowl west of Oxford which was all I could find or afford. And we both caught rainbows! Back in our kitchen as I was gutting them, as I'd learned down at the Arundell Arms – fish belly up in your hand, like a fat envelope: knife point in at the vent, then slide up and away, towards the gills, which you might just need to nick free, then (the bill in the envelope) pull back and towards you from the gills – Max insisted on opening the stomach I'd just removed, of the hour-dead trout. Doing so turned mine. Some of its contents – question marks of larvae – were still wriggling. One tried to take off. I wrote this, as a poem: 'The Catch'.

Even after Dad and Pam had sold Tany, I found a way to keep heading west. Julian, now with a house of his own above the Teifi, let me stay for a hot August fortnight, and I caught sewin at night. When our boys came, I took them, tried. We rented a cottage with a garden that ran down to the West Lyn on Exmoor, and saw a salmon under the sunken roots of a tree in the pool; Connor caught his first fish on the fly from Fox Pool a mile downstream, and remembers it to this day, though there's been much else he has forgotten, including the ultimatum I had to give him in mid-teens. But even that day, on another Devon holiday, our last together as a family, I'd worked out that the best chance of him listening was beside a river, and, now that we've both emerged from the tunnel of those years, the glorious Teign trout that rose to his fly that day, lay in his net, then slipped calmly away remains a stepping stone for us both, an emblem of rare and true contact in lives that have diverged. And for myself, I kept fishing whenever I could. Sometimes it would be a day or two a year I'd manage, nothing more. But I'd keep false-casting – on walks in the Fens, between meetings at work. Most people look at me quizzically. There is one colleague who gets it. He has a cottage above the Tamar. Would I come to fish? It's September 2011.

And then, that next winter, that smudge, that scale of a really big fish, lost.

*

I have to have more of this.

I read more of Ted's diaries. I keep coming across Barrie; the name features again and again. I read a page he wrote for what was meant to be a celebration of Ted's seventieth. 'With Ted Hughes', by Barrie Cooke. They shared, he wrote, a passion for wild nature and violence, and a love of pike. I discover who this man, a painter, is. I write to him, via his gallery – he is still exhibiting – to ask about his memories of fishing with Ted. Could I call, I wonder. But I expect nothing: a leading critic, Ted's biographer, has already told me he never got a reply.

But Barrie writes back. He misses Ted, very deeply. And Nick, too. (It's fourteen years since Ted's death, only three since Nick took his own life.) Would I like to come and stay? To make sure I find him, he sends me the most beautiful vivid watercolour map. So I drive west from the airport. I take a tiny rod with me, a smuggler fly rod, which breaks into six pieces and goes in my cabin bag. Beside Lough Arrow small dragons are dancing: mayflies.

And though Barrie, now eighty-one, has given up fishing, just this last year – he's frail – he tells and shows me enough in the day and night and day I spend with him to make me understand how much a first day and a night and most of a day in his company might have inspired Ted, all those years ago, and drawn him back, with Nick, for more. I haven't yet found Barrie's letter to Ted with details of the pike plug he sent for Nick, but he does show me Nick's own homemade pike spoon, name stamped into the tin or aluminium. He shows me a poem and drawings about pike he and Ted did together. And more. Not just that ancient stone womb at Carrowkeel, that grave at Drumcliff, where he makes a point of standing on W. B. Yeats, poking a stick at the epitaph. 'Cast a cold eye.' But also the time he gives me to browse his bookshelves. I can't believe what, who, has filled the shelf below Ted's. Barrie talks freely of him, too. His other great friend, Seamus. Yes, Seamus Heaney. Seamus is an amateur; Barrie tells me of his disgust that he'd left the rod and reel Barrie had at last persuaded him to buy on the roof of his car on its first outing. But also: 'Outside of Seamus's family, there's no one closer to him alive.'

In everything he says, there's a wildness, an openness, a frank welcome, a sheer commitment to life, and fish, and water, and to art, of course, that I have never known, or at least not outside the diaries and poems of Ted's that I've been reading.

I keep on casting, reading.

Carol Hughes puts me in contact with other fishing friends of Ted's. Not just John Martin, though he, of course, has to have star billing: that salmon! His old friend, too: Bill Tucker, who'd spent long, long hours driving north with Ted in pursuit of Scottish salmon in the eighties and nineties. When, that afternoon on the Mole, John hears I'm seeing Bill the following day, 'Wonderful!' he says. 'Give Bill the fish. He'll have it smoked for you.' They are both as good as their word. And the taste of that wild fish is like nothing I've ever known. It feeds us, body and soul, all winter.

Other invitations, offers, follow. I drive west. Beside the waters I'm asked to fish, with men sometimes as old as Dad, sometimes younger, all of whom fished with Ted, the experiences they give me go deep. They open their rivers and their memories to me. I make new friends of these old men. Men who talk to me with a directness, share their love of Ted – unconditional, they tell me: how could it not be, when what he gave you was what he gave to the fish and the waters they met through? Unconditional attention, intense concentration, commitment, honesty.

And I make discoveries alone. I steal that trout on a May morning; walk the upper Taw in search of that dream waterfall. One mad March, as a Cambridge term draws to an end, I pore over my Ordnance Survey map, plot a route up a farm track, along field edges, over hedges, down through woodland to the upper limit of Ted's fishing on the Torridge. Drive down, stay overnight in the Duke of York, and execute my dawn raid, not reckoning on the frost, the incriminating boot-prints I'd leave in the grass. But I disturb no one – except the stags I startle among the trees of Brimblecombe Brake, or the fox who stares me down across the flood plain meadow from the bank. And he's telling no one. I'm back in the pub a whole hour before breakfast.

Through such meetings, wanderings, readings, I come, oddly, to know the history of Ted's fishing, and his thoughts and feelings and writings about fish, better than I know my own family's. I listen to him, 'Learning to Think', and on the necessary passion of hunting, poaching, fishing, as I drive west. Again and again.

And at last it is Ted who leads me back to my own childhood, restores it to me.

*

It's August 2019. I'd been back up the Taw, leading a group of those who love Ted's poetry; I've spent two nights on the Dart, two on the Torridge. And three hours watching trout rise and water slip over rocks into pool tails on the water Ted mapped for Peter Keen in 1979, inviting him to fish there, on the Taw above Bondleigh. Parking, as ever, where Ted's map told me to park, in an abandoned quarry along a lane from the village. This time I decide against poaching; I didn't want to complicate the memory of the fish I'd heard, seen, felt, down the line and through the rod, even touched, two nights before, on the Torridge.

Back in my study, I read 'Learning to Think' one more time. And suddenly learned to feel – caught the tail of a memory from well before those weekends driving west into Wales.

I, too, had fished in still water. I, too, had spent hours staring at an orange float the size of a lentil. I, too …

And then I doubted myself. Had fishing in Ted's footsteps, willing myself, imagining myself into the waters he'd known and felt, made me dream all this up?

But I remembered a name: the Bottom Pool. I remembered, didn't I, long dusty summer afternoons trailing after taller figures? So I wrote to my brothers.

And: oh yes, Chris said. The Bottom Pool: they used maggots for bait, float fishing for perch.

Julian recalled the Top Pool. Mum had taken them there first, he was sure: pond-dipping. Mum was a zoologist. She and Dad had met at university; Dad at some point handed down to Julian the MSc thesis she was writing when they met, on the influence of hormones in pigeons. Once, later, Julian remembers Mum coming into his biology class at grammar school to cover a lesson for Mr Deighton; she'd brought in a pig's heart for them to handle, dissect. She was brilliant. The Top Pool was where she introduced her own brood to the wonders of what lay below the surface. Julian's inherited that passion. But she then left the boys to it, evidently. The Bottom Pool was closer; it lay at the lowest tip of the woods on the Ercall, the mound where the giant said to have raised the Wrekin with a spadeful of earth scraped the soil off his boots. You could see it across the fields from our garden. It was, for longer legs than mine, an easy walk along the main road, up Limekiln Lane, and then through a gap in the hedge and across that rising meadow. But all that went, long ago, and as suddenly as our family's shift of gravity into Wales. In the early 1970s the earth moved again: two years of construction traffic sliced off Limekiln Lane, blasted those fields, bit chunks out of Ercall Wood. The Telford Bypass, now the M54 motorway, opened in 1975, the summer and autumn of deaths we never mentioned.

But it exists in memory, a pool indeed. Nick rings from Australia: he remembers its steep, muddy banks, the overhanging trees, and watching big fish hovering in the sunlight in the middle – could they have been chub? None of them got close enough to know. Not there, at least. He has no memory of the pond-dipping, or the Top Pool, or even Mum; hadn't Dad introduced them to all this? He'd assumed so. But Chris does remember chub, and then barbel, from the River Severn. He remembers reading Bernard Venables's classic of the late 1940s and 1950s, *Mr Crabtree Goes Fishing*, in which good old tie-wearing Mr Crabtree introduces Peter to the seasons and techniques and waters of the angling year. Chris even finds me a copy in a Suffolk junkshop. Reading it now, remembering I'd seen it myself, I realise Chris knew more of what little Peter Crabtree had learned than I ever had. Because once, at least, on the Severn, he'd fished with his tie-wearing father. Dad had even brought along his own old rod, from his teenage years in Somerset, where they'd moved from Yorkshire. Chris caught his chub that day; but only after – Julian's memory, this – casting so hard and furiously out that he'd cast himself into the water. Dad had had to fish him out.

These emails and phone calls move me. Things kept surfacing, from depths none of us had stirred in half a century. Why hadn't we stirred them?

Well, Dad was not Ted. He was a family doctor, not someone who had to rely on words to heal. He wrote prescriptions, not diaries. I thought again of the evening of Mum's death, and Bob Newhart: someone else's words are better than your own cry, or silence.

I reflected on another absence, which meeting Sarah and her family had long thrown into a relief that the years had made it easier to accept as another inevitable and irrecoverable fact of my mother's death: there was not even a photograph. Not a single one, of Mum, was to be seen in any of the family homes I grew up in after her death; not a single one of me, either, as a boy, in the years before Dad married Pam. Only when my maternal grandfather had died, at a great old age in his and the century's mid-eighties, had Hilda, Mum's surviving younger sister, sent me a selection of the pictures he had: of the two girls, of Gwen graduating, of our family. Mostly Mum, Dad as young parents, with Chris, Julian and Nick. A handful of pictures of me, Dad and my brothers, on visits to grandparents, after she'd gone. The notice of her death, her cremation. Floral tributes, the first from 'Your loving five boys'. Dad must have written that, at least. And yet hadn't Dad taken pictures?

So had he destroyed them? Had the pain of his loss been too great to bear, or his fear of embarrassing his new wife been so much?

Why, I suggested, why not ask Pam and Peter anyway? Julian was about to pay them a visit at their house outside Exeter in a few weeks' time. After some reluctance, fearing the worst – and what would that be? Refusal to part with them, as Dad, ten years ago, when our own elder boys were teenagers, of an age to sail, had refused to let me have the dinghy still hanging, as it still does hang, from the roof timbers of their garage? Or the discovery that he had indeed destroyed, chucked out, pictures we all remembered him taking, while my elder brothers, and Big Al, and Big John, sailed and fished on the waters Dad drove us to – Julian plucked up the courage, and asked.

And Peter, in his thirties now, went up into the attic and found them. Boxes of them. Slides; transparencies. Of course they hadn't looked at them – why would they? But he and his mother were happy for us to have them; why would they not be?

*

Wales, it turned out, was nothing; and the slides from Clywedog, that summer of 1970, and the vast trek up to south-west Scotland, small beer. The Land Rover, and its grey predecessor, had made far greater conquests. Norway, in 1963, with a tent: it swung in a net on its way into the ship's hold in Newcastle docks. Snow on 31 August! Mountains, fjords. The pictures that caught my eye from a holiday they all still remembered were of my brothers hanging over jetty edges staring into fjords' depths. Other European holidays, too, in the late sixties: Austria. In 1969 there I was, holding a rod myself.

But it was Achmelvich that did it. Luce Bay seemed barely halfway. It was 1965. Norway in a tent – that snow! – had made them decide on a caravan. They tried it out in Wales. Lingering shots of Mum in early summer in the Welsh hills; she lies supine, a sleeping princess, her form rhyming the curves of the ridge beyond. Dad in love, I think: good. Chris spinning from the rocks at Llangranog. But then the real plunge, north, up. Pictures of Edinburgh Castle, of the salmon ladder at Pitlochry. Almost there: Chris standing, back towards the camera, in a distant river: campsite at Contin. With a rod? Lots of the Highland Games at Lochinver: Mum and boys staring on from the bonnet of the Land Rover. Burly kilted figures tossing the caber, but also one I missed first time around: 'McLaren, champion salmon caster'. Boys beside wild lochs, staring from rocks over water towards Suilven, the great sudden fist of a peak thrust skywards from Assynt. Boys on the rocks beside the Inver River. Chris with a dogfish! And then one with Julian, too, same fish, holding the rod. A team effort.

A year later they were back, but only after, I now see, more essential groundwork, or waterwork. At Whitsun, the River Severn at Cressage, ten miles from home, is shrunken; Julian and Nick watch from a steep, dry bank. Chris on rocks exposed in mid-river. 'Chris Fly fishing'. 'Chris's first dry fly'. And then, on the same roll, processed in June: into North Wales. At Beddgelert, 'Chris's first trout', though I have to take the caption's word for it. All you see is Chris, and then his brothers, in the shade of a dappled river pool, with rod. And another catch on that same trip: Gwen and Mark. A bundle in a pram.

That July – I was five months – up north again; Achmelvich again. Loch after unpronounceable loch, which Dad does scrupulously transcribe, back home, when the film comes back: Loch Beannach, Loch Roe, Lexey's Loch, Loch Poll Dhaidh. The miles between them. Nick fly fishing.

And then this.

Three boys on the sand by the caravan. Julian and Nick kneeling in lederhosen – tough, rough, hardwearing. From our first Austrian holiday, perhaps. Chris is in shorts and his Norwegian sweater. In other pictures I see the seeds of future sailing – Nick and Julian fighting over a mackerel, or nonplussed by a pollack with which they are asked to pose, sulky. Hormones. But here there's something almost religious, rapt, in their look. A unity of purpose and delight. They've been at the lochs again. Chris's eye holds the camera, two fish in his lap, two in his hands. Breakfast fish, at best. Nick and Julian stare in shy wonder at the two each they hold; the red spots on dark flanks. They've done it; Dad's done it, too. 'The catch: trout'.

Achmelvich; Aughrisburg. The same summer, 1966. Two families fishing, making discoveries. Nigel, Ted; Chris, Julian, Nick; Frieda, Nicholas.

Two years later, in 1968, I'm a real toddling presence in the family, not the larva in Gwen's womb as she lay in those Welsh hills, in intimate photos Nigel took of her that same summer of 1965, or as McLaren shot that line on the field at Lochinver. I am now on my own two feet. I am in almost as many pictures as the new dinghy, named *Annatto*, or maggot. There I am at the playground in Lochinver, and here, one morning walk, 'before breakfast', on a rock. With Mum and Dad, happy, their faces smooth and open in the unclouded light. And then, holding a rod, years before memory, but awakening the dormant passion for the art.

*

Still, though, an absence, in these pictures. The Bottom Pool.

I guess why. Dad was on home turf, duty turf. He needed to drive his boys away from home to find, for them, through them, what he'd not found himself since a boy. To manage hormones at a distance; to allow, but step back from, the excitement which, from a boy, Ted knew involved, and needed, 'the whole body'. And how could he possibly find it here, within a mile at most, less as the crow flies, from the family home on Holyhead Road?

But then I make a discovery. I browse Google Maps. And find that, after all, in spite of all, Limekiln Lane has survived the motorway. So has that spur of Ercall Wood. A dark eye looks up at the satellite camera amid the tree green.

So on an impulse one July morning I drive west one more time, hoping against hope for a hot and dusty summer afternoon. I pack a rod I bought for another of my adventures in Ted's footsteps, and an orange float the size of a lentil, and some light nylon and barbless hooks and shot to weight the bait with. For bait, though I do my research and discover that Wellington still has a tackle shop, I decide against maggots, which since I discovered artificial flies I have never been able to bear on a hook, so take the end of a loaf and a bagel.

Whitelands is still there, too. Almost unchanged, in black and white. The cypress hedge Mum and Dad planted in the sixties onto the main road, quieter now of course, since the motorway. And although half a century of housing estates and cul-de-sacs and bollards as well as the roar of the articulated lorries have chopped and reshaped Limekiln Lane it's still there, too, though my infant school, Barn Farm, has gone. A small boy lolls out of a bedroom window in Barn Farm Close, though, the last turn on the left before the tunnel of the motorway bridge. 'No unauthorised vehicles.' But what about me?

I'd forgotten the cottages, the farm that I discover later, close to what is now 'Limekiln Pool', with the stone outflow from which, yes, Mum would have shown Julian and his forgetful brothers how to catch pondlife other than fish. But there is the opening in the hedge, and that nose of woods beyond the field that rises through another hedge, and if I don't follow that now it's only because there's a sign saying 'Keep out': having come this far I don't want trouble. So I find a footpath up between the cottage gardens, and then a way through the woods. It's been drizzling, and the clouds are low still, and when I find the path dipping and glimpse silver through it I think, first, 'It's all so *close*'; and then, almost at once, prepare myself for disappointment, for the miniaturisation of that great pool into an apology of the puddle. The one time I went back to Tany since Dad sold it the stream was tiny. And as I follow that path down and right I also think of Ted's Crookhill, 'fifty yards across', 'as deep as England', at least once, and in memory: a befouled puddle by the time he took Nick and caught that dream of a perch, and now, in my time, even at midsummer dusk, haunted only by the rumble of trucks on the A1. A pool only of long grass between the fairways of the municipal golf course.

But it's as big as ever.

Here is that muddy bank Nick remembers; here, fifty yards along the path, is the concrete outflow: I look back on the deep water the wall still holds. I turn along the bank closest to the motorway and read MATALAN on the lorries that go past, dwarfing the church spire beyond. And then I'm almost completing the circuit, when I recognise a particular spread of branches, and see a length of monofilament hanging from them. This is the place. I tackle up, in awkward reverence, and something more. After only two tries, the orange float cocks with the shot I've added. I guess at a depth: three feet. There is no way of doing more than guess that

I can think of. I find that crust, wet it with saliva, mould it onto the hook, and lob it out. And there it is. Ten yards away? Well, maybe. But let that not be a distraction. Let not the slither of that sloping bank into water on which, now I come to think, only the exposed roots stop me resting my whole body on that orange lentil, and then my whole being. It's floating in the trees, and the beauty of that is enough.

Nothing else for a long while.

I think: check the bread. Gone: but not a flicker from the float. I'm no float fisherman. Perhaps it's just crumbled. I think I do better with the next paste ball around the hook. Again, the float dances in the reflected oak leaves and the monofilament glistens in the surface.

What did I expect? I didn't buy maggots.

An hour, not hundreds, goes by. What if nothing is in this water but last year's leaves? So I decide to break up that crust, lob chunks of it onto the surface near my float, hoping for stickleback nibbles, or dace. Nothing. This is OK. It is enough to know the Bottom Pool exists, that this place exists, that I did strike, squatting just here, fifty years ago, and that I did land flat on my back and see the little perch that had taken my maggots dangling from what – I look up, as I prepare to cast – just might be that same branch.

The last chunk of my crust goes out, closer in this time, five yards out, if that. The others must have sunk.

So this time I use my bagel, softer, but more readily pliable. And gently, gently, swing it beyond the half-submerged log that's below me there against the bank. I will something to happen; I give all I have to imagine some creature down there in the dead leaves, moving, watching, sniffing.

And then the float twitches. Or does it? And then it twitches again, and then it's sliding firmly down, and I lift – and the water explodes. Whatever this is, it's no tiddler. The line runs away; the long rod, 11 foot, a Mark IV Avon, no less, bought because Ted had on Barrie's recommendation bought one for Irish waters, is bent into the fish. And a mouth shows and I think I know but I have to, have to, get proof, for my brothers, who will otherwise never believe this. The camera's already round my neck, so I lift and steer and fumble and press the shutter and finally bring this – carp! A carp! A CARP! If I'm not mistaken, a MIRROR carp – flapping out onto the leaves and twigs at the water's edge, and press again. And then the line breaks and it's gone.

And when I review all this, and the next I catch, ten minutes later, I see that Ted was right, in those lines in 'Learning to Think' that he wrote and did not change. It's armour-plated, engineered, a hero that came from nothing and will forever be inevitable. Living metal.

I fish on.

7

Strangers

July 1975: the first summer the couple could call Devon home. The old thatched cottage has finally been renovated, and Nethercott Hall is theirs, too: plans for Farms for City Children are taking shape. Michael and Clare Morpurgo are walking some friends down to the Torridge late one evening when they encounter him. 'He was fishing for seatrout ... and loomed up from under the river-bank. I remember a giant of a man who greeted me warmly enough, and introduced himself as Ted Hughes.' Michael knew, of course: as a teacher in his twenties, starting out, he'd loved Ted's broadcasts for *Listening and Writing*: he'd listened, he'd written. Now he'd begun to publish. But this wasn't the time for literary talk. 'I could tell from his demeanour that he wished to be left alone with his river. I learnt later, as I got to know him better, how single-minded he was about his fishing, about his river.'

His river. *His* river.

Reading this, I think: the second of his rivers. But now I know he's added the Torridge to the Taw. That shift in his fishing gravity: Moortown farm is only three miles away, beyond Iddesleigh, where Charlie Weeks, bailiff, local sea-trout specialist, heir to 'Lemon Grey', drinks at the Duke of York. 'The most enthralling moment of all my Torridge fishing' now means: of at least eight years, since 1975.

Then I wonder at this strange meeting. Even a man of Ted's size could have kept low, under the ten-foot banks, 'faded', as he did whenever he wished not to see friends, even those whose generosity had given him the fishing in the first place. Perhaps, in switching pools, in hauling himself from the sunk tunnel of the Torridge and the river's own music, he'd missed the murmur of human conversation until it was too late to avoid them.

More likely, though: Ted saw this young man coming, as someone he had a special reason to court. In 2012, I wrote to Michael Morpurgo. He rang back, told me he never shared the passion he knew Ted had for fishing and his river. He only fished when Ted took him: once for eels, also at night; once for consolation, after *War Horse* failed to win the Whitbread Prize. But all that was still years off. That first late July evening in 1975 Ted knows he needs to introduce himself to the man who's just acquired the fishing rights to a prime stretch of the Torridge. But there's ownership and then there's prior possession. Whose river was it, really? Fishing's about confidence. Make sure the new guy knows you're a part of it. You stake your claim.

In 'Taw and Torridge', Ted's guarded about all this: he discusses *Torridge Fishery*, and cites the success of another sea-trout fisherman 'on what was Lemon Gray's own water', but shrewdly never names that specialist or identifies the hands the river's in now. You keep such information to yourself, and to people you're ready to trust. But it's Mike Morpurgo whose number Ted gives in introducing the Torridge to his friends.

*

May 1977. One hundred and eighty miles north-east.

The day job, or early evening, to catch the punters after work: a poetry reading in Oxford. A joint one, with Ted's close friend Seamus Heaney. In time he'll become famous Seamus, Nobel Laureate. Already a great friend of Ted's, Barrie's, too. Seamus gets the connection between poetry and fishing. His wife comes from a family of eel fishers on Lough Neagh; he's written verse about that dark art. And though he stopped fishing in his early teens, he knows that inside his adult arm remains 'a totally enlivened twelve-year-old one, feeling the bite. And that's enough for a lifetime of poems.' Perhaps in honour of Ted, and Barrie, too – Seamus knows the Island, has spent happy weeks 'Jerpointing', Barrie's current house, also beside the Nore – he reads his poem

'The Salmon Fisher to the Salmon'. The fisherman in Seamus's poem addresses his quarry, knows it doesn't stand a chance:

> you're doomed
> By senseless hunger in your eyes.

Except that, it turns out that Oxford evening, he doesn't know this after all. It turns out that the feeling arm is no match for a knowledgeable head. At the end of the reading, the poets take questions from the audience. A sixty-year-old hand goes up. It's a heresy. But Seamus Heaney is wrong.

Tom Rawling is a teacher. He's spent his whole career in Oxford schools, first teaching English, then – in despair at what he regards as a mechanistic examination system – working with kids with special needs. But he's a Cumbrian, and a fisherman since a boy. Born in 1916, he was, and has remained, a child of his father's war. His father had been the village schoolmaster in Ennerdale, in the shadow of the fells. Known, his whole life, as a pillar of the church. But in a darker shadow, too. Mr Rawling brought trauma back from the trenches and tried to drink his way out of it; he never could, of course, and Tom suffered for it. Daily canings at school, beatings at home.

When the next war came, Tom avoided active service. Worked with survivors instead. Then, with Eva his wife, a socialist, as devout an atheist, their daughters Sue and Jane tell me, as Tom was, he taught. His father's God looked after him: he lived until 1967. His death triggered a breakdown in Tom, a year's sabbatical, then retraining, at a special school for the last decade. He took early retirement. And now, what he's kept under has started to surface: he's been writing poems this past year, about his childhood.

What kept him going through those years? Fishing. He'd always taken himself back to the rivers of his youth. At school he founded a fishing club for the boys, but needed something for himself besides. Each July Tom went, generally alone, to spend a fortnight fishing the famously clear Cumbrian Esk for sea trout and salmon. Thomas Hardy once compared the waters of

Wessex's River Frome to 'the pure River of Life shown to the Evangelist'; Tom found in the fresh fell water of the Esk life and death and fear and power and killing and beauty. And from 1963, he's been finding all that in a man who was everything his father wasn't. Hugh Falkus, ex-Spitfire pilot, charismatic, filmmaker, broadcaster, survivor, charmer, another giant of a man. Falkus published *Sea Trout Fishing: A Guide to Success* that year. Tom let it guide him. He sought Hugh out. Learning his methods from the man himself.

These went well beyond fishing. Days of observation of the fish in the clear water they hung in – 'reconnaissance', he called it: know your enemy, your prey; understand their behaviour, their sensitivity to the slightest change in atmospheric pressure in the air, to disturbance of the water; a human shadow or footfall, or even the smell of fear or injury suffered by one of the shoal, can empty a pool of these silver tourists – equipped you for dark hours of concentrated, confident, solitary casting for the targets you'd just spied. It felt like military intelligence.

Falkus had a plan for the whole night. Made it a game. Like football. The Great Game. First half, from dark to midnight, a floating line, Falkus's own pattern, a slim Medicine Lure, designed to stimulate, to provoke, old habits of chasing silver bait fish out at sea, where they'd put on weight and energy out of all proportion to the river's resident trout. Half-time, around midnight, a surface lure, skated over the surface, to bring the fish up, irritate them. It wasn't hunger that made them grab the lure. It was habit, the memory of feeding patterns out at sea, or in the estuary; it wasn't hunger. That knowledge made the moment of encounter, the take, all the more mysterious. And then the second half, sunk lure, sinking line, pursuing them into the depths, through the small hours. Get your methods right and there wasn't a moment of the day or night when you couldn't catch fish.

Tom's been executing those methods, and the fish they brought him, each summer for years now. His daughters remember him practising his casts on Kidlington Rec, tying and retying the Medicine Lure. He is utterly confident in Falkus, naturalist and fisherman. And he's been evangelising – in prose which Falkus

checked for tangles, ensuring it runs clear as the Esk. Here is Tom
in June 1970, in an article for *Trout and Salmon*. He's peering
through alders at a 'giant flotilla' of sea trout and the occasional
salmon they closely resemble ('you can see the concave tail fin in
this transparent water').

> Insects on the water are almost entirely ignored. So too, are
> experimental offerings of worms and maggots. Occasionally,
> if the watcher persists, a salmon or sea trout can be tempted
> to intercept one of these many offerings – as it can an artificial
> lure. But such fish are rare exceptions. How different from
> the hungry parr and brown trout, snapping at all that comes
> their way. *They* are feeding. But the sea trout and salmon lie
> motionless, save for a lazy fanning of the tail.

Rawling is the state of Falkus's art. And Ted would have known
it by the time they met. Even if he hadn't read the second piece
Rawling published in September 1975, 'Sea Trout by the Book',
Ted certainly owned a copy of the new and revised edition of *Sea
Trout Fishing* it announced.

So when, that evening in Oxford, Rawling points out Seamus's
mistake, Ted takes notice. After the reading the three of them
walk across Oxford. The two real fishermen talk salmon and
sea trout. And then Rawling writes a new kind of poem, about
fishing, about the real marvels of the salmon's life cycle, including
the fatal moment. When something closer to vanity than hunger
is to blame:

> you came to my lure,
> Betrayed yourself
> for a feather.

Tom sends it to Seamus; then, that September, casts it again in
search of a bigger fish.

Ted's been on the radio the night before, reading from *Season
Songs*, that children's book that grew up. That's Tom's excuse for
writing. He bought a copy the year before, read the reviews; he

shares his surprise, now that he's over sixty, that 'other people don't recognize / admit / realise that we're always children. Nothing much changes inside except that the "prison bars" grow bigger.'

Reminding him of their meeting, Tom encloses his poem. Then adds the equivalent of Ted's doctored treble lure to his cast. Drops a line, makes it sound casual. But of course he knows exactly what he's doing. He's about to spend a week fishing with Hugh Falkus, to intercept a late run of broad-shouldered 'harvest' sea trout, and maybe a grilse. He's been out at night collecting lobworms from the grass verges of Kidlington as bait.

I checked the date of this letter. What Tom didn't say, must have itched to say, but in the end left Ted to work out: that meant he'd be with Hugh Falkus on the night Hugh's new documentary on the natural history of sea trout and salmon, *Salmo the Leaper*, first aired on BBC TV. Still, his poem contained a plug, at least: 'Audacious your odyssey, / Salmo the leaper.'

That Sunday night, 11 September 1977, I was eleven; it was my first Sunday night at boarding school. The one TV series the housemaster Mr Gibbons allowed the older boys to watch was *The World About Us*. We crowded into his lounge in pyjamas and dressing gowns. I'll never forget it. I certainly hadn't when, a week shy of a year later, on the last Sunday of the summer holidays, it was repeated. This time I watched it with Dad, and for once he didn't fall asleep. I have no doubt that the sequence in which Big Hugh cast for, hooked, played and landed a six-pound sea trout at night, laid it silver on the bench in the moonlight, was what, six years later, persuaded Dad to send me on that course at the Arundell Arms. Both of us envied that glamour, that wildness, that power and its purpose, in man and fish. And the next summer, for my school leaver's prize I chose *Sea Trout Fishing*.

*

'Are you a fisherman?' By now I've met a second man, the schoolteacher John Venning, of whom Ted asked this question in the years he was writing and revisiting *River*: like the first, Clive Wilmer, John told me how crushed Ted looked when he said no.

So perhaps it's not so remarkable that he responds as kindly as he does at the end of the month to Tom Rawling, an old boy who is teacher, poet *and* fisherman. And who is clearly asking for some kind of help. Ted writes back. He likes the sharp end of Tom's poem, wonders about that Cumberland trip, then shares his own fishing news. Down in Devon they've had their worst ever season. The sea-trout late by a month and, one good May week apart, no salmon to be found, though he knows there have been a few in the river all year. Ted's kept failing to connect, at least with sea-trout: half a dozen dace and a diseased trout from his last night out. But it's not all bad news, even if he has to cast back and abroad for it. He sends Tom 'Earth-numb', with the story of the three salmon it brought him, and rounds off with a tale, itself a few years old, from Ireland. Barrie is the star; Ted names him, as a friend of Seamus, one of the rare times Ted breaks cover with a friendship he kept close. But this story's worth it. Refused cash or fishing as payment for the loan of some paintings for a show organised by an aristocrat who should have known better, Barrie poached his river. Eight salmon landed, one lost, in nine casts.

It's all light enough, this opening onto his world. But Tom seizes it with a sea-trout's savagery. I wonder how I'd have felt, if I'd been Ted, reading Tom's reply – was Tom really so disappointed that he'd only managed eight fish one night on the Esk with Hugh, up to two pounds, fishing hard with a sunk line, which meant after midnight? My guess is that a fishing muscle was being flexed, a point was being scored, if size matters, and it nearly always does. But I'd have allowed him that. Because Tom also wrote this, on 'Earth-numb':

> When a poem is so right, when I wish I'd written it, when it's something I want to write about, I'm almost alarmed that I shall never be able to find my own words for it. Can a 'lure' ever again be anything but a 'prayer'?

He feels the poem in his belly, Tom says. 'The mutual fright + shock of the take especially.' Faint praise this is not. Ted knows better than to respond.

*

But the pool settles. It takes eighteen months. Ted's due back in Oxford for another reading. Tom writes again. He's found his own words after all, and has been 'writing about night fishing, before it all fades away'. He hoped Ted would forgive the intrusion of the three poems he was sending him, 'since it's fishing'.

And Ted agrees. Tom's are the first poems he's read that come at the experience of fishing from within. There's real respect here. And to prove it, a recent poem of his own, which Tom's put him in mind of. Ted puts it lightly, but he must have known it was a proof of the difference between them: 'Night Arrival of Sea-Trout', which Nick had just hand-printed, at home, for the press they'd started. Named Morrigu after the old Irish death goddess, a crow; I've yet to realise why, where she really comes into her and Ted's and Barrie's realm. But there's plenty to keep me sharp in the meantime. Everything in that poem is charged with life: when the sea-trout leaps, 'moon-mouthed, and shivers', even the lobworms drip with passion. And Pan goes wild in the moonlit corn. It will be the moment sea-trout arrive in *River*, too.

Tom knows he's not in Ted's league. His own poems, he says, aren't much more than reports of fishing; but in 'Night Arrival of Sea-Trout', 'like Earth-numb', 'the river explodes'. Still, he is delighted that his own poems 'have hooked night-fishing for you'. And sends more poems.

The friendship grows. By the end of the year Tom's sent him more fishing poems, and then his first little book. And when Ted replies by giving him news of the best late run of sea-trout in the Torridge and Taw for years, and a copy of *Moortown*, Tom takes the chance to make a different kind of cast. He's fished the Taw once, years ago, but doesn't know the Torridge. Does Ted fish association water, or is all the fishing in private hands? How, if at all, can 'off-comers' like him, visitors, gain access? Hotels?

A year later, Tom writes again, a Christmas card: another cast Ted's way. He's decided to book into a poetry course at the Arvon Centre at Totleigh Barton; and though 1980 has been a real disaster on the Torridge, not a repeat of the bonanza, Ted suggests he stays at the Half Moon Inn at Sheepwash. And when it turns out that Ted himself will be in Ireland for a month from mid-March, fishing with Nicholas, he fits up Tom with all he needs: directions from Totleigh to the farm lane where he needs to park, on the Sheepwash bank; a detailed beat map, with two suggested pools, one of them that one near the concrete ramp, and the contact details of Mike Morpurgo and Charlie Weeks. Oh, and Ted also mentions a great recent performance at a Devon hotel of one Hugh Falkus; they'd talked afterwards, spoken warmly of Tom.

And it works. Here, in a letter awaiting Ted's return from Ireland, is Tom celebrating 'a salmon of a time', a nine-pound sea-fresh fish, caught on the first afternoon of his three days on Ted's stretch on a sea-trout lure; he'd tied it Falkus Medicine-style.

Tom's beside himself, feels six inches taller: can't resist telling Ted he doesn't think much of Behind Ramp, Ted's name for it on his map. Another Half Moon angler who buys him a double whisky to celebrate tells him it's really Lemon Gray's Island Run.

And why not? It's a rare event, a March Torridge salmon, and particularly on the fly; after another disastrous year for the sister rivers, for the fish and for the river, pollution as well as estuary nets have sparked fears of the imminent disappearance of salmon and sea-trout from the two rivers, the Water Authority's changing the bye-laws to prohibit spinning, the method favoured by most locals, from all but the early season. And it's all skill, not beginner's luck. Ted has no doubt. Knows where his fish would have been lying, right under the concrete ramp, where the water's created a cave a bit like on the Dart; where he took the lure. And when Tom's poem comes, dedicated to Ted Hughes and Hugh Falkus, Ted gets it right again: is surprised and envious that Tom saw the take, a golden gleam in the stained water.

Tom's proved himself; they make more plans. Another course, maybe, that summer? He could combine poetry and peal, the Devon name for sea-trout. And Ted provides the gen, more local knowledge than Tom could ever have imagined, knowledge that begins to reveal that Morpurgo was right about whose river this was.

He's got plans to persuade Mike to add more big boulders to create more stations for the migratory fish, to stop them rushing upriver into Benjie's water; doing so would be adding to what Lemon Gray had been up to in placing the concrete blocks into the pool below his concrete bridge. Sprackmann's Pit, the long pool just upstream, used to be an even better sea-trout pool, before the Water Board pruned those overhanging trees last year. And at once Tom imagines using it to try Hugh's surface lure at midnight, only to doubt whether he's too old to be wading at half-time on a strange river. And wonders, too, about the stain in the water: does the Torridge ever lose it?

And then Ted goes further. Sets the hook deep; saves the best till last. Looks upriver to beyond Mike's upper boundary: the junction pool with the Okement. That's the real sea-trout pool, the richest on the whole river. Lemon Gray was right, even though of course he was promoting his own hotel, trying to hook fishermen, too. In that third of a mile, deep pots in the still water beyond hold really big fish; at night they move back into its beautiful spreading tail. The Half Moon rents it. And in July Ted should be around.

Which sets Tom thinking: perhaps Ted might join him on that water, and Tom might join him on Sprackmann's Pit and Island Run. They could have both beats together, the whole stretch. But it isn't the whole mile of fishing Tom wants. It's company: Ted's. 'I hope we fish together.'

Early that June, plans for Tom's stay advancing, more news from his Torridge correspondent. Of the dozen salmon Charlie Weeks has just seen in Concrete Pool; meeting Charlie one evening, mad at having lost a seven-pound sea-trout, and then an even bigger one, both hooked on the one fly he ever uses, despite Lemon Gray's suspicion of it: a size 10 Peter Ross, dark mallard wing, red body, with white and silver ribbing, tail fibres. Ted himself favours a small Silver Stoat's tube, fished fast; and he can react fast, too, when he hears the sea-trout are in, the kind of approach only a man who lives twenty minutes from the river can adopt. Just that week, when the fish have been in the river only a few days, their sea-strength still on them, the habits of feeding still vivid, Ted has had three half-hour visits: on the evening he'd met Charlie; and on two successive dawns. Four fish, averaging four pounds.

Two hundred and fifty miles east, in the Fens, thirty-five years later, I spend my dusks and my dawns dreaming of such fish.

But now I see another reason for these stories of Ted's, those deft, quick raids. Tom's grand plan for them both is like Hugh's. It would need a whole night, a campaign meticulously planned, confidently executed. And drafting 'Taw and Torridge' a year later, Ted will give at least lip service to 'Falkus's dictum', intended to urge fishermen to fish beyond midnight and through to dawn, that sea trout 'can be caught at any time'. But, Ted goes on in that essay, nights of midnight mist are nights to retreat to bed. The 'real artists' find their way of catching Torridge in coloured water and clear – remembering that unlike the Esk, in its upper reaches 'the Torridge acquires a stain it never loses'. None of this is sea-trout fishing by the book, of course – if you mean Falkus's, or even *Torridge Fishery*, which he urges Tom to read.

Still, for all that wariness of a grand plan, he genuinely wants Tom to taste at least some of this magic for himself. Perhaps the more so now Ted knows that, once more, his visitor will be tasting it alone. Ted's not going to be there to fish with Tom: he has the chance to join Nick again in Alaska. And by now he knows he's finding his way towards his own book: *River*. So he slips two poems into his letter describing that Okement junction pool and those deep pots above. 'An August Evening' and 'After Moonless Midnight'.

'After Moonless Midnight' isn't a poem a disciple of Falkus could have written: it's no report, no how-to guide. But you can tell it's Ted: 'I waded, deepening' for a moment takes me back to 'Stealing Trout', to the Taw at dawn, Ted's first deepening into the charging water. Then I yield to this blacker Torridge depth: all that matters is the world he wades in and what happens to the self when he does. But this time it's not the gift of that headlong rout of the river to conjure him a trout. Here, now, all the force lies in the fish: watching, listening, in numbers he can't know, but which he still imagines in all their extraordinary power. Their 'magical skins', their feeling gills, their eyes. Their charged senses, their power. 'Their mouth-aimed intent', their 'torpedo / Concentration', all of it held in suspense, in service of a true wildness. 'Their savagery waited, and their explosion.' Tom would have detonated it. The bucking rod.

Not Ted. Not this time. This isn't about catching a fish. It's about fish and river catching the fisherman. 'We've got him.' And it's about Ted's sense of the fish. I remember Falkus, in *Salmo the Leaper*: 'He'd be a bold man who pretended he knew anything about the psychology of these fish. But we can observe something of their behaviour when the level falls in these clear water streams.' That makes Ted a bold man.

Or just a man who knows the river and its moods. And one who's prepared to withdraw from it when he feels he needs to, when the river needs him to.

'An August Evening' casts a different light: the new moon that bathes it, perhaps because autumn's in the air, too. It doesn't last long: a wet fog that descends at midnight, clamping his head, stiffening his fingers; he retreats. But he's had more than enough time to watch, feel the river, and have some contact, at least, with its strange visitors.

The fish Ted remembered at Crookhill were 'too immense to stir', but you knew from the outset they were pike. But this evening, the 'star-touched' river is touched, and only gradually can he bring himself to say what by, to name them. Journalists have a glib, slighting term for them, 'the silver tourists', as if these night fish were on as much of a jaunt as the visiting anglers down for a particularly exciting evening out on their summer hols. Ted knows otherwise, knows you have to edge towards them. These are 'sea-tribes', and they deserve an anthropologist's respect: 'too serious to stir', or even to name – you keep them on the tip of your tongue – until the time has come for them to fulfil their purpose: they're 'up for their weddings', 'The carnival on the gravels'. Or perhaps it's something in the water: perhaps their mood has been coloured along with the river, 'still beer-stained after the barley disaster'.

Whatever causes it, Ted knows that theirs is a sensual vocation, a calling that humbles the modern fisherman's version of the Great Game. 'They will not play tonight.' Their 'longships' have

'Holds crammed with religious purpose', which Ted knows it's his privilege only to glimpse:

> Robed in the stilled flow of their Creator
> They inhale unending. I share it a little.

And the experience moves him, shakes him:

> Climbing out, I make a silent third
> With two owls reassuring each other.

*

Tom stayed and fished at the Half Moon that July. But he had no luck and missed Ted – who arrived back from Alaska too late to do anything but ring the inn to find out how Tom had got on. And though Ted alerted him, in 1982, to the fact that he'd bought another rod for the Nethercott beat, and would be advertising the farmhouse at Moortown, with fishing, in *Trout and Salmon* that season, it wasn't until October 1984 that the two of them met again, sharing an evening of talk at Totleigh Barton. Tom had published his first full collection, *Ghosts at My Back*, and was now guest reader. Tom's daughters Sue and Jane showed me a picture of the two men talking together. Poetry and peal, I'm guessing. A couple more times they discuss a joint outing, the last of them on the Exe in 1988, on which Ted then had a rod. But the ledger doesn't include Tom in the list of those Ted fished with that year. And I've found no evidence they ever fished together.

But Ted kept writing to him. The last I've seen is dated 1994, two years before Tom died, only four before Ted. They are great letters: copious, passionate, generous. And it turns out their secret is simple: to remain pure, exclusive, true to the terms of that first abrupt meeting and talk afterwards. They're about nothing but poetry and fishing. And they reflect, and resist, sometimes by force of will, the ill health of the rivers he loved. They tell the tale of the disaster of the Torridge: agricultural pollution, water abstraction, low flows and algal bloom and spinach-green sluggishness, as well as the rare but blessed days when it flows full and true. The letters soon settle into a rhythm: annual or six-monthly fishing reports of all his trips abroad, drawing together the loose-leaf diaries I'd been reading and revelling in. Ireland, Iceland, Alaska. Scotland, later, too, from August 1981: Lewis and Harris salmon, and the Spey's marvellous sea-trout in 1985. By then he was Laureate, and spending more money as well as time on privileged waters. But he never forgot who he was writing to: made sure to say how the locals on the Spey had free access to the sea-trout every evening from 8.00 p.m., once the paying guests had retired to their hotel dinners.

The last item in this bundle of correspondence – Tom's daughters wanted me to have copies, but the originals are still in private hands, which is why I have avoided quoting them – was the reason I drove to meet them well after the end of the season, one winter's day, at Sue's house in Lincolnshire. I'd seen it before, photocopied in the British Library. I saw at once why Ted made that copy. It's a letter of condolence to Tom's daughters Sue and Jane in December 1996. He had come to know their father well. Against expectation, Tom had written poems he had spent a lifetime needing to write. And then: 'he had the key to Paradise. Knew where it was, how to get into it, and what to do when he got in there.'

Ted makes it sound real, three-dimensional. Getting there sounds possible; operating in it, too, if you were suitably equipped. And the words at once rang a bell: I thought of that wonderful moment in 'Taw and Torridge' which describes that 'almost hidden world' you enter when 'you let yourself down … into the cleave of the river' 'in green Devon evening light' and know you're entering 'a paradise – the sort that survives in few places'. It made me long to enter it myself.

*

I'm back at Rose Cottage above the Tamar. This time I've brought my rod. It's the May half-term holiday, and I've heard that the big sea trout have arrived, and Underhill, the best pool on the Tamar, is available.

It's a warm night. And there's no moon: good. Moonlight frames human profiles, scatters these wary fish. But I'm rusty, and self-conscious: casting a fly at night when you're excited or unsure can snarl your invisible line. I've climbed back out of the river and am fiddling on the bank near my car, head torch safely off the river. And then I hear a rumble. I extinguish my beam. A deeper darkness looms along the bank. And it's not a cow, or a deer, or any other creature of the night. A white pickup, lights off. And my heart sinks. Was I not meant to be here? Is it bailiff or poacher? I've been longing for this night.

But then a friendly voice speaks out of the darkness, warm Devon: 'Hi, Mark, I'm Gerald. How you getting on? John told me you like Ted Hughes. What's your favourite poem? Mine's "October Salmon".'

And even as my mind reeled with wonder, the charm of it, I knew the answer: ' "Strangers".'

*

In the British Library there is a folder of Ted's 'poetic portraits'. All but one is of people, and they go no further than sketches. But here's something different: an untitled group portrait, in real time, three full pages of reporter's notebook, all verse. And for once water conditions and light mean that he can sketch them. It's early June, mid-morning, 'Spring side of midsummer' and the day's brightness probes the river bed's gravels, picks out the shadowy forms of minnows, and

> The big heavy strangers,
> The sea-trout, in flotilla.

Time is measured in slow light. 'Sun inches.' The sea-trout defy it. All day, they embody 'Night-cool'; all day, whether he's beside the river, watching damselflies emerge in all their metals, or back at home, Ted has them in his head; he revolves around their still centre.

> Wherever
> I walk today, they are there. Whatever
> I happen to be doing, they are there, watching,
> Unmoving.

But these 'seven longships', 'Each one concentrated, like a shell in the breach', are full of the charge they've brought with them, power he knows he might just be able to provoke. At the end of this draft they

> Still struggle with their sea-strength,
> Ready to explode at the touch of steel.

You can feel 'An August Evening' and 'After Moonless Midnight' stirring in this portrait. And it's the closest the Torridge ever comes to the conditions Tom Rawling and Hugh Falkus took for granted: clear water, when you can see the fish, measure them, have time to find and discard words that respond to the play of body and water and light and the mood these fish inspire in you at different times of day or night, in different years. I suspect Ted wrote it about Sprackmann's Pit, before the Water Board hacked back those branches in 1980. Perhaps in 1979, when the memory of Rawling's own poems were fresh: Ted had praised them for the feeling they evoked of the hook's steel on tooth.

'Strangers' is the poem in *River* that slow, day-long portrait in early June became. But it settles for the first moment, a brief encounter at dawn. There's no question now of taking these fish from the river. It's enough just to watch, wonder at these rare conditions: 'There they actually are under homebody oaks'. He won't have long before some false human step or clumsy movement on their skyline – his or a companion's – sends them scattering, like the trout they themselves were before some sexual imperative to feed, breed, silvered them at sea. It's enough to 'see the holy ones', the priests of that sea-tribe.

Ted concentrates. Not, now, on their future, in the autumn. That's too far off. He gives all he can to their attitude, their poise, their focus. He relishes 'the slight riffling of their tail-ailerons', wants us to share it, feel it, say it aloud: as he'd known full well when he met the new owner of his fishing, it's not a raised voice that spooks them but a clumsy step. Stillness helps him catch every detail of the river as it takes these sea-tribes, strangers, in: using the word he'd have come across when he and Sylvia were in America, he notes 'water-skeeters / On their abacus', 'the buzzard's slow hand'. But above all, he concentrates on the sea-trout. They ignore anyone or thing who watches them, targets them – the sun 'so openly aiming down', and looking up with a serenity that only Ted could have defined as he did. These extraordinary fish

> Absorb everything and forget it
> Into a blank of bliss.
> And this is the real Samadhi – worldless, levitated.

Samadhi is a state of superconsciousness. Ted owned a book by a Hindu spiritualist, Mouni Sadhu, called *Concentration*. It's an essential, rare stage on the path to self-realisation, and it requires years of disciplined self-training. Ted had to explain it to the editors and critics who asked him what it meant. I stumbled across it in one of Ted's fishing notebooks, among lists of sea-trout flies. The sea-trout are emblems, exemplars, of a consciousness he aspires to. The ultimate insiders in a vision of Paradise only Ted was equipped to see.

*

Gerald Spiers and I have spent some great days and nights on Ted's rivers: Ted's way with sea-trout made such sudden intimacy between strangers natural. We've hunted them on the Dart below Dartmeet one midsummer night of torrential rain; its leaf-spattering sent us home early, and drowned out the soul and body music of 'The Dark Violin of the Valley' that Ted heard all night long. On the Tamar, on a night of glittering moon, Gerald watched while I waded, deepening, and was seduced by the dazzle of the silver calligraphy my line made casting into the tree-shaded darkness of the run below the tail of Underhill Pool. The water had crept to within two inches of the top of my waders when my foot slid off a rock and I lunged, wobbled, just recovered. They almost got me then. But we've also searched for spawning gravels on the Inny, a tributary of the Tamar, where it runs thin and clear high on Bodmin Moor, between Christmas and New Year.

Gerald's eye pointed out a great fish, a seven-pounder, he guessed, deep in a tree-shaded pool on the West Dart, thirty-eight years to the day and date that Ted walked and fished that same beat: Saturday 14 June 1986; 14 June 2014 is also a Saturday. The Dart is famous for its clarity, even in flood. The moor peat is a fine filter. Even in water so clear, it was only the smudge of what looked to me like a tawny leaf deep in that pool – but it was a leaf that held curiously still against the current, then, there! moved over that rock: a fungus on a green head – which gave that seven-pounder away. And only one small peal came to us that night, down on the lower Dart, at Staverton. But the fly Gerald had given me that first night would catch me a bright silver three-pounder on the penultimate night of the season the following September, back at Underhill, just in front of the glimmering white rock at the pool tail he'd told me was where big sea-trout lie. It was, and remains, one of my two biggest.

The following afternoon I waded quietly upstream from the run below, looking for trout or whatever would take my dry fly. The water was low, clear. And when I approached that same rock, I looked down and saw, only a step away, a smooth, grey torpedo of great beauty. Calmly she hung there; as calmly, as I watched, under the pressure of my eyes, the shadow of my rod, she moved away, upstream, into patterns of glitter and shade my polaroids could no longer resolve. But for the moment – how long? Ten seconds, twenty? – of that encounter, time slowed; light slowed. I was no threat to her; I was merely sharing her world for a little. The fish was letting me in. But that night, at ten o'clock, after rain, casting towards the rock, she was grabbing me. Savagery, not hunger. My second three-pounder, her flanks silver on the wet grass. It was a triumph then. Now I'm not so sure.

*

Charles Inniss, now in his eighties, with an MBE for services to the Torridge, still runs the fishing for the Half Moon, and visiting rods can still fish the beautiful stretch of river above the Nethercott beat: a half-mile of the left bank of the Torridge above the Okement junction, and Monument pool below, and a run below that. You can see the cross in the meadow opposite. The big white house, Bondstones, looks down on you; so does David Ward's farmhouse. But there's Beam, too, a twenty-minute drive downriver, just below Torrington, and above the tide: the one place Ted mentions fishing for sea-trout on the Torridge in 'Taw and Torridge', where at eleven one sunny Friday morning in 1980 he started casting across the tail of the weir pool, and discovered the 'extraordinary intercommunication system' at work in a shoal of peal. Eight small fish caught, and released, but only after swapping from the silver-bodied fly that caught the last. Word had got round. Killing them would have let him catch more. But experimenting, and the ways of the species, interested him more.

So I had the keys to Paradise. I knew where it was, and how to get into it.

Still, though, it took me four summers. In 2015, my eldest brother Chris and I travelled south-west. He is eleven years older and a lawyer: though we live in adjacent counties, he and I inhabit different worlds. How would we see this astonishing secret corner of North Devon? And how would our nights be? Though he has always imagined himself a fisherman, he hasn't cast a fly in at least fifteen years. Ted once took his own brother, Gerald, to the Mole for sea-trout one evening, and cast out for him, letting him retrieve. I needed too much from this visit for myself to be Chris's guide, but was at least confident that I'd put everything in place as far as I could. The rooms at the Half Moon, the emails to Charles Inniss, hoping for particular beats. It was a mid-July weekend; it should have been perfect.

But our hearts were elsewhere. Dad was ill. He lay in one of the wards named for the region's rivers at the Royal Devon and Exeter. He was weakening. We spent too little time with him, but this was before we'd found the photographs, and of course by then it was too late to ask Dad. At any rate, we didn't say much: ours is a family which has never found anything speech-easy. It was enough to report, and for him to know, that I'd taken Chris sea-trout fishing. Brought him within reach. And it was good to spend what time we did together.

On our last night we fished the beat Charles said that he was keen for me to know he rents, not the hotel, in some private arrangement with an owner he never names. I know that 1982 was the year in which the Half Moon lost the right to rent it, and Ted called its off-comers 'the opposition' when he saw them on the far bank: they made him feel crowded on the river, rushed. Charles calls it Okement Foot, but it's the stretch Ted described, sure enough. That junction pool with the spreading tail. The still depths of the canal-like 200 yards above it, with what looked like miner's ladders down the cliff of the bank. No sense of how deep the wading was.

We did our best, but nothing. Not a splosh. Were the fish here? We regrouped at midnight, under opaque cloud. Moonless. The beginnings of a mist. We felt cold. Just before one, owls started hooting. We called it a night, pleading the long drive home the following morning.

I returned to the Half Moon the following July, with David, newish husband of an old friend: originally from Lancashire, he's now based in London, fishes his home rivers whenever he can and the capital's ponds and reservoirs when not. He'd arranged a visit home to collect his waders. We met at Exeter station, drove north-west, deepening. We tried Beam first. I'd done my homework, knew for sure, from Ted's letters to Tom and from Henry Williamson that, yes, that pool below the weir was indeed where Tarka the otter was born, under one of the huge beech trees on the far bank. I'd also come supplied with as many small Silver Stoat's Tails, Invictas, Butchers, Peter Rosses and Alexandrias as I could justify, and with more of the Bumbles Gerald had given me. And this time, at 11.00 a.m. or so, the hour of Ted's experiment, I cast across the tail of Weir Pool and hooked a sea-trout with my first cast, and lost it within seconds. I could have cursed; I wanted to whoop with delight. But remembering Ted's experiment and the intercommunication system, I made sure to change the pattern I was using. Not another touch. Something better, though. A minute later, in the sunlit brown of that tail water, a silver moon of a fish flashed; I caught its eye, but that's all I caught. That afternoon, I saw a salmon enter the pool over the lip from the rapids below, move gently upriver, black and huge in profile, but unimpressed by any of the lures I swung past its snout. And that didn't matter either. Up at the neck of the pool, under the weir, and ten yards down, salmon leapt and crashed or swirled at the surface. They were there! Just to know that was enough.

At dusk, I was back again, and swinging a team of three flies round this time hooked and played a sea-trout, of a pound, for a minute or more. It swam, flicked, held itself in the current a yard from me; I reached a hand to my back for my net; the fish surged, and was gone. Once more I was elated.

And then the next morning, water falling and clearing, Charles came into breakfast at the Half Moon. What did I fancy? I was becoming his most incompetent regular. Okement Foot? Yes, of course, he said. Described a new, real hot spot, right at the bottom of the beat, where it touched the Nethercott water. He and Adam, another sea-trout specialist who mans the bar when he has to, had lugged boulders out into the river to make a workable croy you could pick your way across into position. Should we start there at dusk? I asked. Start there this morning! Flick a fly into the run, right at its neck, from the island you'll see in mid-stream – go easy, mind, across that croy – then work down. I followed his advice. And fifteen, twenty yards down, at the limit of my cast, a firm take, a wonderful fight, and this time Gerald's old net opened and claimed a fish that, as I watched it in the water, became water: grey, slate, invisible. Only when I lifted it did the flank flash silver. A peal! On a Silver Stoat's Tail, Ted's fly. It was beautiful, and right for the pot, and would have been good eating. But Ted's poems stopped me; their reverence became mine. It was a stranger, without question a member of a sea-tribe. It was vulnerable. I slipped the hook from its jaw, eased it back into the water.

That day I spent time staring from between the branches of an oak into the tail of the junction pool, but there were no sea-trout I could see. I waded upstream, catching four trout, two of them full-grown fish, from the yards below the inflow of the water the Okement brought off Dartmoor. Was this where Ted watched his strangers at dawn, and through the day? And that night I slipped into the river a hundred yards upstream, where the water is still and smooth. I waded, deepening, down towards the tail, past those holes where I knew big fish had lurked, in his day – still did, said Charles. I slid into uncertainty; but the mud that sucked at my ankles in by the bank stopped when I stepped out into water waist-high. I stood. Looked downstream, and into the shadows of the far bank. And – splash! – something leapt, an upside-down heaven, from just before the bone-bright branches of a dead tree. I saw its silver-grey, sensed it surging around the pool, cast towards it in complete confidence. Again, and again, and again, searching the pool. Three, four more times it or another fish leapt in the next hour, as I fished steadily down. Never have I felt more certain that the next cast could produce a fish; never been more sure that the fish that came could be the fish I have hunted all my life, or a school peal. But nothing came to me.

I tried in the fast run where I'd caught that morning's fish, but caught nothing. Walking back upstream, opposite the monument, I watched as the moon emerged from thin cloud and made the lip of the junction pool glitter and gleam, golden. I re-entered the water upstream, fished down again, casting under moonlight but into the dark its light would never reach, still hooked on the drug, the adrenaline, terror and excitement. But nothing. Certainly not disappointment. I knew Ted had it right. Their magical skins, their eyes, had the measure of this intruder and his friend down at the tail, who had fish crash around him but had not a touch. That night we fished until 1.30, happy, rapt, sharing their world, and felt no evil. A blissful blank. I guessed that if, like Ted, I returned at dawn, at four, I might just see them, aliens; might worship them, this species that kept their secrets tonight. But I didn't return. It was enough to know that Ted had, here.

*

It's the last night in July 2019. This time I'm alone. My heart sinks a little when Charles isn't there to tell me what's what at breakfast, but Adam sees I'm fixed for flies – size 12 Peter Rosses, he insists, no bigger, certainly not that hairy job that works so well on the

Tamar. He talks me into position, from behind the Half Moon bar.
Don't bother with that deep water, he says, beyond the junction.
You have to be in place opposite the inflow from the Okement;
whatever you do, don't miss the first half-hour of real darkness,
he tells me. Cast towards that tree on the far bank, gentle as you
can manage. Inch it back. Two casts before you step downstream.
And if nothing's doing there, be prepared to fish the tail right to
the lip of the weir.

   And now I'm in place. The light drains to grey, then darkness.
The river thickens. My blood with it. A great splosh, a ghost
gleam, out in mid-Okement. Something's here, then. I do a soft-
shoe slo-mo shuffle of wading, but the bottom's true here. I take
my time. Lengthen line. Cast towards that black shape looming
from the high bank; cast again. And I have one! No mistaking
it: the leap, the savage power, for all it's no monster. I'm seventeen
again, except that as the pale flank glides over my net and I lift,
I know this beauty, well over a pound, is going back. And so does
the one that follows, how long later I don't know, but from the
same dark water this side of that tree. I hold each of them, planning
to ease them to and fro to revive them, let them go, but each takes
off at once, like a bird from my hand. More than swallows, not
yet tigers. Flying fish, night swifts. Whatever, they plunge back
into Paradise.

8

Great Irish Pike

Only now do I see it. Why Tom Rawling never got his wish, to fish with Ted, to claim a second father, or a third; why Ted was never as impressed as he might have been with the gospel according to Falkus; why, when Tom wrote his first letter, early in September 1977, Ted at once replied as warmly as he did. Naming Barrie Cooke, and Ireland. How could Tom have ever competed with what Barrie was about to do for the Hugheses, father and son? The die was already cast, the ferry crossing booked.

*

It's shortly after noon, that half-term. 27 October 1977. Fifteen-year-old Nick is rowing a borrowed boat, back up the twisting reed-fringed arm of a lough they've been exploring this morning, on the third day of their first pike trip to Ireland. They're on Castle Lake, Co. Clare. What has just happened has left him and his cameraman gaping with wonder.

Nick's adamant. They need to find Barrie, back near the island at the opening of the twenty-acre circle of the main lake, fishing water 140 feet deep in a fibreglass coracle the size of an armchair. He'd designed and built it seven years before, knowing any number of such dark waters that might hold a twenty-pounder, or even yield him his ultimate prize, 'a beautiful thirty pounder in a glass case'. They need to ask how he's been getting on, pretend that the fish in the bottom of the boat is only a decent one, not the twenty-five-pounder Nick has been preparing his tackle for with military dedication on each of the last three evenings, and then dreaming of. They need to see the incredulity on Barrie's face – even Barrie, who has caught hundreds of Irish pike, has only ever seen one bigger fish alive, and they know when: a fish he'd encountered three years before, laying siege to it for three months in its weir-pool lair on the River Barrow back in Co. Kilkenny as close to home as the Torridge was for Ted, then losing it round a tree ('A tragedy', he'd told Ted. 'A magnificent great sow of a fish with jaws like an empty coal grate.')

Barrie's done more than share his vision. For the last six years he's been laying patient siege to his friends, too. Enticing Ted as well as his boy to think, feel, dream again of pike. Of course Barrie knows Ted's poem 'Pike'; has probably guessed, even if Ted hasn't told him, the depths of his friend's fascination, the darkness it had come to hold for him. But Barrie's an optimist as well as a fisherman, who knows how to control his impatience. So having once mentioned his own plans for a book on pike, he lets that bait alone, lets it lie. That's when he sets to work on the boy. Barrie has three daughters, but no son. Nick will be as close as he gets to one. Hence that pike plug Barrie posted him, at nine: a wooden lure of his own construction, teeth-marked from its first pike to prove it worked. Then passed on pike-lore, stories of real as well as rumoured fish.

Crucially, Barrie has made sure Nick's growing 'mania for pike-fishing' was far more knowledgeable than Ted ever was at Crookhill. He imparted 'information' alongside fishermen's tales. Ever since, in his first years in Ireland, Barrie kept an income coming in when he wasn't selling paintings, by writing for the English angling press – Bernard Venables at the *Angling Times* encouraged him – he'd kept pace with the new methods developed in fenland drains and English gravel pits but brought to Irish loughs by a new generation of English pike fishermen. These travelling pike men had sent him back to the fish that he'd caught for food and painted in his early winters in Co. Clare, when the trout of the River Fergus stopped rising to a fly, before he had turned his painterly and piscatorial attention to salmon. In 1962 Fred Buller formulated his theory of great pike, the greatest of them fattened on Irish loughs by runs of trout and salmon.

Pike (1971) featured his list of historic mammoth pike, ten of the fourteen biggest from Irish waters.

For the past decade, one of these itinerant English pikers, Barrie Rickards, another boy who had never quite grown up, has been writing about how to find, fish for, catch and handle and release big pike. Double-figure fish, yes, but twenties, too, even approaching the mystical thirty-pounds mark. Rickards has developed a 'lair theory' for big pike. They lurk, he's discovered, in 'hot spots', rather than spread across the vast waters these monsters swim in. To find them needs observation, local knowledge, and such dedication that pike men he knew were contemplating abandoning jobs and moving to Ireland, to find them and then to catch them. And a peculiar care for this predator once you have caught it: don't follow the Irish example of destroying it as a trout eater. Removing the specimen will mean more but smaller pike. Instead, return it, to grow even bigger. Another thing: never, ever let on exactly where you met your leviathan, lest it fall next time into the wrong hands, murderous hands. You have to cherish your prize. In 1976, in an update to his *Fishing for Big Pike*, the chances of the experienced piker approaching thirty pounds were only 'moderate', 'your chances of a 30-pounder quite low. You need that extra something called luck ... What is abnormal is the capture of a 30-pounder by a piking beginner; or the capture of a 40-pounder ... These captures are things of dreamland ... things sent by the gods (like fossils) to puzzle and bemuse mere mortals.' But Rickards was a Cambridge paleontologist when he wasn't out on his fen drains; as it happens, his office was about a hundred yards away from mine, which means, from that room where Ted once dreamed of that burning fox. For whatever reason, Rickards brought the long, lofty view to his piking. He knew that 'something headier and above the normal has to exist or we'd all stop fishing tomorrow'. Knew that 'The tremendous emotion involved in these captures has to be experienced, or seen, to be understood.'

And here Nick and Ted are, experiencing just that, and wanting it to be seen, too. Ted already feeling it: 'How complete + final the feeling, as I lift its curve in the net.' No fantasy forty-pounder, this.

But no mere beginner's luck either. And that's why they need to share it with their Barrie, because he has made it possible: plotted it, orchestrated, informed, even, this morning, drawing the rhetorical flak of the Irish colonel's wife, a battle-axe with an English accent, whose house overlooks the shore while his friends slipped by with their trolled rudd and half-herring. (It was the rudd, not for the last time, that scored.) Barrie must therefore be a part of the triumph he's set up. It is a triumph of will.

So Nick is rowing, despite the fact that blisters earned on a gale-torn lough the day before have burst during a fight which bent the handles of his reel, let alone the old greenheart rod – Gerald's gift to Ted, years before: it's never seen such action, the rod tip dragged underwater, the line wrapped round the anchor rope twice, forcing Ted to cut it, free the line, retie the rope. They plan their lines: they 'think they've found a hot spot'. They speculate on the weight. Ted's convinced that it must be thirty pounds, but Nick is more modest. Already they've learned this, from both Barries: 'The compact to tell nobody about it, locally, + elsewhere nobody where it was caught.'

Barrie's face, when he sees Nick's pike lying there in the net across the bottom of their boat, 'is one of the gratifying moments'.

And it's Barrie who decides the pike's fate, sets up the day's clinching miracle. 'Nick wants him stuffed', and though Barrie sees the difficulties, 'if he's thirty pounds, he has to be stuffed'. How can Barrie prevent his young friend doing what he'd longed to do himself, with a fish of that size? But the weighing scales settle things. Twenty-four and a half pounds. Ted notes Nick's 'Desperate desire to stuff it, quickly modifying to great desire to let it go.' But that's easier said than done. Surgery follows, using long-nosed pliers to remove from the pike's deep throat the rudd he had towed or 'trolled' in search of bigger prey up that twisting, narrowing arm of the lake, and the elaborate hook on which the little bait fish had been mounted.

Only then can Ted take the last of his many pictures. I've seen them: he sent copies to Barrie, who stuck them in his Fish Book. The decades have gilded them: an orange patina. And then, that evening, he found a better way to record it. His first fishing diary, even if it's not with the rest of them. I found it only when I'd searched all the rest of the dedicated fishing diaries and turned to the personal journals. Blame that on the date, and all that meant. Nick had caught his pike on his mother's birthday. Not that Nick would have known this: she took her own life, and so much from his, in his thirteenth month. So: a father's perspective. But potent, uncanny stuff still. How can he not include it in the poem he'll draw from these adventures, but, mindful of Rickards' advice not to reveal your hot spots, won't publish until long years later? How can he avoid the memory of Nick's cradling of 'Lough na Cashel's great queen', and – that miracle – of 'giving her the kiss of life / In the cat's tail shallows'? He calls this poem 'Some Pike for Nicholas'. But they're also, already, for Ted, for Barrie, too.

And as Ted records all this, it's clear why he turned to the page not the shutter. The camera 'removes me noticeably from the action, + from the mood of responsible participation'. But it leaves him free to watch, wonder, with a feeling that isn't so final after all. He writes it all out twice, urging himself what to remember: a strange kind of double exposure. Confronted at last with the enormity he's dreamed of catching, written of catching, the reality Nick has brought to the boat leaves Ted uncertain. Wondering, still, what to make of it: him: her.

> they carry him in the shallows, push him gently to + fro to get the gills going. She takes a moment or two. Rose coloured translucent immense fins, giant head, deep white belly. The most beautifully shaped pike I've ever seen – or Barrie. She rolls + snakes, exhausted but recovering. Film runs out. Did I see less or more, with the camera. Less. She writhes ponderously among the eel grass – coppery gold under six inches of water. Then she's gone, and it's over.

*

But, of course, it isn't over. It's only just beginning again.

The next day they return to Castle Lake – and are almost charmed by the lake's formidable protector, who has herself fallen for Barrie's story that they are scientists from the Inland

Fisheries. She even calls Ted Dr Hughes. They spot an otter, see
and hear a loon. Both make it into the poem; so will the twisting
arm of that pristine wilderness, which becomes a cat's tail curling
off the crouching body of the lake which the poem dresses in the
lightest of Irish disguises, Lough na Cashel, but otherwise catches
as sharply as any map. They'd launched their borrowed boat from
a pumping station at one of the ears.

That winter Nick's force of will prevails. He has, Ted tells
Gerald, 'an unusual talent for forcing his dreams to materialize'.
But his father evidently doesn't need much persuading: his own
first cast from Barrie's coracle on that trip's first morning on a lough
Ted heard and spelled as Cortmacoragh had seen to that: swift,
definitive and, it turned out, haunting, taunting contact with a
pike with a throat longer than the ten-inch wire trace designed
to prevent its teeth biting through the nylon. A four-foot-long
crocodile kept leaping clear of the water for the rest of that day,
trying to shake free the hooks.

So they tackle up: new Mark IV carp rods and Abu Ambassadeur
reels, as Rickards recommends. All this will, Barrie confirms, be
'terrifying to all pikes'. In due course, an echo sounder, a boat, a
van, too, where they can cook and sleep beside the water. And
in time Ted and Nick will also use those rods on Alaskan king
salmon.

But the following March, 1978, on their 'second great pike
attack', comes a humbling. It could have been much worse: they
almost founder in a storm off Saint's Island on Lough Ree (where
Rickards had, one still dawn, glimpsed its monster); son points
out to father that he is not wearing a lifejacket. They catch almost
nothing in ten days, despite daily phone calls to Barrie, who
directs their operations remotely from his home beside the Nore
in Kilkenny. In Mayo, Barrie has told them Fred Buller caught a
thirty-three-pounder from the River Aille feeding Lough Cloon,
where the pike from neighbouring Lough Mask go to spawn.
And, sure enough, they find that river, sprawling in flood out of
its banks, and drag a 13½-pounder from a tangle of weeds and line
under the boat. Then they catch the great man himself, following
directions provided by a contact of Barrie's to Buller's own

pike-fishing cottage near Lough Mask. But Buller knows it is the close season, at least in England. He has his own compact: 'doesn't fish for pike in March', Ted notes. Buller suggests they try Lough Key, fifty miles north, evidently to protect his Mayo pike. And they follow that lure. But nothing doing there either.

*

That summer, their only 'summer campaign', they began with a two-day stake-out of the pike and salmon of the River Barrow, a slow riverbend and a long straight upstream of Graiguenamanagh, and only twenty minutes from home for Barrie. Its own story. Then they head north-west, to Sligo, and Loughs Arrow and Key. Back in Devon, Ted emulated Barrie's ingenious dedication in pursuit of the prize. Got devious, indeed. He persuaded Keith Sagar, his closest critic but a resolute opponent of fishing on ethical grounds because a keen keeper of marine tropical fish, to send him as many brightly coloured corpses as he could. Ted never told him why, of course. But encouraged him to ask his tropical fishkeeper friends to join him. Even supplied details of how to pickle them in formalin. When I asked Barrie in 2012 he knew at once: they made glittering deadbait for pike, in case they couldn't catch rudd or rainbow trout escapees from the local trout farms.

*

In the October half-term of 1979 they're back in the north-west. They're staying in a fold of the hills on Lough Arrow's north-eastern shore. A cottage belonging to another friend of Barrie's that looks down on a small lough which Ted's diary Scottishes as 'Loch Och'; no map agrees. But it's a place of fascination for Ted: he's heard that Paul Cullen, who owns the cottage, once saw a thirty-pounder follow his bait into the shallows before she lost interest.

One morning in May 2014 I asked at the farm next door to the cottage, and immediately discovered the name works through the air if not on the page. I get directions, down a tree-shadowed tunnel of high-banked track to a reed-fringed eye of a lake. Then look again at the fishing map of Lough Arrow, and see what the literalist in me had managed to overlook: Lough Agh. Ted spends 'two visionary hours' there.

*

In the week they spend here, they begin to hear it, feel it: even the air's full of pike. Locals report that one fifty-six-pounder emerged from the depths of Lough Arrow with a dodgy swim-bladder and was shot by an English army officer's pistol. Another pike as long as the post office van. And, from the vast and bleak Lough Allen, twenty minutes east, even darker stories which they had to believe. Thirty-pounders are being caught, yes, but by visiting German anglers who are beheading them, for trophies, leaving the boats they rent from Barrie's friends the Dwyers awash with blood. Can this be borne? But also: why not them?

While they summon up courage, they're relishing wild and dangerous weather on smaller waters. On Lough Key they'd watched two solid double rainbows form as 'the whole lake surface flashed with the blown smoke of the rain'. Barrie is 'transfixed', 'Keystruck'.

Two days later, on 1 November, they rise to the challenge; so does Lough Allen. Amid wild waves, in depths their echo sounder makes 179 feet, Nick casts another rudd, and all three of them in that plunging boat see leap, rear, a fish Ted reckons at the time as thirty pounds at least; Barrie and Nick aren't so sure. The loss induces despair, of course, but, Ted notes, that's good for a seventeen-year-old. And it's good for Ted, who completes a draft of a poem whose closing lines, that man-size rearing gills, bloodlit, that tail like a hurricane lantern, will reappear in the poem he would eventually draw from all this, 'Some Pike for Nicholas'.

The memory of that man-sized fish rearing, its giant tail, glowed for Barrie, too. A fortnight later, he sent Ted a 'memento'. I guess it's a sketch: one of Barrie's sketchbooks is devoted to images of pike, among them Nick putting his whole body into a cast, Nick's rearing pike on Allen. Barrie keeps for himself a fine charcoal drawing of the Hugheses in the stern of their boat, drawing a fair but not great pike over the net. But the brief encounter with that real specimen evidently went on haunting him: that autumn Barrie looks further into the past for inspiration, and completes his masterpiece, 'Lough Derg Pike'. It's a six-foot-long gold and green portrait of a ninety-pounder caught from the largest lough on the Shannon system in 1862. For the last century, the leviathan had hung as a stuffed and fading trophy in a Clare pub. But Barrie, who early in his own pike mania had risked all by crossing Derg in his own pike-sized coracle, spares no expense in rekindling the glory of that fish: the gold on the flanks of his pike is gold leaf. He even writes to Fred Buller about it, acknowledging the 'impetus' the old master's 'splendid big pike book' had lent him. Buller visits the gallery where the 'fine' picture, mounted above boxed 'relics' – old tackle, a reel, a gaff – is hanging, and asks to include a black and white image in his next book, *Pike and the Pike Angler* (1981). Sensing piscatorial immortality, Barrie waives a fee.

*

But forget, for the moment, the monsters who depend on poundage for their value. In his diary of that autumn half-term trip, here is Ted thinking about a pike of his own, a comparatively modest specimen that took a small pike they'd mounted live on a hook on another local lough, Meelagh. The surge and flash of this six-pounder below his boat, the three-quarter-pound fish across its jaws, 'Renewed very sensationally my feeling for the uncanny ferocity of intent + the machine-like power of pike'.

Another small back-country lough they fish that week – I found it up a twisted nearby lane, tucked into the hills, its far bank a cliff face below a thick wood still darker in the morning mist – magnifies vibrations, careless boatmanship or casts. It's like an eardrum. And these waters amplify, magnify, thoughts and questions, too. His admiration for the solitary cogitating predators he knows these mysterious little loughs must contain. Why aren't they catching them? It's a question of their faculties and the conditions and the way they interact. He comes to their defence. Sounds just like them. Their imaginations meet. They are, he realises, far warier of noise + novelties than we give them credit for – and, being predators, + therefore given to solitary cogitation, listening, watching, calculating, + in general more play of imagination than simple flocks of gullible feeders or greedy opportunistic trout + more given to stealth + precautions, more aware of carelessness, more alert to alarms, I imagine they are, possibly, uniquely shy. Like wolves. Among fish.

When they are hunting – attacking – that's probably another matter. But when they are simply dozing, or meditating, I think they are at least as sensitive as salmon.

That's the real lesson of a holiday that, Nick's lost 'giant' apart, had been disappointing in terms of numbers and sizes of pike caught. Ted concludes:

In future my pike fishing will be stealthier and – without sacrificing strength – finer.

*

A memento wasn't all Barrie sent Ted that November. He also had news. Rang to tell him. He'd discovered 'the perfect lake'. Lough Gur, a crescent of water wrapped around a limestone outcrop called Knockadoon, twenty minutes south of Limerick. As he told Ted, it oozed 'pike-ness': was just right for autumn and winter pike. And Ted knew why. It had a history of great pike: Buller had two Gur fifty-pounders in his historic list, and Tom Carroll, the farmer who let them launch their boats from his land, claimed to have caught a thirty-eight-pounder himself, sometime back in the mists. Gur also had a healthy population of rudd, and conditions – weed that grew thick in summer, from eutrophication – that deterred casual bank fishing, whether by locals or the Germans. (It was, Barrie pointed out, a long way from 'the Hun zone'). But when the weed died back in the colder months, it was also shallow enough to pursue their quarry with every method known to modern pike men. But with a conveniently small number of deeper but not bottomless holes and trenches where the big pike lurked; holes you could get to know. 'It just <u>might</u> be Hot Spot!'

Ted came at once, for two days of reconnaissance, and then returned with Nick. In four frost-furred days in late November and early December 1980 – a treat after Nick's Oxford entrance exams, and to knock his school days on the head – they broke through ice at Gur's margins and found them: caught twenty-eight pike, nineteen over ten pounds, one, Nick's, twenty-two pounds. Ted's first pike, which grabbed a herring head after they'd moored to have lunch off Knockadoon point on the second day, was, at fourteen pounds, two pounds bigger than any he caught at Crookhill. And they were strong: Ted remembered the astonishing power of a nine-pounder as he lowered it back into the water on the scale hook the pike broke as it twisted, wrenched itself free. Best of all, they saw grim proof that greatness lurked in those waters. Five of those double-figure fish had flanks scarred by enormous teeth.

*

Gur was where Ted and Nick came as close as they ever did to perfecting the art of catching great Irish pike. And they did it on the two visits they managed on their next trip, criss-crossing Ireland for three weeks in March and April 1981. That was why Ted wasn't on the Torridge to see Tom Rawling catch his salmon.

It was a mad trip, not least for the miles they covered – from east to west and back again and again in search of fish. They tried to match species, priorities, locations. Salmon for Ted (no luck at all, on Beltra in Mayo or the Cork Blackwater in Waterford, whose empty waters at least yielded him a poem for *River*, 'Eighty, and Still Fishing for Salmon'), pike for Nicholas (Lough Cloon again, then Gur, then the River Barrow in Kilkenny, then Gur again, before a final rendezvous with Barrie and his daughter Aoine on Lough Carra, back in Mayo).

But on one of their Gur strikes that Easter it's about more than fish. Seeing the fields around Cloon ravaged by EU-funded dredging works to improve agricultural land by lowering the water table, and then seeing the chalk streams a few miles from

Gur suffering the same fate, leaves Ted and Barrie horrified for the fate of the trout and pike that have swum for centuries in these rivers and lakes, which progress seems about to ruin for ever.

The stakes mount even higher on the evening of 24 March, when they meet Gur's guardians – Michael Quinlan, schoolteacher, all pebble-eyed intensity and intelligence; Francy O'Loughlann, 'like a gigantified Charlie Weeks' – at the Heritage Centre they've just opened to show off Gur's archaeological heritage. Quinlan plays them a video of the archaeological treasures, from Neolithic stone circles to medieval castles, that the lake is famous for. He talks of developing the area.

But that will bring visitors to wonder at the haul of axe-heads, combs, recovered from its waters and its shore since the water last fell in the nineteenth century. Francy farms near the lake. He's the leading light of the local gun club, and genuinely cherishes the lough's amazing bird life when he's not blowing it out of the sky or stuffing it (he is a taxidermist); he has fears of his own. Ted and Barrie urge them: protect the lake and the pike from the Germans.

Ten days later, after another trip back to Kilkenny, and Jerpoint, Barrie's fine Georgian house on the Nore, a couple of miles upriver from the Island, in which Ted and Nick had managed another camping trip beside the Barrow (and another story), they're back at Gur, with nobody but each other for company.

It's a big year for Nick. He already knows he's got a place at Oxford, where he'll read zoology, and now he's just landed a research assistantship in Alaska this coming summer, inspired by their light-filled weeks they spent hunting salmon and sharing rivers with bears the previous June and July. (Read 'That Morning' in *River*. It's another 'what happened yesterday' poem. As Ted had told Barrie that September, it wasn't just the fishing: 'It's just the most beautiful place I've ever been. Nicky's smitten too.') Now his future's beckoning. He's coming into his own, growing into his strength.

But all this casts a shadow on Ted's diaries from this trip. In passages written at or after midnight, first at Jerpoint, then at Gur, he is doubting his own purpose, as poet, father, man. In the twin-bedded room he shares with Nick at Jerpoint, as Barrie's greyhounds howl and his son sleeps deeply, Ted despairs of his degraded, decultured audience, and resorting to cliché in concession to their diminished understanding. Worse, 'Thoughts of how I have handed my life over to others. How I am no longer living my own life. In almost everything, I have stepped into the background – with Nick, with the farm.' In a poem Seamus had published six years earlier, abut his own life in rural Wicklow, he'd described himself as an 'inner émigré', taking refuge from the Troubles back in the North, which he'd decided to leave for his own and his family's sake, but still feeling terribly exposed. Here in Kilkenny Ted describes 'My absolute inner emigration' from the social life organised for him in Devon: he has become 'something beside myself, disarming myself', having 'relinquished every enterprise of my own self-satisfaction – or of real exploration. Every lonely path.' He has 'lost the thread of earnest dealing with myself'.

Back at their bed and breakfast at Holy Cross, a mile from Gur, also after midnight, Nick asleep beside him, Ted complains of 'this year's visible deterioration', in his own weakening eyes: 'at 30 yards + more, all small images double.' It's the year he's turned fifty. And Nick's growing strength, 'so like his mother facially, + in his expression, that it is uncanny', drives Ted to 'strange meditations', 'quite fruitless' but 'irresistible', at what Sylvia's absence and Carol's role in his son's upbringing has meant. 'How I deliberately suppress + efface my self, to give him play, to lift my pressure off him.'

For a moment, reading this, it's impossible not to consider my own life as a son, a stepson: what did I take from Mum, from Pam? Did I ever think for a moment about what I gave either of them? And my own life as a father of three sons, too. The youngest of them seventeen now; our older two, adopted sons, with more troubles than fishing can heal, have passed that milestone in the years I've been fishing in Ted's footsteps.

But then the moment passes. And I see what Ted writes here as just that, a moment. The small hours are full of them. And I see that he's as prey to them as anyone, even if he's better at catching them. Ruthlessly honest.

I see what he's already forgotten: what took him to his diary that night in early April; what he had just written. And that's just as clear and sharp, but this time devoted to the weird, compressed poetry of pike fishing. 'Nick put on the big rainbow, summoning the 30 lber. It spun heavily. I had a herring, twirling delightfully.' Even if you are a fisherman, you need to remind yourself that the rainbow is a trout, that in a boat from which Ted 'spun around the clock with everything in the box', it's the bait that spins, not the angler.

It's been one of three great days, in which his fishing had risen to match his writing, his thinking. He's fine, stealthy, intuitive. 'Something about the light put me in mind of' a particular chartreuse lure, which he'd cast, and 'a great double swirl-rise took it': water and fish are one. It becomes his biggest pike yet, rearing and shaking its head, bigger even than the eighteen-pounder he'd caught on their first stay here in late March: Nick reckoned twenty pounds, though this time the scales didn't figure: Ted 'Brought the plug back through its gills. Slid him back + he was gone before I realized we'd caught him'.

Even better was to come. At lunchtime they'd walked on Knockadoon, admiring the archaeological remains that had impressed Ted in December, and of which he'd learned much more on their visit to the visitor centre two weeks earlier. Nick, returning to their beached boat, and a rod with a mackerel deadbait out, found the line running, the bent handles of that old Aerial reel rotating. He ran for it, grabbed the rod, ran twenty yards back up the hill before striking. 'The moment of moments.' But only the mackerel comes back, gashed from end to end.

And then another moment, the real moment of this day, which is the one that makes me want to reach back across the years and stop Ted's midnight pen. At 4.00 p.m., Nick asks for his father's advice, at how fast to retrieve the lure and spinning rod Ted has just laid aside to replace the deadbait he'd been fishing on his other rod, 'feeling the roach's helplessness', with 'a half-mackerel, to sink + draw in its place' – and immediately hooks a 23½-pounder, which 'when I saw it I thought "thirty pounds"'. Nick manages to draw it to the net without tangling on other lines or anchor rope. Whatever else this tells you about a father and a son, you realise how expert they've become, at the logistics of modern piking: expert boatmen who have mastered the art of the drift, managing to fish, between them, two trolled baits and two flung and spun lures on four rods from the same boat.

The following evening brings simpler satisfactions, and now the diary's full of them. Companionship, after hours spent happily apart. Ted books their ferry tickets home for a few days' time, then they visit the seat of Crom Dubh, one of Ireland's old gods, in the stone circle between the lake and the Limerick–Holy Cross road, while Nick lazes in the sun. The best kind of double exposure. They fish until dark, and then enjoy the landscape together. The moon is still new. Ted quotes his son: ' "Fishing the moon under the moon. Lough Gur + the moon smile at each other – 2 big grins." Nicky, being happy.' Ted adds a dimension of his own: 'If Gur had been moon-shaped, as now, 5000 BC, it would have been ten times as holy. But then it was a ring.'

Their last morning brings a misty calm that Nick knows 'the almighty Barrie Rickards specified as the best conditions for a dead bait'. And more proof that old dogs have their uses. It's a suggestion of Ted's that a bait might be a bit closer to the boat that piques another enormous pike, at twenty-two pounds, to take Nick's float-fished herring head, 'just after, at N's insistence, I sang On Ilkley Moor, to encourage the pike'. At some point Ted returns to his earlier note to prove Nick's prowess: '23½lbs, 22lbs.' But Ted for once has the last laugh, even if it comes with a catch: a ten-pounder, its pectorals shredded, its abdominal wall pierced by a pike that had evidently swallowed two-thirds of this fish before letting go.

And another resolution, too, of something a long way back. Ted notes, at last, what Nick and Barrie must have told him, along with Fred Buller, that 'a male pike over ten lbs is very rare'. On this trip Ted keeps a tally of the sex of the pike they catch. But there are still more males than females on that list. He was clinging to that chance: kept seeing signs, possibilities, of that rarity, of his own dreamed grandfather pike. Barrie and then Nick had helped him see it, here, at Gur, beyond and within Gur and moon: he felt at one with this fish, this place, his son becoming entirely himself. For the moment at least, all the other dangers they'd registered, all their fears, of past and future, fell away, and for once the pike, and that ancient eye of a lake, 'stoniest, oldest eye of reality', looked kindly on them, gave them both what they wanted: as Nick put it, '2 big grins', and as Ted, in 'Some Pike for Nicholas': 'my boy, my dream alive without distraction'.

*

That December they return, Ted's fishing finer than ever. It's freezing, too cold for Christmas piking. But on an ice-fringed Gur, he outscores Nick in number and weight of fish, and celebrates with a drink at Reardon's with Michael Quinlan, whom he presents with a copy of *The Iron Man*.

*

So Ted was ready, when Barrie finally moved his own long-cast bait closer, to rise to it himself. He wrote the poem Barrie showed me, along with his illustrations of it, when I visited him above Lough Arrow in May 2012. 'The Great Irish Pike'. The predator misunderstood, but imagined, protected from all the accusations and bait fish hurled against him over the years. 'The pike in his cell', meditating like the fish of those great and hidden hill loughs of Co. Sligo, here, in a lake that smiled like a dragon, and whose ice-fringed eye was easy enough to recognise if you knew what you were looking at. But still, safer all round, for angler and pike, not to name. Safe, that is, until 'the watercolourist of human progress' drains him out; safe, until 'the hired German beheads him'. Poem and drawings took the two friends a week to produce in April 1982, at Appledore, on the west bank of the estuary the Torridge shares with the Taw.

*

In mid-December 1982, they're back at Gur for their annual winter pike attack. Could this go on for ever? One omen seems strangely propitious: Ted's bedtime reading is 'Jungian analysis of Kafka as textbook case of puer eternus chronicus'. Another boy who never grew up? Then I read it, and discover that Kafka was more like Tom Rawling, who left it until the last years of his short life even to try to escape the prison bars of his youth. Out on Gur, Nick, not yet twenty, is in the thick of real deep life. He immediately catches a seventeen-pounder, 'Fearfully savaged very recently by something – its belly sack almost pierced in two places, its back scarred + cross-cut'. Violence, that longed-for menace, still lurks beneath the surface. And it's a good sign: at least the poem hasn't killed him off. Could this even have been the prelude to more hunting magic? At Mrs O'Neill's they meet 'Jim the terrorist', Ted's nickname for a rough-looking seller of aerial photographs whom they'd first met over breakfast two years before. On the 15th, sheltering from a fierce westerly wind in a bay closest to the Limerick road, they moor, and for an hour watch three otters playing ten yards away. Ted squeals, bringing one of them within six feet of the boat.

At the end of a day fishing in violent wind, two youths approach Ted and Barrie as they are unloading the boat. They peer into the boat, saying nothing. But they know the lake 'a bit', know 'There are big pike in there'. Ted says he's seen nothing, but when asked whether he's from here volunteers that his friend is from Kilkenny. By then Barrie's back is to them; he's packing up, his last afternoon.

The next morning Nick and Ted resume their fishing, and birdwatching, after a walk on Knockadoon. They row into the wide bay inland from Crom Dubh's seat. There they spot a pike float in the water, and row across to it, thinking they might find a weary pike beneath it. In fact, a doubled length of algae-covered bailer cord descends into the depths; when he hauls on it, hard, at Nick's insistence – it might be an eel trap! – Ted discovers thick rope, then glimpses through the sunlit depths a woven bag, full of a weight he knows to be metal. Either loot from a robbery or guns. He drops it back.

By the time they are blown off the lake by a squall that afternoon, Ted has resolved what two of his friends have described to me as his 'moral dilemma'. To tell the Gardaí as Nick is urging would have involved them, even as informers. It would also have blown their cover for good. Back at Mrs O'Neill's, he hitches their boat to the car, having decided to head for England the next morning. In the night, Mrs O'Neill's dog barks into the small hours; next morning she reports that she saw two figures, young men, on the road above the house well after midnight, staring down, as the snow fell. '(Temporarily?) we have exhausted our pike-lust.' Replaced by a new, darker curiosity: his diary ends by remembering the boat they'd seen on the bank directly below the stone circle, 'the one boat on the lake', which must have been used to drop the 'loot'.

*

Reading those last vivid pages of fishing diaries I knew I had to see Gur. I could be free on 17 December 2013, the thirty-first anniversary of their departure. It was a revelation: cold, if nothing like as bitter as some of the Decembers, but keen on the slopes of Knockadoon, or the dragon's open mouth, where I made a point of scrambling over gates and wire meant to forbid wanderers. I stood and stared across at that bleak bay where they'd found the pike float.

The Heritage Centre's crannog hut now has central heating. I asked after Anne O'Neill and Michael Quinlan, leaving my details with the teenager on the till, who'd heard of neither. But I didn't try fishing. It wasn't worth it. 'Can he still be said to exist?' Ted's poem had asked. A 2012 Water Framework Directive Survey of Lough Gur undertaken by Inland Fisheries Ireland seemed to have the answer. It had found small populations of rudd, perch and eel, and only five pike, between eighteen and forty-eight centimetres in length – the biggest of them a little over two pounds, then. Eutrophication and phosphorus levels had taken their toll; Ted and Barrie's fears for, and in, 'The Great Irish Pike', had been realised.

*

Early in the new year, an email. From Aine Barry, of the Heritage Centre, who was sorry to have missed me on the day I'd called. But she could help. Anne O'Neill and Tom Carroll the farmer were, as she put it, 'dead at this stage'. But she knew Michael Quinlan, rather well: he was her father.

Michael told me in March 2014 of new plans to revive the fishery and its stocks after years of decline. In due course, I sent him an essay I'd written on all this; he reciprocated with photographs of Barrie's watercolour, then, to my delight, asked me for a shorter version of my essay for the Lough Gur Historical Society journal. Given other local sensitivities, maybe it might be better without that last grim twist in the tale. I agreed, slightly reluctantly, but with a sharp sense of how much history and politics ran just under the surface still.

*

In late January 2016, I emerged from the Manuscripts Room after reading Ted's account of the capture of the great queen of Castle Lake, to find another message from Michael. He had sent me a photograph. Just before Christmas, a local angler had taken a great thirty-pound pike from off the shore of Knockadoon, where I'd wandered two years earlier: and his name was Hughes. Blood was dripping from the pike's jaws – hers, I assumed. He was grinning. I wrote back by return, just on the off-chance. Might someone – even, perhaps, Mr Hughes – be persuaded to take me fishing?

*

And so I found myself flying out again. It was 3 December 2016. I had a window seat. Above the wing, and hovering over the patchy cloud that bright December morning, an entire circular rainbow led me over the channel and across Ireland. Only when we dipped for landing, banking over the distinctly smiling dragon of Lough Gur, did it fade, and by then it had done its job, heralding improbabilities. And thanks to Pat Shanahan, who had bought Mount Cashel Lodge off the redoubtable Mrs Dighton, I was at his jetty on Castle Lake at 10.30, in bright sunlight, and tackled up and breaking the thin ice in the bottom of the boat. First I followed Barrie's route, and method – one of the fish he'd caught on 27 October 1977 was a Big S, lent by Ted. But it brought nothing from that deep outer circuit of the main body of the lake. I passed the crannog island, too thickly wooded to permit a landing; I rowed, then drifted, down that wild idyll of the cat's tail, in hot sunshine, right as far as the channel where the river fed the tip of the lake.

I switched to a fly: I love to cast, and draw, the rhythm of it. I worked my way, drifting, along the reeds. And there a savage take led to an irruption of a serpentine pike, black and gold in the net, an ancient head, and best of all gold-gilled and writhing as it leapt from the water into the low sun in a clear sky. My tinsel fly in its jaws as it flapped and hung in the boat looking as though it had swallowed a Christmas tree. Not great, or not if size matters. I'd estimate four pounds; I declared five when I got home. But this was a fish twice as angry and more vivid than the first fen pike I'd caught, on Ted's pike rod, and a Big S; and leaner, rougher, darker. A male, I'd guess. It was more than enough. Without exactly shaking hands, I freed the hook from that deep throat, all seven hundred angled teeth, without mishap, or wounding, mine or the fish's. It went back with a python writhe.

As dark fell I was on the road south, crossing the Shannon into Limerick, heading for Clancy's Bar in Bruff, and Michael Quinlan. And the next morning I was finally afloat on Gur, with a friend of his whose name I caught but couldn't spell: Donncha MacGabhann. A retired lecturer in art, and now an independent scholar of the Book of Kells, Donncha is a delight: courteous, deeply knowledgeable, and a man of these parts among others. Mr Hughes was, Michael had decided, unavailable, or otherwise unsuitable, so Donncha would accompany me out on the lough, and even offered to be my boatman, allowing me to concentrate on the fishing. We agreed to meet after breakfast outside the church.

Only then did I realise. This wasn't just December. It was December 2016; as I waited, I read the monuments, bright still, seven months after its centenary, that had been posted by the memorial to the heroes, the martyrs, of the Easter Rising. Their bravery in the face of enemy fire as they fell. Enemy fire: in my innocent pike-smitten ignorance it took me a moment to realise – the British. Now I understood Michael's reticence, was glad I'd taken his advice, and resolved not to tell Donncha of the pike float and what lay beneath it as we ventured onto the lough.

It didn't matter. We had a marvellous three hours under quiet grey skies, righting and unlocking local farmer John's small ten-foot dinghy, the one boat I saw on the shore, from its home in the reeds just down from the stone circle below the Limerick road. We circled Garrett's Island. I tried to remember Ted's transcriptions of the result of his echo sounder and concentrated my attentions there. I sought out Barrie's hot spot, realising that our small boat, cosy enough, was still twice the size of his coracle. In the choppy waters, which we shared with huge flocks of swans and geese, I was glad of that. As we talked we drifted under Knockfennell; once there was a stop, a pull, as the fly felt something, was grabbed by something. I cast again. Nothing. But that was enough, too. I wasn't greedy. I had my great (diminutive) Irish pike. And I'd felt one in Gur.

Late that afternoon we reconvened at Reardon's, the pub where in 1981 Ted and Barrie had met the locals. Michael had brought Barrie's watercolour. For my part, I read from my transcriptions of Ted's diaries; we discussed Anne O'Neill, and Tom Carroll, and then the local competition for Ted and Barrie: the gentle giant of a man, the shooting enthusiast-cum-taxidermist who offered to stuff any pike they caught to clear them from the lake. Francy, I read. Michael turned to the man on his right, the man who'd been at Clancy's the night before. 'Francy O'Loughlin', he grinned. Thirty-five years on and still sitting in the same snug. The tales spun that night – tall stories, by turns Guinness-dark and bright as bronze axe-heads – are not for sharing.

*

One more thing I learned from that trip. I hesitate to admit it, but there are few limits to the lengths a man won't go in pursuit of pike. I realised that you could, if you were mad enough, and prepared to suspend all thoughts of carbon footprints, do this trip in a day. Just give me the right day.

The right day comes: the last Sunday in October 2019, the 27th. This time the plane from Stansted takes a more direct route into Shannon, and I look down on the body of the cat, its tail.

Pat Shanahan's out for the day, but he's happy enough to leave this itinerant Englishman to his lake, and his boat. So once more I complete this circuit. I don't do dead bait, and I can't risk wasting the day fishing for rudd, but I do have a rod that will troll a rubber half-herring as well as my fly rod. So I retrace my steps, retracing theirs, forty-two years ago. I row past the crannog, down into the cat's tail, the rod tip pumping, juddering, sometimes wildly, sometimes with a steady rhythm. But when at last I strike, reel in, all I see, looming from the depths, is that rubber half-herring cloaked in such a mass of weed that, as I fumble with the rod, try to decide whether to bring it in, the bloody thing breaks: the rod-tip that is, not the herring. Somewhere, someone's laughing at me.

So I revert to the fly, cast as I did two years before into the reedy margins of the cat's tail shallows. I spend a happy afternoon there, until the knot in my new-fangled wire leader gives way and the fly goes, too. Still, it's blissful. And the lake is glass, beneath broken cloud. No otters or a loon, but there are compensations: a kingfisher, crows, herons. The only one who doesn't seem content is a single heifer in a lakeside field. She's been bellowing like a creaky hinge for hours, and she's still at it as I retreat towards the mooring, in time to catch my evening flight.

9

An Ancient Thirst

It was my first evening with Roderick and Caroline Murphy, at the house they'd taken for a fortnight with friends from the North. Isham lies on the eastern bank of vast, black Lough Mask, and the limestone pavement between the house and the shore was, though fascinating – the grykes between the limestone slabs teeming with delicate flowers sheltered by the stone, clinging for dear vivid life in the little, sometimes circular, infinitely delicate pots of limestone they grew from, shaped by rainfall, which had also filled or half-filled them with a centimetre or two of soil – nothing, they told me, beside the real thing, the Burren, an hour or so south.

But Mask itself is nothing to the Murphys beside its smaller sister lake, Lough Carra. They wanted me to fish with them, because they'd been coming here since the seventies, more often than not with Barrie, and because Barrie had brought Ted and Nick here, too. Carra has the most exquisite trout I've ever seen – silver, black-spotted beauties, which if you're lucky or very skilful you can lure from waters that shimmer the palest luminous green. I rely for that knowledge on a photograph Caroline took of Barrie with a fish I'd assumed was a sea-trout. He wrote up its capture in the Murphys' fishing diary. He'd edged into a clearing in the reedy margins of the lake, waited for it to rise a second time, pounced. Of course, when I tried that the following day, I managed to be too late with the cast, too quick with the strike or bewildered by Roderick's barked instructions from the stern. Once he lost patience, cast over my line. But still, I marvelled at the water. It's the lake bed that does that, they tell me: crushed shells. And hearing that I've come across a reference in Ted's diaries to a spot which it turns out the Murphys, too, know as gentian point, where tiny sapphires more often seen in Alpine meadows grow, they take me there for lunch.

Even before all that, I was bewildered that first evening: thrilled, moved, saddened, tantalised. The day had begun three and a half hours south-east, and thirty-two years before. Since I'd last met him, frail health had forced Barrie to move back to Co. Kilkenny, not to the banks of his beloved Nore but to a place I'd found it easier to rely on the satnav's autocorrect to complete than to risk saying myself: Graiguenamanagh. There, the evening before, I'd left a battered old stuffed trout with Julia, Barrie's middle daughter. She'd rung him where he was living in a kind of independence, in a warden-supervised maisonette a couple of minutes away, but had warned me he might not remember he'd agreed to meet me. But, yes, he was happy to meet; so at nine I'd turned up – you could spot his maisonette by the paintbrushes in jamjars sprouting from the window sill. He was still getting dressed, but welcomed me in, made me tea. Then listened, intently, as I read him my transcription of a 200-line fishing diary Ted had written in 1980. What I'd heard from Julia – his confusion, his distress, and his daughters', that in his frailty, with dementia diagnosed, he had somehow lost the collection of letters from his poet friends, Ted among them, that meant so much to him – made me nervous as I started. But I also thought: all the elderly men I've met who fished with Ted have had fond memories stirred when I've told them they'd been mentioned in Ted's dispatches. So why not try?

Barrie had rung: there was a great run of salmon on the Nore. Ted had to come; no time to lose. And because this was salmon, and because it was in school term, Ted took him at his word, and came alone, and at once. Caught a tiny plane from Plymouth to Cork – had he chartered it? – rented a car, brought prawns, the lot. It made my Stansted day trip look restrained. And even sensible. For three days, thousands of casts, they fished the Nore together. Nothing. Five thousand casts of nothing. But then, a last throw of the dice, Barrie took Ted back west, to Clare. Not, this time, to Kilnaboy, but to Dromore, a lough laced by the Fergus a few miles downstream, a place Barrie knew and loved. And there, at last, 'solid communication with the prize', at the place where the river connected two arms of the lough. The fourteen-pound salmon that came to Ted's flung Toby was in wonderful condition, thick-shouldered, fresh-run: ' "The most beautiful salmon I've ever seen!" said Barrie.'

I looked up at him. He was leaning forward, rapt, in the one armchair in the place, staring at me on the one kitchen chair. And at once: 'I did say that! And it was!' And then: 'Would you like to see the letters?' He turned, pulled aside a curtain that hung across a cubby hole behind him, and pulled out a cardboard box. It had once held leeks.

Among the treasures I saw that morning was a rough photocopy of a cartoon, of Ted, in ermine, leading a procession of fishermen, carrying all kinds of kit. I asked Barrie who they were. He added names, in shaky pencil. Paul, Barrie, Roderick, Mike. Would that be Roderick Murphy, I asked? Paul Cullen? Yeah, Barrie said, nodding. I told him then I was heading up to meet Roderick and Caroline that evening, but that I'd be driving via Thomastown and the Nore, and wanted to try Dromore. Before I left, he reached for two books of his paintings, inscribed them for me with love. But needed me to remind him of my name and the date.

I left Graiguenamanagh, stunned; drove west, through countryside that I began to realise was quietly very beautiful. I stopped at Thomastown, peered from a bridge over what turned out to be a side stream at darting trout, then drove into town, found the Nore itself, glittering. I looked upstream from the town bridge to The Island, shading my eyes against the sun's glare on the water, passed the ruins of Jerpoint Abbey and realised that I must be close to Jerpoint itself, the HQ for those fishing trips. But I had miles, hours, to go before I got to Isham, so headed on. I crossed the River Suir, one of the Nore's sisters, famed for the size of its trout; drove west again, slowly, and eventually found Dromore. A ruined castle loomed from the woods at one end of the lake. A boat was pulled up between trees: I let myself imagine that Barrie and Ted had just this moment hauled it out. I found a low bridge, a short section of stream between the lake's arms. Could it really have been here they fished? I indulged myself a while, knowing I'd never get closer. And then I headed north, through Clare, faster than I knew Ted and Barrie would have done: I had the N5 to follow, the dual carriageway built at great expense with EU money and providing an almost straight run from Limerick to Galway – almost, because of an Irish care to avoid an inconveniently placed fairy tree – and I wanted to get to Mayo, all new territory to me, before the day at the wheel and the emotion in my head caught up with me.

Drink had been taken by the time we began to talk, and for a while it was what all fishermen begin with: what had, or hadn't been caught, and the reasons for it: air temperature, water temperature, wind direction. But then we turned to Barrie, Ted. And turned back, too. Only then did it dawn on me that the Murphys had themselves followed my route, just the journey I'd completed, but more slowly, because towing their nineteen-foot fishing boat; only when we talked a bit more that I understood that their home near another place much longer to say than to drive through, Skeaghvasteen, was near the third of those sister rivers, the Barrow. And so I read the poem Ted wrote about it, 'River Barrow', as we sat, or began to sprawl, at table after dinner. And began to realise, once it was in my mouth, what a world it opens.

Half of me, the scholar in me, wondered, too, if they might answer a question, living above the river themselves. I'd thought they'd know 'the skull tower' that looms over the river on the hot evening in deep summer of molten reds and greens it describes. That skull is the one note of coldness in a poem that oozes a mysterious pulsing heat; I felt that heat as I read it to these strangers aloud. They could tell, surely, how moved I was. But astonishingly, they claimed not to know Ted had ever written it, nor did they know which skull tower. What they meant was: they didn't yet know me.

*

It's early April 2016, a bleak Saturday afternoon. And now I'm at Tinnakeenly, the beautiful former ruin of a family home Roderick

and Caroline bought and restored and extended forty years ago.
By now we do know each other, Roderick, Caroline and I. We've
been silent together, casting for trout. We've also talked. Roderick
has told me his life story as we drifted on Lough Arrow; I've
told him more of mine than I would have done closer to home.
Casting, watching the waves, has helped. So have the greens, the
spent – fishermen's bluff lingo for the closing stages of the life
cycle of the mayfly that does those mayflies no justice at all. And
Roderick has seen me catch a trout. He'd seen how moved I was,
how much it had marked me for good. Now we'd just watched
the Grand National together. He asked me whether I wanted to
see where Ted and Nick and Barrie camped beside the river. We
just had time before a dinner date with the Kavanaghs.

We drove in convoy. I followed him across the main road then
down a lane that snakes along the valley, rhyming the river's turns
a hundred feet below. We passed an ancient ruin of a chapel, then
farms and fields and cottages. Roderick stopped for a chat with
a teenager, who waved at me, curious. We drove on. Stopped,
started. After a number of false alarms he was sure. Pointed
me down between a farm and a new house under construction.
Was as sure this was the place – he'd visited them, brought more
supplies – as he was that he wouldn't be joining me. I also had the
feeling that his reluctance was more than just the steepness of the
field. 'Take your time. Back by 5.30?' No one was about; there
was no one's permission to ask. So I picked my way over two
dry stone walls, down a steep slope, through the thickets Ted had
cursed, then onto the flat riverside meadow where they'd pitched
their tents.

They came in July. The summer after Lough na Cashel's great
queen; the prelude to their first Irish 'summer campaign', as Nick
had been calling it, according to a letter from Ted which Barrie
had showed me that morning in Graiguenamanagh.

As it happens, more glamorous destinations – Iceland in 1979,
Alaska in 1980 and 1981, Kenya in 1983 – conspired to ensure
it was their only one in Ireland. Ted's diary of that trip in the
British Library records it as 4 July, and it's in prose. It doesn't give
a year. Three months after that April Saturday, I found another

version, this time in verse, three-quarters of the way to the poem he finished – that one is dated July 12th 78. Still on manoeuvres, then, but in that week he'd come to know there was a poem in it. Good: Barrie wasn't the only one with a book to write.

Roll on almost thirty-eight years. This was April; rain turned to sleet, and, briefly, to snow, while I walked up and down that flat, which July would fill with orchids. Still, though, it took hold of me, that stretch of the Barrow. Drew me in. It seethed: welled up, turned in on itself.

The water was high, turbid, dark; engine-oil green, brown, under heavy cloud, not the sunlit pink of a sliding ballroom glass dancefloor on which, in the poem Ted drew from their July camping trip, 'River Barrow', 'Tiny sedge-flies partner their shadows'. Far too cold today for that glamour, or for the midges that have the poem's last words, leaving Ted's skin itching and swelling. But here I was, and for the moment it was enough. More than I could have dreamed of. Contact:

Future, past,
Reading each other in the water mirror
Barely tremble the thick nerve,

Ted had written in 'River Barrow'. Now that nerve was flexing, stirring, with spring floods, but still to the deep power of its own logic. Even in the wrong season, I thought I could see what Ted meant in its slow power, even so: if ever there was a

Heavy belly
Of river, solid mystery
With a living vein

this was it. They – 'we' – sprawled on the grass, with rods for antennae, listening hard for the bream-shoal; I knew from Ted's first diary that they'd fly fished, too, for trout. Nick had caught pike, Ted and Barrie perch. Anything went, or came to them.

I walked that riverside field for ten slow minutes and stood and summoned, and could imagine – even without a sight of the skull tower, though I scanned the woods that rose high beyond the feed lane of the current towards the far bank for a glimpse of it – the sense of ease, fullness, perfection, Ted saw in the reflection of those same trees in this sliding place. And – something rarer – a spotless spot in time: 'All evil suspended.'

And then my time was up. I drove back to Roderick and Caroline's, ten minutes away if that, as Ted and Nick and Barrie had done after two nights beside the river, to return the water container they'd borrowed and to borrow more kit – an outboard motor – for their next stop, Lough Arrow.

The next morning, I was following the route they'd driven once they'd picked up that outboard, to Jerpoint. It only took me twenty minutes, but I drove with some trepidation.

Jerpoint – not, as I discovered, Jerpoint House or Jerpoint Abbey, which I tried first before I found it – is about ten minutes and two miles upstream of Thomastown. Barrie lived there for fourteen of his twenty-four years in Co. Kilkenny, from 1972 to 1986, until Sonja, his partner of twenty years, moved him on, first into his studio in one of the barns, then to a house and studio right beside the river in Thomastown itself. In 2016 Sonja was still living at Jerpoint, as she did until her death in 2019, in one half of a house designed by their only daughter and Barrie's youngest, Aoine, in the garden of the grand Georgian mansion they sold some years ago to a Camphill Centre for adults with learning difficulties. Aoine lives under the other slope of the gable. But Aoine wasn't there on the weekend of my visit, as she had been on the morning Ted and Barrie and Nicholas returned from the Barrow to prepare for the next leg of their trip. So I had Sonja to myself.

Sonja was used to talking. She was Ireland's finest potter, and Holland's, too. I'd read interviews she had given to Irish journalists, seen the rich earth firings and glazings of her round pots. I knew that Seamus Heaney had written her a poem, 'To a Dutch Potter in Ireland', and she told me she was with Marie, Seamus's wife, within hours of his sudden death in 2013. I saw the pots behind her as we spoke. Was in awe of their beauty. And, as she told me of her life, was in awe of that, too.

But I was also prepared to be cautious, nervous even: over breakfast that morning, Roderick had spoken of his own clashes with Sonja at the Kilkenny Design Studios, where they'd both worked from the 1960s. That was how he'd got to know Barrie. When they started fishing together, he had stories to tell of dropping Barrie back, in what should have been shame, after trips that should have been two days long had become two weeks, to face what was never going to be the music. He could hear it from the car.

I came with particular questions I thought she could answer. Questions I wished Barrie had answered differently when I'd met him first above Lough Arrow four years before, and which his failing memory had prevented my asking at all in that spartan maisonette. One above all. Ted, he'd told me, was a fisherman; they talked fishing. I could believe that, from my days on Carra and Arrow with the Murphys. Their bond was deep, but fishing and water was at the heart of it. Seamus, though, his books the shelf below Ted's: Seamus was the man with whom he talked art, aesthetics. Could that really be right? I asked Sonja. Could a man who clearly loved poetry as much as Barrie did really only have talked fishing with Ted? And was Barrie really as close to Seamus as he'd claimed?

But though Sonja told me much about that love of poetry, she was more interested in her own vivid memories. She began with a night during one of their stays at Jerpoint where Ted had not retired to bed to write his diary after midnight. Instead, she and Ted sat up till dawn, discussing anthroposophy. Did I know what that meant? Well, I didn't, so she told me about Rudolf Steiner, the Christian mystic, educationalist and philosopher of 'spiritual science'. Sonja's German mother had actually known him, early in her life, late in his. About the principles of the schooling that had blighted Sonja's own education before the war, when she and her parents had moved to Amsterdam, and after it. About the year she'd spent away at school in Germany, after surviving the war in Amsterdam. When they'd got together in the early 1960s, both in flight from first failed marriages, Barrie had been intrigued, curious about it, asked her so many questions that she'd returned to it. He hadn't the patience for Steiner. (That's why he left Ted to it, and Sonja, that long night.) Barrie preferred to read books which you really needed to study – Sonja had founded a group for the purpose – as though they were the detective novels he read in his studio as he painted. And in the late sixties and early seventies he was more interested in making those bone boxes I had seen in the books he'd given me. Ted, though, already knew Steiner. Was fascinated, and was just as open, to Sonja's own path to spiritual science, biodynamic gardening.

And Sonja told me more, much more. Something that surprised me. Hitherto I'd thought that fishing as Barrie and Ted did was emphatically men's work; you needed to be a fisher*man*. Now Sonja told me stories of her own fishing with Barrie. But to get there she spoke, first, of visiting him and his first wife and their two daughters in Co. Clare, her shock at the roughness of their country living. Of the day he'd given her in the Burren, wildfowling, in 1959. I guess, now, also at Loch Gealáin, the Lake of the Flesh. Of his abrupt and unexpected appearance in Amsterdam, three years later. Of her own love for nature, first in the German forests, then, when they both moved to Kilkenny in the mid-sixties, on Irish loughs and rivers with Barrie, fishing for trout – the madness of those fishermen, those *men*, shaking the bushes to make the mayflies dance: 'Crazy!' – and sea-trout, and the salmon that swam the Nore beside their house. And, finally, she spoke of the wrench when, pregnant with Aoine, she realised that one of them would need to give that up when Aoine came along, and that it wasn't going to be Barrie.

I was late for lunch that day. And reeling. But still I had not found, or heard, quite what I was hoping for.

And then, a few weeks later, I met Aoine. It was over dinner in Cambridge, but as soon as she began speaking we were back in Ireland. Ever since we have been talking, emailing, visiting, exchanging discoveries, questions, memories. Through these conversations I've come to realise what Barrie and Ted might have been talking about during that strictly unnecessary but really essential camping trip beside the River Barrow that July, twenty minutes but a world away from Jerpoint.

*

The spelling of her name – somewhere between the goddess of Lough Gur, Aine, for whom Michael Quinlan had named a daughter, and the phonetic version Ted used in his diaries, Onia, to describe this 'sweet kid' they met on their return to Jerpoint that April afternoon, and who then joined them on their long journey north-west to Arrow and Key – isn't the only unconventional thing about Aoine. She may rhyme with her mother. (Another odd half-rhyme: Aoine and I were born only two months apart.) She's the child of two artists, each so dedicated to their medium, so immersed in it, that she had to make her own way through her early years. And that meant being a child of The Island, too, the great old mill house beside the Nore to which her parents moved just before Christmas 1965, within weeks of her birth. Almost at once the Nore came to meet them. Sonja had told me of the floods that swept downstream, the first within days of their arrival: she'd had to caulk the doors and windows with river mud to keep the water out, but when it started spurting up between the floor tiles they retreated upstairs with eggnog to ride out the storm. They floated paper boats on the waters lapping at the stairs. When the waters subsided, they found salmon caught in the netting in the rose garden. More than once, a pike took up temporary residence in the hall, before moving to the kitchen. In that leek-packing box, Barrie showed me a poem Seamus Heaney had sent him, 'The Island', to record it.

And in undue course, in quieter, drier times, Barrie and Sonja lost their daughter; then lost her again.

As a baby, first: Barrie sounded the alarm when, returning to the house from his first-floor studio over an archway by the mill, there was no sign of her. Distraught – had she somehow got out, fallen into the deep sluice channel of the old mill workings, drowned, while they worked? – he and Sonja, who had been hard at work herself, searched for hours before discovering that she had crawled upstairs, exhausted herself, was curled asleep under their bed.

But then as a girl: even after they'd fenced the garden, Aoine was drawn to the water. She knew that's where she would find

Barrie, when he wasn't painting: when he fished from the strip of land that led down to the weir a hundred yards above the house, he had a bell he rang when he'd hooked a salmon to summon Sonja or Aoine with net or tailer. She learned that if she wanted a father, she would need to have one on his terms, in his world.

That bond between father, daughter and fish grew in the months and years after he laid her out, as a baby, beside a salmon at least three times her length. Aoine let me see Barrie's Fish Book. It's full of confirming treasures. Four pages full of the pictures Ted took on the day Nick caught that great queen on his mother's birthday. Pictures at Gur, too: of pike, one of Ted's delight as he weighed one; one by Aoine of Barrie and Ted, Barbour-jacketed. Leaning between boats, Ted's orange fibreglass deck, Barrie's coracle, as they came together for lunch. Huge sleek catches of tench. That stunning Carra trout I mistook for a sea-trout. The Sheelin monster, 5¼ pounds, that Barrie had cased, and started his desire for a specimen pike to match it.

But the most moving is a picture captioned 'Aoine, Self, and 22lber', in March 1972. The fish dwarfs her, the rope around its tail wrist level with her head. Barrie's squatting, but the top of his head is missing. That's not the point. The point is her eyes. Wild, defiant, self-possessed; but possessed, too, by that giant fish. She's clutching a withy, a long branch, to rhyme with Barrie's rod.

Her own bond with Barrie and the fish deepened. Literally.

Her father warmed to it, let her in. Through the seventies Barrie took her with him, after tench, bream. He painted the tench lake, not his daughter. And was, Aoine told me, in his studio, as her mother was in hers, when in her early teens, downstream, on the river below Jerpoint, spates brought trunks down and they wedged over the gap in another weir. She told me she'd go out, alone, unsupervised, tie a rope around the log, the other end about her waist, and plunge into the water, with a homemade snorkel, two halves of a tennis ball, one mounted above a length of polythene tubing, the other sliding up it to provide the seal, so she could hang for as long as she could beside the salmon in the flow, breathe with them. Total immersion. Mad ingenuity? Or just practising what her parents were preaching?

In August 2016 I sent Aoine my transcript of a letter I'd just read in Atlanta, where Barrie's letters to Seamus and Ted are kept in a high library tower. It was from the year of that proud picture with the salmon, 1972. Barrie was full of praise for what he'd read of Ted's work in Persia with Peter Brook. Ted had invented a new, visceral, primitive language of expression for the play they'd made together, *Orghast*. Barrie couldn't compete with that. But he had, for three years, been devising a system. An installation of valves and pumps, to prove the identity of water and blood flow in river and body. Everything flows. It was more than metaphor. It was confluence, of Barrie's world of fish and water, and Sonja's.

And more besides. In the year they'd moved to The Island, 1965, the Steiner press had published an English translation of a book by the German engineer and Steiner disciple Theodor Schwenk: *Das Sensible Chaos*, or *Sensitive Chaos*. The forms of water, above all its response to disturbance, the curls and backchannels and reverse pressures and currents, were, Schwenk argued, at the heart of all natural processes and spiritual, from river meander to fluency of thinking to the formation of organs, even bones. It added years of observation to an old Heraclitean truth that Barrie painted on his studio wall, at Jerpoint, then on the quay in Thomastown, in a studio he made from a handball alley, which he roofed in Perspex. Everything flows. The closer you got to this truth, the more exactly you saw it, the more fully you understood the world, and your place in it. Barrie was excited in that letter. After working on it for three years, he said, with an engineering friend, a competition in Belfast gave them the chance to submit plans.

Nothing came of it. Their pumps wouldn't work: they'd failed to understand the negative pressure, the backflow, that was as crucial to the way the heart's pump works as it is to the vortices which the water in a fast current makes when displaced by the gills of a trout, keep curling back, then forward, keeping them in the stream. Another disciple of Steiner, the forester Viktor Schauberger, knew that, designed a trout turbine.

But Aoine told me she knew all about it, as a girl. How could she not? And then – the answer, after all these eddies and rapids and runs, to my question – she said, also: of course Ted and Barrie discussed this. And Ted and Carol would have discussed it with her, too. When she was old enough – or, at least, nine – Sonja and Barrie sent her to a Steiner Waldorf school. Which happened to be in Gloucestershire. She'd catch the train to Rosslare, the boat to Fishguard, the bus to Stroud. At nine. And then spend the half-terms, at Court Green or in Moortown, with Ted and Carol. Ted took her fishing, and nature-watching, at dusks and dawns. She remembers him telling her: 'Fishing is my way of breathing.'

Who better to understand that than this child of the Island, of water? I thought again of Ted's poem 'Go Fishing'. Its imperatives:

Join water, wade in underbeing […]
Gulp river and gravity
Lose words

I thought of its amazing imagining of fish, 'That materialize in suspension gulping / And dematerialize under the pressure of the eye'. I'd always and only associated that with the rapt self-communion Ted found in fishing, in the world of water. The intensity of his admiration for those seven strangers, the sea-trout, his concentration, peering down on the bank, reaching, reaching, for a state they achieved and held until he gave himself away. Those Sligo pike, contemplative, the sensitive predator he knew he could be, too, disturbed at last by his lure. Now it gained a dimension. Its imperatives became an invitation Aoine had accepted. I saw her roped in the Nore gap, in the coiling currents of the cold, invigorated water, her homemade snorkel the only thing that stopped her gulping river, to be with the salmon.

And then I thought again of 'River Barrow'. That three-day camp beside the river, for once not in different boats, but listening, not just through the antennae of their rods to the bream shoal, but to each other. Without Sonja, without Aoine, without any risk of losing Ted to anthroposophy for the summer evening. I began to see and hear all the things that Barrie and Ted would have talked about, or everything that could have seeped into their time together, so near home but in another world. Barrie's total absorption, his work on water and the body, Schwenk's way of reading sensitive chaos, the vortices he saw in the in-turning 'down-roping' of its water. I began to see it everywhere: the seductive urgency of water, pulling you down into it. The body of water speaking to the body of the fisherman, one seducing the other. Greedily. And I heard it in the lines Ted began taking from that time by the river with his son and his old friend:

> It's an ancient thirst
> Savouring all this, at the day's end,
> Soaking it up, through every membrane,
> As if the whole body were a craving mouth
> As if a hunted ghost were drinking – sud-flecks
> Grass-bits and omens
> Fixed in the glass.

However many times I read this, I couldn't be sure if this was the river's thirst alone, the river's body, or the fisherman's, staring into it as into a pint, into his future and past. And I wondered: how ancient was it?

*

Over the course of ten days in May and June 2017 I began to find out. After four years of flying visits, leave from work gave me the chance to spend more than a weekend in Ireland. I brought the car, spent a long weekend with Roderick and Caroline on Lough Arrow, then moved half a mile back down the Annaghloy peninsula on the north bank of the lough to a cottage by the shore. Roderick lent me his outboard for the boat that came with the cottage. Or lent us: because my wife Sarah and youngest son Ben spent the school half-term with me. Ben, at fourteen, finally began to tolerate his father's obsession, and began fishing himself; Sarah joined me for afternoons on a glassy lough when sky met water and exchanged places. We landed on Lyttle's Island, watched mayfly dancing in woodwind airs and landed on deserted jetties of grand, abandoned houses from another time. Ballindoon on the promontory overlooking Lyttle's Island. The eerie estate of

Holybrook House, for sale now; it was here, in a side lough I failed to find, Paul and Barrie and Barrie Rickards and the man who introduced them, Douglas Palmer, another palaeontologist who spent years on both sides of the Irish Sea, caught double-figure, even twenty-something, but not quite great pike in October 1980.

I took them up to the Carrowkeel tombs on the Bricklieve Mountains, where Barrie had taken me five years before. Arrow, Sligo, Roscommon, lay before us. Then we all crept into that ancient corbelled dark, and felt as though we were creeping back into the calm of a stone womb.

And then we drove back, as Ted and Nick and Barrie had done, over the Unshin, the river that flows out of Lough Arrow, a river, Ted told another Irish friend from his student days, 'I dearly love', for the huge trout that slipped down into it from the lough; he fished for those Unshin trout with Barrie in 1982, and I'd found out where the year before, following Roderick's instructions to the stretch below an old rabbit farm ten miles downstream. It's chalk-stream clear, and it has been running clear ever since the Morrigu, ancient battle goddess of the Tuatha de Danaan, coupled with the Dagda before taking to the skies in the form of a crow above the second battle of Moytura, which saw the Tuatha see off the Fomorians once and for all, centuries before the Milesians saw off the Tuatha in their turn, drove them into the barrows and clefts and cracks in Irish ground, the barrows, the Sidhe, from which they sometimes still emerge.

That battle took place on the plateau just above Barrie's house, the boulder-strewn hog's back of a hill we walked that week. We'd climbed to it through the deserted grounds of a luxury hotel, Cromlech Lodge, which Barrie had waved at five years before as we'd headed in my hire car for the Carrowkeel tombs. Overpriced, he'd said then, though the food's OK. He was right. Now the place was done for, doomed, even, if architecturally intact. A pandemic might have struck. Above it we followed an eerie path through a pine plantation; a bleak wind soughed in the dim light, and I thought, 'What in God's name am I putting us through?' But then we emerged into a grassy dell dominated by a huge, cracked stone, ten feet high and wide if it was an inch, somehow lodged on its edge across the path. Balor's eye socket: the Fomorian invaders' giant king, a glance from whose venomous eye could kill, was finally blinded in battle by his grandson Lugh, felled here. We felt alive, pressed on across the gorse bloom of the plateau, brushed through long grass, buttercups, daisies and sudden concentrations of bog cotton. More massive warrior-stones: against one, Ben posed as one of the Tuatha. Lough Arrow winked in the distance.

We came down off the hill's flank, walked back along the road above it, passed Barrie's house, and I thought again, the more vividly for being there, of the curious moment of unexpected intimacy he had insisted I witness, just before we'd set off for the Carrowkeel tombs. Rather than eat out at Cromlech Lodge, he'd been preparing dinner, a rice dish, which he heated on his stove in a lidded pot and then – 'Come with me,' he said – placed to warm under his duvet while we walked. He'd learned the method in Borneo in 1975, he told me. I was more taken with the vast Mediterranean colours of the canvas behind his headboard, and a much smaller and more curious relief, all grit and gravel between what looked like two clay banks. Or – rearing legs? Could that be, I wondered? Yeah, said Barrie. 'One of my Sheelas.' But though the letter of Ted's I found in the selection on the shelves and read aloud eagerly to him seemed not to ring any bells with him, when we returned from the tombs we ate that rice dish, delicious, off plates of Barrie's design that turned out, themselves, to be two blue rearing legs. Splayed, distinctly female. He licked his clean. I couldn't quite follow suit, but sneaked a picture, wondering at the time whether I'd just been set a test, and guessing that if I had, I'd failed it, lost something, by not asking about the design. But I was too British, too polite. I'd known him only a few hours. The bottle of Barbadian rum he'd asked me to bring him was still half-full. That night I'd flicked through the book of pictures he'd given me: saw another two Sheelas, and the watercolours, the bone boxes, the knots, of foliage and naked human limbs, and female forms, always female, Barrie painted, made, throughout these years, long before and after the gold and green magnificence of his 'Lough Derg Pike'. Felt awed, out of my depth.

We had a mile or more, Sarah, Ben and I, still to walk along the road back to where we'd left the car. But we'd gone no more than a couple of hundred yards from the turning down to Barrie's place when Sarah touched my elbow, pointed. Fifty yards away a big dog fox, really luxuriant in his coat, was staring back across at us. This was late afternoon; we were hours before dusk. It must have been a good ten seconds he stared – more than enough to let us know whose patch we were on – before turning, shrugging himself between hawthorns. Whenever I see a fox I think of Ted, and feel, as I felt then, on the right track.

But it would be three years again before I came to realise why I saw that one. Then I saw something Barrie had kept from me, reasonably enough: the guest book he and his third wife Jean Valentine had kept at Ballinlig, but which had fallen shut for good when their marriage ended. I saw how Ted rounded off his and Nick's visit to their old friend in October 1992. He had returned to the pike poem he'd written to thank Barrie for their first Clare pike trip with Nick, then written out from memory when Barrie and this guest book were still beside the Nore. There was a cartoon Dagda, in the form of a pike, what else, swimming willingly into the open mouth of a Marilyn Monroe of a crow: 'The Dagda meets the Morrigu, on the Unshin, near Ballinlig.' There was a fond reference to that other perfect lake – 'Without Gur, God would have given up.' There was proof of another walk Ted and Nick must have done, perhaps – who knows – after Barrie had set another Sarawak rice dish to warm under the duvet. For here was the battle of Moytura. 'Through the bottom of Balor's broken eye-socket, the Dagda's cauldron', famed for its power to restore the wounded, was said to have 'tumbled and was lost'. And finally proof that some rumoured losses can be reversed. 'They lied. The cauldron of the Dagda survived, returned, and steams / On the Cooke's table.'

*

At the end of that early June half-term, I said farewell to Sarah and Ben at Dublin airport, then drove three hours back, into the west. To the Burren. I had another appointment to keep. With

Barrie's first and oldest model, the inspiration for those Sheelas of his, the source, as Ted saw at once, of Irish mana. Ted's source, too, for a poem it took him almost twenty years to deliver to his friend.

In doing all this, heading west, I now knew from Aoine, I was following in her father's footsteps. Right to the end, for as long as he retained his memory, he never forgot the Burren, or Kilnaboy, or the Kilnaboy Venus. She's there in a vivid watercolour map he did of the place in 1984. And he renewed his acquaintance with her after he left his house above Lough Arrow for the final time. In September 2012, Barrie spent two nights in a house he'd first come to in 1954. The schoolteacher's house, then: Michael Kelleher let him stay a night or two as Barrie, with his help, found a cottage to rent in the field behind the church. He took Barrie wildfowling, introduced him to the Lake of the Flesh, became the subject, with his fellow gun Corey, of one of Barrie's earliest portraits.

It's still the schoolteacher's house, or the retired headteacher's: Declan Kelleher, Michael's son, followed his father into the profession. But Fergus View is also now a lovely bed and breakfast, run by Declan and his wife Mary, and they were pleased to welcome Barrie back. Now they have a Christmas card – of wild geese, of course – that Barrie sent Michael in 1962 framed above the bed in the bedroom Barrie stayed in that September. It's the couple's tribute to their old friend. Mary told me to have a look – American guests left the door open as they checked out.

But Declan also showed me more. He pointed me to the old cottage, now almost entirely reclaimed by ivy, a hundred yards across a cow field from the gated lane behind the church, which Michael persuaded his farmer neighbour to let Barrie have in 1954; Barrie would have walked that lane on his way to fish. Flies were buzzing on the cowpats. I spent an hour in and around that cottage, completely happy. Seamus Heaney once called Barrie a Green Man. This was a green man's green home.

You'd have mistaken it for a bush. But I went in. Saw, on those sections of its walls not yet livid with moss, proof, in wild triumphant rhyming couplets very few British teenagers I know could have managed, of recent couplings. Names were named, too. I couldn't help thinking Barrie would have approved. And then I walked the first part of Barrie's walk, through that field, along that lane, and then went through the gate and into the churchyard of the Kilnaboy old church. If you didn't know where to look you'd miss her, but I'd seen photographs, and found her all right, the Sheela above the door on the south-western door. Indistinct; limestone or granite, I couldn't be sure. About a foot high, no more. Wizened. Shrunken stone tits. But hands, there, clear enough under the lichen, down between her legs, pulling herself apart. I did know where to look. So, I'd discover, did local women; till well into this century, approaching a millennium since she was placed in that wall, the childless wives of Kilnaboy would be known to come and seek her help, look up to her. Whatever the Church pretended she was doing – a crude warning against lust and the sins of the flesh – those women knew what Barrie knew. Then I turned and looked away, and followed her hard gaze across the valley. The Fergus, Barrie's first river.

And on my first evening, in the last of the light, I walked from Fergus View down to the river myself there, cast a little smut of a fly upstream through the arch of the bridge onto the meniscus of the water and caught fourteen red-speckled troutlings, none of them worth a photo, but beautiful in themselves and in their abundance, before darkness came.

Next morning Declan lent me a map, showed me the Lake of the Flesh.

I walked that lake, imagined which of the slots of rock Ted and Barrie would have lain in to hear the wild geese come in. An eerie, pale, calciferous water, fed by the stream that flows off the sugar-loaf limestone of Mullach Mor and that will one day, surprisingly soon in the spans of geological time, and with the help it can rely on from expected quantities of Irish rain, eat its way through it.

*

I was staying with Roderick and Caroline when I heard from Julia Cooke. Second babies are never quite as exciting as the first or last, and as a newborn baby in 1960, Julia had had to compete for Barrie's attention not with a salmon but with that beautiful dead rain-grey heron, and with his growing obsession with what he called Sheela-na-giggery. He knew he should be celebrating the new birth, but couldn't bear not to paint. He was an artist before and after he was a father. So he could at least paint fertility, Fergus-style. River clays, river gravel. Waters of life, spilling from the womb. Aoine wasn't the only one to have to take Barrie on his terms, then. Or to lose him.

But whatever pain he'd caused by leaving her mum and their two girls for Sonja when the youngest of them was only three, Julia, like her older sister Liadin and like Aoine, had still been there for him. And she was the one who was just round the corner, really, in the months he completed the last leg of that long journey south and then east, from Kilmactranny via Kilnaboy to Graiguenamanagh in September 2012, took up residence in that spartan bungalow, faded and needed help. She was the one I told that the letters were safe.

Now, two years after his death, she'd come across a new letter from Ted in Barrie's papers that she wanted to show me. It was June. As I drove I recognised the turning to the old chapel Roderick and I had passed that April afternoon, and I stopped and looked down at the flats beside the Barrow, then drove on, uncertain how far my detour had taken me out of my way. Not at all, it turned out. On the contrary, I had time to kill, so I parked in woods above the river just before the town, walked down a path, and discovered a massive rock, an old oak growing from its fissures. The skull tower? It had to be. I looked upriver from the boardwalk, got a distant view through the trees of the flat fields camping ground. Flies were dancing over the water. I disturbed a bird, a flash of electric blue in the trees. Kingfishers never disappoint.

The letter Julia showed me was Ted's thank-you letter, written weeks after that visit to the Burren in September 1962. Full of the Burren, the Sheela, and hinting at plans for a collaboration, a joint publication the following year. Eventually I'd find Barrie's letters to the prospective publisher, a blurb, even, which Barrie had persuaded Jack Sweeney to draft, and then roped the first of his poet friends, John Montague, into enhancing. It spoke of Ted and Barrie's deep correspondence, even when they were miles apart. 'For although both Hughes and Cooke are naturally solitary workers, both are immersed in a detailed attention to nature where flux, and even violence, seem a lawful order.'

And that, when I discovered it, struck me as true, still. It sent me back to 'River Barrow': poet and artist, rods out, engaged, not just with the fish, solitary fishermen coming together, 'all evil suspended' in the flux of the river.

*

On my way back from Julia, riding the exhilaration of the discovery of Ted's letter, I wanted to find another source. It was a balmy early evening, so, skull tower lurking in those woods, I drove back along that road above the river, parked, and let myself down into the cleave of the valley, over those stone walls, found the path snaking through the brambles, and down to those two flat fields. The orchids weren't yet in flower, but this felt more like it. I could have pitched a tent here. I lost myself in the river, ceaseless emerald and gold, grasses and trees on the far bank. I had *River* with me, and my camera, if not my rod, so I read 'River Barrow' to the place. And it was as beautiful as it had been when I'd first read it to Roderick and Caroline at Isham three years before. No, even more beautiful. That 'dog-bark stillness'. A dogwalker's companion, on the towpath opposite, delivered on cue.

*

Beautiful, yes – and I knew then that a talk Aoine had asked me to do in a few weeks' time about Barrie, Ted and the river would give my PowerPoint slides an abstract expressionist backdrop my audience could lose themselves in as they drifted off – but not quite right. An unease grew in me. The poem mentioned a foam line near the far bank, a weir. But it didn't mention a towpath. These two fields were perfect for camping but didn't fit the bill, by which I mean the text. And as I'd finished my reading and headed back, a rowing eight rounded the bend below that wood where I'd seen my skull rock and the kingfisher. Even for a floor of ballroom glass, it felt too smooth, managed, domesticated, tame.

Another thing, more basic: sitting beside the river that July evening, the sun sets, like some molten glass orb still red from its own furnace, into 'green ember crumble / Of hill trees, over the Barrow'. But this stretch of the Barrow above Graiguenamanagh runs north–south, so to have seen this sunset over the river wouldn't they be needing to be on the east bank facing west? These fields were on the west bank.

So in the weeks before I was due to return, I bought guidebooks, maps of the Barrow. It's one of Ireland's longest rivers, and was for decades a major arterial route for barge traffic: now most of the boats on the river are leisure cruisers, as they are on the Shannon to the west: the nearest lock, I saw, was only a mile or so upstream, at Clashganny. And Clashganny had a weir, too; that's where the river turns south. Best of all, there seemed to be another candidate for the skull tower just downstream of the weir, Clohastia Castle, on the west bank, too.

I learned something of its long history, as well. And its prehistory, its founding myths. The Morrigu, the crow-death goddess for whom Ted and Nick were about to name their printing press, has a son, Meiche. Was he the product of that union on the Unshin? In Meiche's heart are buried three serpents. If they burst out of his heart they will lay waste to the whole of Ireland, so Meiche has to be killed, and burned, to prevent it. When the ashes of his body are poured into the river, the river boils, and all the fish are killed. In old Irish, Barrow means the boiling river.

I go back to the poem, see the sky through which that red globe sinks above the restored, fish-rich Barrow rather differently: 'the flushed ash-grey sky lies perfect.'

In late July I returned, armed not just with my own new Mark IV rod and quiver tip extension – if I was going to engage the bream shoal, I reasoned, I needed my own suitably sensitive antenna – but with an ambivalent assistant: Ben, now sixteen, had been sufficiently intrigued by what he'd seen of Co. Sligo to give Ireland another go. At dinner on our first evening at the Murphys, I sketched my plans. Roderick was withering. 'Bloody Englishman: I showed you exactly where they camped!' But I need to be sure, I said; need to work out that they could have walked upstream – I had a memory of a wall of brambles as well as the usual barbed-wire fence on those flats. 'Well, in that case, you'd better be careful,' Andrew, another guest, advised: 'some of the farmers round here have been known to shoot trespassers.' From the other end of the table, my assistant glared and went pale.

We tried, the next evening. We struck off the main road down a track in what should have been the right position. We clambered over gates, with signs threatening trespassers – but only, law-abiding me told Ben, with prosecution. A crazed terrier flung itself at the glass of a sitting room of a deserted bungalow. 'What if they come back while we're by the river?' Ben asked. We pressed on, to where the track entered thick woodland; we knew, knew, that the castle ruins should be here. We even heard – I wanted to hear – the sound of running water. But woodland doesn't do that jungle justice. No one, now or, I guessed, then, could have made it through to fish there, even if the bank was the kind of place you could cast from. And though we made it to the weir pool at Clashganny, and though in evening sunlight I tried spinning – a Big S again – casting across the weir's foaming foot, and persuaded Ben to film me in what passed for action, the anglers from the far bank, above the weir, must have been thinking 'Bloody Englishmen', too.

Despite all this, the talk went well. Julia, Sonja and Aoine all came; so did Roderick, Caroline, Andrew and his wife Tina, who I knew had been close friends of Barrie. There were artists who were devoted to the Barrow and the Nore, whose subject was the river. The river dazzled them in the gold and green of its June glories. Once more I read aloud, and lost myself in the marvels of 'River Barrow'. On the drive to Thomastown afterwards Ben did want to check something: 'You don't think Barrie was a good *father*, do you, Dad?' 'No,' I replied, 'not the kind I'd like to be.' But I'm certain his daughters all loved him for the man he was. And at Jerpoint that evening Sonja served us ice cream and gave us a tour of her studio, before Aoine walked me down to the Nore, at dusk. Trout were rising.

But still. A mystery persisted, a dissatisfaction. Almost a year passed. And then I saw that 4 July, the anniversary of the day after Ted's account of lugging kit down over those walls, through those brambles to the riverside camp, fell on a day I could make it over. And rereading my transcription of that diary I discovered a sentence I'd missed. On the second day, the 5th, 'Farmer ferries us across.' All my efforts, then, had been on the wrong bank.

I had to have one last try.

*

My hosts, the long-suffering Murphys, claimed to be glad to see me. But they chose not to at this hour: 5.00 a.m. on 5 July. By 5.15 I had parked at Clashganny. A limpid, clear river. I walked downriver; that is, down the pond-like canalised navigable slow water below the lock. Trusted myself: kept going. I heard, gently, flowing water, faster, through the trees on the far bank. At last I came to another lock. Looked round. Nobody, of course. Wobbled across the swing bridge. Saw, on a tree trunk, 'NO ENTRY. TRESPASSERS WILL BE PROSECUTED'. I thought: if challenged, I am a hired German, with no English. And followed a path through longish grass round the end of that wooded island, and suddenly there it was.

A long swift run. A broad, surging river, a wild thing, with rocks you could step on to get closer to the main flow. At its tail, an old weir, not of the Clashganny kind, but a salmon or eel-weir, funnelling to a gap you could fill with a net. I had my fly rod, a nymph. I leapt from rock to rock, saw in one mid-stream stone a hole as round as any I'd seen in the limestone at Isham, and in that hole a golf ball, snug as a bun. I caught a dace; just smaller, I reckoned, than the roach at Aughrisburg, but delicate, exquisite. I turned and faced the rapids upstream as the mist rose off the river in the strengthening sun – and beyond saw an ancient crumble of stone rising on the far bank. The skull tower! I retreated to the bank, headed further upstream.

And there it was. A still, gliding, deep pool, with a foam line near the far bank. Just below the still impressive edifice of Clohastia Castle. Invisible from that bank, here it stood, proud. The pool stretched a hundred yards upstream. Even this early in the morning, flies danced. Long grass stems overhung the water.

I posed my fly rod, imagined this was a humid evening forty-one years before. Watched the whorls, the glides, the muscle, the nerve, the belly of this place, and two fishermen talking, and one sixteen-year-old upstream casting, casting, casting.

I spent an hour there. Completely happy. I'd slaked my thirst for this place, satisfied the itch. Trusted, found, Ted's 'River Barrow'. Trespassed to delight.

But I knew, too, that I wouldn't be there that evening. Andrew was off for a night's sea-trouting on the Slaney, forty minutes away over Mount Leinster. It had been fishing well. Why didn't I join him?

10

Visitations

When Nick 'cast his rainbow for the thirty pounder' as the opening salvo of the latest assault on the pike of Co. Limerick, he wasn't commanding the skies. He was just making the most of what he'd caught that morning, ninety miles east. Before breakfast (trout he'd smoked in the van the evening before), two more rainbow escapees from the trout farm up the side river flowing into the Barrow had taken his Rapala lure, the largest of them two pounds, blackish, missing its pectorals.

Three years have passed since that first idyllic camping trip five miles or so downriver. This is the moment before the moment of truth, when the Hugheses embark together, but for the first time without Barrie, on the challenge of Gur and its monster. It's the interlude between those nights in at Jerpoint and their return to Anne O'Neill's. And we know that Ted took doubt with him. Just as well, then, that, boy becoming man, Nick took trout.

It's Monday 6 April 1981, part of that great Irish month of fishing. And this interlude had begun on the Friday, a day of blue warmth. Only five miles or so upriver from Graiguenamanagh, twenty-five minutes from Barrie and Sonja, but on the opposite slope of the valley from the Murphys' house at Skeaghvasteen, and another world. Their destination, the Barrow at Borris. Their hosts were the Kavanaghs, themselves old friends of Barrie's. Andrew, my sea-trouting host, Ted recognised – he'd seen him on TV the year before, in a horse race. He offered them dinner that evening or lunch on Saturday. Tina was about to give a ewe who had 'lost her insides' when she had split, giving birth to a big second lamb, a dose of milk and four eggs, then showed them their horses. Racehorses, that is, and a boy whose nose a nervy stallion had broken.

It was, Ted noticed, a 'giant' house, 'colossal'. And with the trappings of ancient wealth. But worn lightly; as lightly as Barrie and Ted wore their own old Barbour jackets. Tina led them inside, and it could have been a hard-nosed farmhouse, except for the family motto in Irish, the massive doors of fine walnut. Tina translated the motto, 'Peace and Plenty', and then gave them the unauthorised version, 'Fucking and Farting.' She'd been brought up in Lincolnshire but now only knew England through its racecourses. Ted was intrigued by her confidence, the talk that came from her like a swift river, confident, mannered, over a substrate of what he knew was feeling, considerateness. He couldn't imagine such a combination in England.

Then down to the river at last. Tina led the way through sheep-thronged parkland – Ted reunited lambs the wrong side of a fence with their mothers – down a rutted lane through ancient woodland, which must have required some care: they were pulling their boat, battered now, behind the van – to 'the broad brown Barrow', and left along the river to a small, rather grand sandstone arched bridge over a side stream, but itself the size of the Taw, and notably clearer than the main river. The sandstone had come as ballast in one of the barges. Ted noticed kingfishers hurtling down this stream, out under the bridge and into a wood on the far bank of the Barrow. Tina and her flock of children hung about a bit, then left them to it.

Now they took their time. They assessed things: which is to say, watched what the locals were up to on the river. And it took all comers on its broad brown back. Another car arrived, having just lost its exhaust on that track through the woods. The English driver laughed it off, then lobbed his worms towards where a salmon had shown yesterday. His passenger, a young Irishman, slipped away with his fly rod. A third angler cast a Devon minnow, 'as idly as a man might go for a stroll'. Ted and Nick fished till nightfall, spent a steely cold first night in the van, parked beside the bridge over a side stream they'd crossed just as they left the grandeur of the park. At Jerpoint Ted's sleep had brought him dreams he needed to think about and to write. Now he dreamed of three bears – Alaskan or fairytale? As he woke, Nick met him with another suggestion: 'Come on you Himalayan honey bear, get up.' Nick's Oxford zoologist friends remember his jars of Court Green honey.

The Hugheses spent the morning trying a method that should have worked, easing their boat downstream between the weirs behind naturally drifting dead baits under floats. Should have. It didn't. At midday Ted left Nick to it – which, it transpired, meant catching escapee rainbows from Andrew's trout farm higher up that side stream, smoking one in the van – and went up for drinks – the Murphys, already old friends of the Kavanaghs, joined them – and lunch. Wine flowed as well as the talk, about the anti-pollution conservation committee Andrew was on, and the need to inform farming practice with the latest research.

Then final proof of that ancient wealth, not so much lightly worn this time as just, well, accreted. Andrew takes Ted down into their vast cellars. Ted admires the stalagmites, each a stringy foot long, each with a drip on its tip, and helping in their way to control the damp. He notices chalk boards with cellarage details, some dating back to the early 1800s. And empty champagne bottles strewn everywhere. The stair down, too, he notes, is cluttered with rubbish.

Then back to rejoin Nick, beside a river that, as night comes on and mist clings to its surface, keeps its secrets, like some book they found much harder to read than its woodland banks:

Broad flat river we cut through tonight, turning aside the pictures, turning the pages.
Primroses, violets, milky maids, celandines, wood anemones.

But though they were both sure the method was right, 'lovely', the Barrow yielded nothing. So they reeled in, kept that trout for later, packed up, called in at the house to bid their farewells to their hosts and collect bait from the freezer – it's odd the things a fisherman-diarist neglects to mention in the first place, but this was clearly a basic human right for the itinerant piker – and fled west.

*

The first evening I spent in their company at the house beside Lough Mask, the Murphys may not have remembered 'River Barrow' but they had been sure of this: it had been while walking with some friends of theirs that Ted had seen his first kingfisher. They also knew, from what Ted had told Barrie, and Barrie passed on to them and these friends, that he'd written a poem about it shortly after. 'Oh really?' I think I said, but 'Bloody Irishmen', I may have thought. When I returned to Ted's essay 'Taw and Torridge', and studied its drafts, my scepticism increased: he wrote of that wonderful stretch of the Torridge as it slipped downstream from Nethercott and the valley closed in, that it was an unusual day when you didn't see a kingfisher.

Then I found, and read, and reread, Ted's diary of that weekend at Borris, a diary fishing for people as much as pike, and spotted those kingfishers hurtling out under the bridge from the Taw-wide side stream, and I thought: never.

But then, in early April 2016 – the first Saturday of the month, to be precise, and a couple of hours before Roderick will take me down to those flat camping fields five miles downriver – here is Roderick driving me through massive stone gates and into the stable yard of Borris House. It's a day short of thirty-five years since that hot blue afternoon when Ted and Nick arrived here. But we drive on a little further, to the beautiful modern house tucked, with plenty of room to spare, within the walls of the old kitchen garden – which had served the main house and estate until 1956 – and with its own fine aspect over the Barrow valley. Spaniels emerge, rather friendlier than Roderick's, and here is Andrew Kavanagh, a trim figure still, if no longer racing horses. Andrew and Tina gave us tea in a kitchen of such proportions that the vast canvas over the dining table – one of Barrie's, of New Zealand – looks right at home.

And then we are driving back past the seventeenth-century crenellated confection of Borris House. Their son, Morgan, one of that throng of children back in 1981, lives there now with his own family. They've taken on the farm – more often than not when I've seen him, he's cheerfully mud-spattered – and the responsibilities that come with such an extraordinary place: while they live in one wing, the rest of the house and parkland, including ballroom and family chapel, across the inner wall of whose gallery Andrew and Tina commissioned Barrie to paint a mural – he chose the tree of life – earn their keep as a venue for weddings. (As they already were in 1981, Tina insists, when I mention Ted's diary: that explained all those empty champagne bottles.) But those were in the days before websites: now it makes commercial sense, adds a personal grace note to those crenellations, and so the bookings, to mention the history responsible for that motto. The McMurrough Kavanaghs can trace their lineage right back to the Kings of Leinster, the lost royal family of Ireland.

For the past few years there's been another annual source of income, and one that adds literary royalty to the scene. The first weekend in June, Borris House hosts a Festival of Writing and Ideas; Roderick and Caroline's son-in-law is its director, and their old fishing HQ from their own fishing trips, many with Barrie, some with Ted, becomes, for that weekend, a car-a-vin.

Tina Kavanagh still knows how to talk, but now it wasn't horses but the Opera: the Met, Covent Garden, Verona, sopranos and baritones, stars and friends. And then she was leading me as she had led Ted and Nick past the chapel. We drove across that sheep-grazed parkland, grass as startlingly green and then, abandoning the car, slithered – recent rain and copse-clearing had left the track a quagmire – down into rough woodland, along the track that led past a large, modern house by what she called 'the mountain stream'. Salmon still run up it to spawn on the slopes of Mount Leinster, though in nothing like the numbers they once did. The rainbow trout went years ago, when – just here, by that house – they gave up on the trout farm. I noticed that the water was startlingly clear.

We left our cars there and walked downstream, along a pitted overgrown track, dogs plunging into deep piles of dead leaves and charging up the hillside after scents. Tina's talk did the same. A lowering sun lanced through branches in strong new leaf, the mountain stream charged, twisting, down the tight valley that twisted with it, and stands of larches and pines on the far bank, their darkness in strong contrast to the openness of the older oaks on ours, made me ask another question. Packing on their last morning, Ted had noted the 'jungle of laurels (every logged stump, an eruption of stems, every sod sprouting its laurel sprigs, + the uncut woods and impenetrable criss cross mass of laurel stems') – that was before Andrew and the boys had spent the whole of one winter clearing out the undergrowth.

But I also tried to listen to the water, keep one eye out. A faint hope: amid all this easy operatic chatter and dog-crashing heartiness as we made our way down the stream, any self-respecting kingfisher would be holed up somewhere three pools away. But I brought the subject up: I wanted to hear it from Tina herself. She couldn't remember exactly where it was, but she was definite: Ted had seen a kingfisher fly past, and had said:

'That's the first kingfisher I've ever seen.'

She remembered it particularly, because the claim had surprised her, too.

*

When do you see a kingfisher? What does it mean to really, actually see one? And how do you write about it when you have? It depends on your point of view, of course, and Ted couldn't have been better equipped. But he had competition. For the last hundred years or so, a single phrase of the Jesuit poet Gerard Manley Hopkins, writing from a seminary in the Vale of Clwyd in 1877, seems to pose the problem and answer it in a single breath: 'As kingfishers catch fire, dragonflies draw flame.' And until that walk down the mountain stream with Tina and Roderick and the dogs, I'd never questioned the rightness of that insight, as swift as its moving target.

All that most of us ever see of kingfishers, I suspect, is just that definitive tracer-bullet moment of spontaneous combustion, when light reflects off their astonishing blue backs in flight and

scatters: attracts our attention and then confounds it, slips out
of our sight and into reflection, memory, analogy. It's crowning
proof of how nature engages our senses, illuminating truths about
the creatures we see but then making us look again.

And I know, from cold experience, what it takes to convert that
brilliant, electrifying blue blur up- or downstream, mid-flight, into
a reading, a more exact visual encounter. For months, one winter,
in the mid-1990s, I walked the dog along a half-mile of asphalt
bicycle path beside a playing field on the outskirts of Cambridge;
the path followed the twists of a trolley-strewn, bramble-tangled
stream. That winter a kingfisher was in the habit of leading me
upstream: a few inches over the water, jet-straight, for forty or
fifty yards, before I'd lose that blue. But with practice I learned
where it came in to land, what to look for: the shit-spattered
leaves below a favourite twig. Sometimes I'd get close, watch the
bird in profile, at rest, or at least, waiting for me to get that close,
no closer: because whenever I stopped my hesitation would seem
to prompt the next dip into flight, like a jet off an aircraft-carrier
deck, and the surge away until it reached the next twig. On several
days that winter, I'd manage to follow the kingfisher; it would
guide me, for three or four such bursts before it banked away
over the stand of low trees and bushes that gave, on the far side
of the stream, onto a gravel pit owned by a city fishing club. That
was a dark winter as well as a cold one, but my spirits were lifted
by that flashing guide.

In the after-image of iridescence's dazzle other thoughts and
feelings may spark. Physicists may wonder about the energy
that organises it, wherever it lies, in the fibres of the feather;
metaphysicists like Hopkins – who researched optics while a
Jesuit novitiate – may see in the light show the God who 'fathers
forth', whose beauty is without change. But I've come to see
that in making kingfishers and dragonflies actors in this larger
drama of flickering light and heat as well as language, dazzling
specimens of 'the one thing and the same' that 'each mortal thing
does' – that is, 'selves, goes itself' – Hopkins converts these
predators into prayers: overlooks their prey that fuels their fire.
The poet's vestried interest is ingenious, determined: from a line

that began in natural movement he leads his readers through a series of perspectives and faces that take us to God the Father and back again.

As I grew away from a faith I found at boarding school, I found it easier to admire than to share Hopkins's conviction. And that Cambridge winter, when spring came and the foliage burst and the banks of that stream became green and crowded, I missed it, never caught sight of a kingfisher; perhaps because its own pickings were easier. But that loss has itself trained my senses to catch what I can of these amazing birds.

These past years, of fishing on the Torridge, the Tamar and the Dart, or walking, whenever I can at first light, beside the fen lode that runs a hundred yards from my house, I've come to learn that the sharp midshipman piping that cuts through a conversation or a drifting silence could and should give me notice of a blue streak that – there! – I was primed to see. Once, on the bridge over the Okement at Monkokehampton, that piping brought my gaze into focus at just the moment a kingfisher spotted me: I'll never forget the veer up in horrified redirection at the figure only feet before it, wing feathers outspread like bright fingers, the ochre breast flipping up and away and the sudden shock of light-scattering blue from its retreating back.

I know how privileged I've been to have these meetings and near misses, however hard I think I've worked on myself to earn them. But I had never actually seen a kingfisher fishing, let alone catch a fish.

*

Tina's still talking this Saturday afternoon in April. Now we're getting close to its confluence with the Barrow. Tina's tumbling operatic performance holds centre stage, drowns out the murmur of the mountain stream.

I keep my eyes cast to the right height as a pool on a bend gives way to a run of downstream rapids. And a kingfisher catches them, draws them with me: my attention comes to rest, as it does, briefly – a matter of two seconds – on the lowest twig of a bush over a pocket of water at the foot of this run; it holds my eyes while – there! – it dips down, breaks the water, comes up again, the slant sunlight glinting on a silver sliver in its beak; then shoots – hurtles – away, towards the confluence with the Barrow. All before I can, or want to, say a word.

*

I go back to Ted's poem, the one that, Ted told Barrie who told Tina and Andrew, who told Roderick and Caroline and me, he'd written after his own conversation with Tina that Saturday afternoon. 'The Kingfisher'? I have nothing but Tina's memory of what Ted said to make me think so.

But now I see it. It must have come to him quickly, while he was in Ireland: a last call for a place in *A Primer of Birds* that his friend Leonard Baskin finished setting and printing that June. It's in good company: Ted had found other bird poems – 'The Rival', about a cormorant, 'Whiteness', about a heron – in encounters at dawn on the Torridge the previous September and May, consolations for when those other, stiller strangers eluded him. Like 'The Kingfisher', they found their way into *River*, too.

'The Kingfisher' is here, now: it could suddenly be nowhere else. That 'raggle-taggle tumbledown river' must be the mountain stream, charging past ancient wealth so lightly, roughly worn. But it's not just this river, it's what happens on it, the sequence of events. The studied perch; the bird's hi-tech lens-assisted X-ray penetration of what, even to a fisherman with polarising, glare-busting glasses, remains 'a tangle of glooms'; the straight dash downstream through the light. He – and it is a single bird, a real fisherman, royal, too, a capital fellow, Kingfisher, 'beak full of ingots' – 'Leaves a rainbow splinter sticking in your eye'. However hard or fast you look, neither language nor any human sense, hearing or vision, can keep up. And you're not the only one. The 'oafish oaks' seem to be looking in the wrong place, too, for things they assume only to be stones, while he has lifted all its jewels, 'Shivering the spine of the river'.

But there's more to 'The Kingfisher' than this smash-and-grab raid. Ted's learned from Hopkins, from first to last one of his favourite poets. He, too, wants to say more, slyly. Remember: scion of Ireland's lost royal family has just shown him what lies in and beneath that old house: the gap between theory and practice on pollution. Farmers whose practice lets them down. The easy chaos of old money, but what the ancient wealth sits on, too: that amazing clutter of the Borris cellars, stalactites and champagne bottles. Now he spears this other spry royal of a bird. In 'The Kingfisher' fisherman Ted answers back to Hopkins, reverses the direction of light: 'Through him, God, whizzing in the sun', source of solar light set tumbling, 'Glimpses the angler'. 'Through him' – and whether 'him' means the kingfisher or angler doesn't matter, because, as Ted once wrote, 'Fishermen understand why Christ was said to be a fish', 'Fishermen worship water' – God's in for a surprise. He has his nose rubbed in another kind of genesis, the 'fishy mire' few humans ever bring themselves to imagine. We're in the tunnelled bankside burrow where life and death get churned, swallowed and shat out, once the spine of that glittering ingot caught so expertly in the water of the mountain stream has been snapped, its spark of life extinguished. What did Ted say about the stairs down to the Borris cellars, just inside the main door? It was 'as cluttered with rubbish as the wildest dump'.

*

I return alone, the following summer, to this same bend and riffle and pool and a plank bridge beyond, which I'm guessing wasn't there in Ted and Nick's day. By then I've heard from Roderick and Caroline that Tina frankly didn't believe what I'd felt safer telling them of my vision that April afternoon, any more, really, than she'd believed Ted. I can't blame her. Nor, this hot June day, can I find her to convince her otherwise, because this is the Sunday of the Borris Festival of Writing and Ideas, and the house and grounds are teeming with writers and guests, and Tina must have other people on her mind.

But between sessions I can slip out of the chapel and walk past the marquees and Roderick and Caroline's repurposed car-a-vin, where first thing that morning the three of us sat, remembering, imagining old days. I walk through that great green meadow, the grass already hazing, long-stemmed, towards hay. I cross the bridge, pass the house and the site of the old trout farm, then head down the mountain stream. And there, on that plank bridge, seal my compact between poem and place. In bright tree-filtered sun I read 'The Kingfisher' over that raggle-taggle river and the pool's smooth depths. Both run clear. I even try taking a photograph to prove it. Try. The camera's whizzing lens focuses on the page and turns brown water in the background dark. Or it goes for the water and leaves the page a foreground blaze of white. So I put my camera down and concentrate on reading *River* by this river, do my best to catch both.

*

I've yet to return to Lough Carra, and on my one visit there with the Murphys I couldn't stay long enough. I had appointments to keep in Connemara. So my other regret, beside not catching one of those marble trout, is that I never made it to the Keel River: Caroline pointed out its mouth as a dark smudge in those distant reeds.

It was the last morning of that great Irish Easter trip, 12 April. From Gur, ferry tickets bought, they'd decided they could squeeze in one more leg, a return visit to Carra. This time Nick lay in: Gur had satisfied his ambition for the year of a twenty-pound pike. But Ted and Barrie were up at six, and eager for more.

They went downriver. Ted taking the east bank, Barrie the west; Barrie had found three-pound trout there the day before. It's another lovely river, and with surprising depth after Carra's shallowness, full of twisting channels and clear water running over holes. The tall rushes growing out of boggy margins made fishing tricky, but this morning as Barrie ranges ahead Ted 'raised + touched one fish'. Later, he realises that if they'd only examined the stomachs of yesterday's river trout – preparing them for breakfast, they would discover they were full of black alder fly, and shrimps – they 'might have scored'.

Still, though, that dawn left its mark, on diary as well as Keel mud: 'Otter prints everywhere – deep deeply divided pad prints.'

*

Ted's love for otters was even deeper, clearer, twistier than the Keel River. Ducklings imprint on the creature, whether avian or human, they see first. So with a boy and a particular otter. Remember his early love affair with Henry Williamson's Tarka? That marked Ted's territory as a poet from the start. At seventeen, he saw a poem of his, 'The Recluse', in the school magazine, *Don and Dearne*, named for Mexborough's two rivers. That poem imagines an old man wandering a wild shoreline of wet, black rocks, but makes room for Tarka in all but name: 'The otter comes here in the winter but even the shells are empty, – / … And the otter goes inland hungry'. This is not Don and Dearne but the shared estuary of Taw and Torridge, as Henry Williamson had given it to him. In Cambridge in his twenties, miles from all four of those rivers, he wrote, from memory and somewhere else in him, 'An Otter', itself in two divided parts. Ted claimed that the Greek god Pan gave him the first part, during a session with a Ouija board; the second appeared to him, intact, a fortnight later, from the air: he merely had to copy it down. And though Tarka's at the heart of it, the otter's eye at water level is also Ted, at least for a moment. 'So the self under the eye lies, / Attentive and withdrawn'. In the meniscus between air and water, 'the limpid integument / Reflections live on', otter meets poet.

But by the end of the poem the otter has gone. 'Crying to the old shape of the starlit land', he has become its own lament: he is 'a pelt' hanging over the back of the chair. The hunter hunted, prey at the last to the hounds, packs of which still splashed howling, teeth bared, through British rivers, humans charging after, wild for blood. Otter hunting would not be outlawed until 1979. Eating in the bar of the Half Moon at Sheepwash before heading out after sea-trout, it's always a shock to see an otter head looking down on me. 'Haldon Otter Hounds, River Torridge, May 15 1957'.

When Ted met that otter at dawn on his first trip to the Taw, on 15 March 1962, what else was it but a confirmation? He had 'ended up

in my childhood dream, on Tarka's river'. He wrote this a quarter of
a century on, in 1996, when a young friend, knowing of his passion
for Tarka, sent him a copy of the same first general edition. Ted told
him: 'the typeface brings it all back. I still recognize every sentence.'
Ted's life had come to twist itself into Tarka's. They haunted each
other. He wrote of where else he had 'ended up – later – with the
fishing on the Torridge, which included the trees under one of
which he was born'. Later meant 1980; those trees still overlook the
weir pool at Beam. So when, that May, a spill from the creamery
at Torrington upstream and pesticides killed a hundred salmon and
five hundred big sea-trout, and Ted spent the next decade 'fighting
... to save that river', it was a deeply personal fight. Read '1984 on
the Tarka Trail', and there's no mistaking his horror. Ted told that
young friend, in 1996, 'I never saw another otter, down here, till
four or five years ago, when they started to release artificially bred
otters into the Torridge.' So: not until the full story of *River* was
itself played out. But in the meantime there were the wild others, the
otters he'd found ways of summoning to him.

*

One May morning, on the west coast of Ireland, three schoolgirls
bring their priest a package: a black waterproof folder full of
poems. They also bring the tale of how they got it. A stranger had
appeared suddenly beside them where they'd been playing among
the rocks. He'd asked the names of the mountains strung across
the horizon beyond the lough, and they knew that. Then if they'd
ever seen a miracle. No, they said. So he gave them one. Pursing
his lips to the back of his hand, the noise he conjured was uncanny.
'A peculiar, thin warbling sound', 'like a tiny gentle screaming', 'It
was like a fine bloody thread being pulled through their hearts'.
But it worked. A creature emerged from the water – all they could
say was that it was like a big weasel, the size of a cat – and came on
and on, over the rocks, towards them, till it was crouched beside
the man and ready to leap into his lap. The girls could smell the
lough's fish on the creature. When one of them flinched, it reared,
erect, and they thought an attack was coming, but instead it turned
and was away, back into the shallow water, gone.

The parish priest scoffs at the stranger's definition of a miracle. What is the bringing of an otter out of the water beside the great world itself, which God summoned from the waters of chaos? But that priest evidently doesn't know his Irish legends, whose sides otters are on. In one old story Ted knew for sure, Seamus and Barrie, too, an otter rescues a priest's Bible from the lough where a deranged king of Derry, roaring naked against the very thought of the Church, has thrown it.

And, sure enough, soon this priest on the Atlantic coast finds himself swimming in his own torrent of words, a sudden rapture of description, and that otter merges with Creation itself, 'an infinite creature of miracles', its eyes ever more 'dazzlingly-shining'. The girls, disconcerted, leave him to it, leave him to return to himself, his memory of that morning's otter, and the poems in the waterproof folder. He begins to copy them out.

We are in the strange double world of *Gaudete*: the novel, between verse and prose and those final poems, Ted published in May 1977. That stretch of straggly coastline, that encounter with girls and priest and stranger and otter, is where its epilogue unfolds. I recognised it only because it was on that stretch of straggly coastline that I had an appointment to keep the day I left the Murphys at Isham. But because I kept that appointment, I know exactly where it is: in Connemara, between Cleggan farm and Lough Aughrisburg, where Ted took Nick and Frieda fishing for the first time, returning to camp, and fish at dawn, in June 1971. In August 1977, Henry Williamson died, on the morning they shot the last scenes of the film of *Tarka*; that October, at Castle Lough, in Co. Clare, an otter would applaud the capture of Nick's great queen, on his mother's birthday; on 1 December, Ted spoke at Williamson's memorial service. Loss and hunting and creation, heart and nerve and spirit. Catch it, glimpse it, mourn it, summon it whenever you can. And I remembered that Gur diary, the day before they discovered that pike float in the bay, Ted talking otter, bringing one of three they saw then to within six feet of the boat.

*

But of all these otters, this is the one I love. Those river prints, at dawn on the Keel River. Deep, deeply divided. Otter pads. Not just on the mud, but also the ones Ted drew above and below the poem he wrote, and Nick printed, within fifteen days of their return from Ireland. Its own mystery. One set of four pads point east between title and first line; another, turned west. Each pad and toe printed, as if the creature it supports is standing calm, still. Beneath the last, Ted's pencil signature. Call it a footnote.

You'll find it in *River*. It isn't obviously Irish. It names no places, never even names its subject: the closest it gets to the creature that has left its mark, 'one dawn in a year', is a hint, almost a misprint, 'a dark other', a guess – is that branch below the water really a …? The play, in and out of river, that had filled the night, along with the hunting; all this can only be imagined, a creation story traced in 'mud-margins, / One dawn in a year, her eeriest flower'.

And for a decade it made its own way, slipped quietly into *River* a wary distance from the fisherman's other dark rivals: the cormorant, the mink.

But then in 1993, with no photographs to compete with it, Ted gently restored 'Visitation' to its rightful place. Now this Mayo otter, the cry that might have filled the night, 'half sky-half bird', follows 'The Kingfisher', echoes it. The week that gave him them both has left its marks, there, black and white, on both sides of the same leaf.

*

The March week I spent at Rose cottage reading *River*, I walked the Cornish bank of the Tamar. Spring sun shone. But debris from winter spates still festooned the oaks and alders marking the river's high banks, ten or twelve feet deep in places: twigs and branches, yes, some worn smooth as heron bones, but also high-water marks of silt and river sand in unlikely armpits of the trees that had withstood it, and the odd shred of nitram fertiliser bag. Some were at my eye height: a seventeen-foot flood. I'd just been reading Ted's 'High Water'. I imagined the valley full of the charging torrent of giant mud pigs. And then I came across something I didn't need to imagine. Exposed roots of an oak gave me handholds: I scrambled down to a beach of grey river sand, ten feet long, above a slab of black rock. And there were the neat five-toed stars I'd seen first on the print of 'Visitation'. Hours old, no more. I spent some minutes there beside the waters, watching the steel grey of the waters and glint of light on it, wondering whether I was being watched from some holt under the roots.

That October, I was back on the Tamar, right at the end of the summer, no, beyond it. After salmon in the last days of the season. A miracle: this time I caught one, a six-pound cock fish from the neck of Black Rock pool. His flanks were the colour of the leaves my fly dropped between to search the depths he came from. Late the next morning, preparing to fish a wide and deepening run below rapids, I was checking my fly when a sharp, high, piping cry – one blast, then again, caught me. I thought I knew this cry – a kingfisher – but was surprised at its volume above the river's talk: I looked up, eyes focused a foot above the water. Nothing. I lowered them.

But it wasn't a kingfisher. And it wasn't an otter. It was two: biting and playing, twisting, two bitches were skipping and diving and surfacing and rolling their way up the rapids, out of the pool I'd been about to fish. They looked over at me as I watched; they let me film them, even. Entirely at ease, at what must have been play. Those five or six minutes were among the most marvellous of any I've spent beside water. At the end of it, they just disappeared, became river.

11

Milesian Encounters

Tuesday 4 August 1981. Ted leaves North Tawton at noon, in blazing sunshine; by 10.30 that evening he's pulling off the road north of Fort William, having driven 650 miles. But the lay-by he's chosen, gratefully, wearily, turns out to be the entrance to yet another of what he calls the 'campinggrounds' – an odd usage, until you know that since getting back from Ireland in April, Ted and Nick have spent four weeks in Alaska in June and July, and stayed in several. He's been passing them for some time now. Canny Highlanders have opened them along the main A82 as it winds through the mountains, for the benefit of 'the English Caravan'. The proprietor challenges him: come inside, and pay, or move on. Ted moves on.

He sleeps in the car, under trees. Fitfully. 'Wakened by shot-showers of drops on roof from soaked oaks above' – Ted Manley Hopkins Hughes – he moves again. Oversleeps. But he still has enough time, waiting for the morning's first ferry at Mallaig, to admire the wildness of the pass he'd driven through to get there, and to look ahead. Across the current-torn water of the Minch lay a sight to lift even bleary eyes. Rocks and soil and water and the heavens: every element was on the move. It's his first encounter with Skye, its 'Steep olive body' scored with water and bracken, its rounded 'tops rubbed to the rough bare grey under-crag', and what he writes there on the quayside responds to the great seething friction of it all.

Cloud-shadows flowing across it also Northwards
Steam raw + then dragging the tops, blue beyond.

Ted is heading northwards, too, into that blue. That afternoon he has another boat to catch, from Skye's northernmost tip, another more serious ferry journey from Uig to Tarbert, on Harris. And it's a long, long island. And there are those English caravans to contend with.

But Ted's never been one to play safe. He has also calculated that he could squeeze in an adventure – or, perhaps, business: he still has *River* to write – en route. And he comes prepared. Glen Sligachan, and the Sligachan River, lay thirty-three miles away up the east coast, twelve short of Portree. 'On Fishing Map had seen it was accessible fishing water.'

Fishing maps are, of course, designed to sell fishing.

But Ted is never going to be deterred. And, anyway, you don't carry the memory of a fishing map unless you've been tipped off in the first place. It turns out Ted's acting on the most curiously intimate of local knowledge. But it isn't obviously local to this wild, wide-floored valley, running between 'hills', as his diary put it, and reminding him at first glance of Iceland, where he and Nick had fished in the summer of 1979. This local knowledge was born in Devon.

In those days the Sligachan Hotel sold day tickets. Ted parts with his £4; a boy vacuum-cleaning the hotel lobby tells him that 'the Pools' actually began two and a half miles upriver. He sets off, pressing through 'a scatter of walkers and tourists'; somehow, he's neither. His business has begun. He makes his way as best he can along the bank of the rock-strewn river. There are two side streams he needs to cross, tufts of heather and grass to plunge between, and bogs to splash into, 'never too deep'. And then he comes to a drain that may have been: at four or five feet in depth, and muddy. Though he could probably clear it, he decides against. It is now 11.30; his boat is at 2.45. The clock is ticking.

Ted takes stock. The river has changed character and is meandering. He thinks he's reached 'the last of the pools. The accessible ones'; at least his humour is still dry. But they've been worth the effort. Both are 'luminous over pink granite gravel'. One is a long, straight run, really the tail of a pool whose 'head deepened' above the drain; above it, the other flows vividly clear and deep. The water's 'Lucid amber'. Amber: translucent ancient tree resin: many ages ago, it oozed into this peat. Now it preserves what it holds. Here a ram's skull – 'bighorn', this being the wild west – lying ten feet down: he christens it Ram's Horn Pool. But its shape, 'a giant ear', feels familiar, 'very like the Concrete pool on the Torridge'. And that gives him the confidence first to locate his targets – Ted knows 'exactly where the fish would be' – and then to try other methods. When none move to a fly, he switches to a spinner, which works its charms, in the water and on the page – sounds almost human: 'Tiny Toby rose + hooked a 5 lb fish. Lost it.' He doesn't say whether he saw the fish, whether it was just a flash or surge in the water as his flung slug of metal fluttered by. He doesn't even name the species. But he records the aftermath, and it's already beginning to grow. In the casts he had time for after he had 'lost it', Ted 'brought him, 3 or 4 times again, or others'. *It, him, or others.*

And that's that. The deadline of the ferry looming, he prepares to retrace his trudging steps, 'a tower of melting sweat'; only now noticing a track along the valley floor he'd missed. Following it up would have given him longer fishing. As it was, he begins the descent into Uig just as the boat's coming into the bay, and makes his rendezvous with Simon and Hilary Day, and friends. Soon he's on the sundeck, chatting to Hilary, one of the party he would be joining on North Harris, forty miles north across the Minch. But he also meets two more fishermen – 'one big-eyed portly lisping fellow, one small neat quiet fellow' – bound for what they call 'the Grimster'. Fellows, he calls them, 'chaps'. Not the kind of word he'd used for the owner of that lay-by.

And then disembarking at Tarbert he joins this curiously exclusive version of that English caravan, following the switchback road west around the coast of North Harris, to a natural amphitheatre of a bay. It boasts views south to the great sandy beach of Luskentyre and west to the very edge of things: the 'high pyramids of St Kilda, fifty miles away, seeming five.' And it has its own royal folly: Amhuinnsuidhe, a 'tall grey fairytale castle' of granite Ted thought had been built for Edward VII. In fact, it's a mid-nineteenth-century construction, for a tweed baron. The king never came. But there were cannons pointing out to sea, and jewel-fringed lawns: red and purple fuchsia, copper montbretia. Beyond the garden wall the river tumbles down under the road to the sea. And where fresh water meets salt below the falls salmon and sea-trout are shoaling, their backs showing, waiting for high tide to help them run upstream to the estate's lochs inland, where in the days ahead the castle guests will attempt to interest them in a fly. Ted doesn't wait, can't. For the second time that day he turns to Tobys, 'touched 2 or 3', likely foul-hooking them – Ted calls it 'snagging' – on their treble hooks. Of course, all this is against the estate's strict sporting ethos: fly-only. It should go without saying. Ted mentions the 'custom' here: easier to ignore than rules. Then a boozy dinner and more talk, till well after midnight.

Only then does he write all this down in his diary. At speed. Promises himself that details, personalities, will follow. He's fishing for men, as well as with and against them.

*

And then he wrote the first part of it up.

I don't know when – it was certainly at some point between 5 August 1981, and the spring of 1983, when, 700 miles south, the staff and parents of Blundell's School in Tiverton, East Devon, opened the latest issue of the school magazine *Enter Rumour* and found they had entered a different universe. By then, too, Ted had made sure that his version of events would help give *River* another dimension, too.

If the parents of Rupert Day had invited P. G. Wodehouse to join the family for his first visit to their favourite Hebridean links course, I can be fairly sure what kind of short story he'd have produced. But this is a poem by Ted Hughes, and though it does claim to be for Rupert's parents, 'for Simon and Hilary Day', my guess, having met them both, is that neither of them knows quite what to make of it even now. Simon has confirmed – though surprised when I asked him – what Ted's diary had noted in passing: yes, the Sligachan Hotel had a unique hold on his heart if not his memory. His parents had conceived him there on honeymoon.

The hotel turns out to be the one element of Ted's diary entry not to make it into 'Milesian Encounter on the Sligachan', though what Simon had told him clearly plays its part in what Ted wrote. Instead, this astonishing poem is about an experience only Ted had, and only Ted could have told it in the way he does, staring back and through that diary as he had done into the river's luminous water. Whenever he returned to it, the diary became an enlarging lens. The poem devotes all its energy to catching and then strangely releasing everything that happened from the moment Ted followed that advice about the pools and headed two miles upstream.

If you ever want to see what can happen to a fish touched, lost and brought again, or have ever wondered what bog tussocks look like in verse, or how a great poem can come at you out of a whorl of truth, find 'Milesian Encounter on the Sligachan' in *River*. And then take a deep breath. Ted knew that title was a mouthful, and in his short script for the readings he gave on *River*'s publication two years later he tried to keep things straightforward. 'The Sligachan is a river in the Isle of Skye, and the poem simply describes a brief visit to it, and the encounter with one of its inhabitants.'

And he's right, up to a point. His poem mines that evening's diary, that first impression of Glen Sligachan. But he makes you shake its hand, too, the valley as well as the river. Or get shaken by it. The journey upriver is nowhere near that insouciant stroll of that Irishman on the Barrow. The chunks of text Ted makes his readers leap between don't just look like the bog-cotton squelch that lay between the hotel and that 'accessible' fishing. They make you feel it. Its real depths. Its edges: 'the razor-edged, blood-smeared grass'. Was the blood Ted's or another victim's, or a trick of the light? Whoever's it was, it's not just a trick of the pen. An undeniable note of menace has entered: those two streams he crossed have each become a 'clatterbrook' as acid-pale as the slant light.

Other forms loom, sudden, beside this 'bogland river'. Here's the first of the valley's inhabitants: a snipe rips up off the valley floor. The shadow of more: eagles in the hills it lay between. At least, the diary had called them hills. Here, in the poem, they're

body parts: shoulderblades turned into stone, or individual
vertebrae in some great spine; or 'horn-skulls'. And the sum of
the parts: the Cuillins. For many visitors to Skye, the ultimate
climbing challenge, but Ted's happy to leave them to the birds. He
also does his best to bring the Cuillins down to size, or perhaps he's
just looking at them from over a bite to eat. In the blue brightness
of that August noon they shimmer like 'wrinkled baking foil' in
the heat haze. (I remember something John Martin told me that
first day with him on the Mole: Ted's idea of the perfect picnic
was a slab of baked salmon in foil: why bother with bread?)

And then he's back to it, urgent again, late, hot, bothered. Still
'a good half-hour more' of flailing like some daddy-long-legs –
elated, yes, but so ungainly – across an altogether wobblier mass,
'a quaking cadaver' beneath his own body. And now – revenge –
he's swallowed, right in its maw: 'up to my hip in a suck-hole'.
The gear he's hauling with him doesn't help. He's 'melting
suddenly': bogged down.

Not bad for a prelude. But now 'the shock' of the encounter is
on us. Under him.

I wish I'd heard Ted read this in person, been in the audience.
'*Simply*' a description? I'd love to have had him plunge me, in real
time, into the 'shock' of what follows. Depth, flow, body, current,
and a silent piling otherworldly force a million miles and years
from the fairytale castle that awaited him at the end of that day.
Water, yes, but how much more than that? And where on earth
did it come from?

Keith Sagar, Ted's critic, bibliographer, non-fishing fishkeeper
(and that innocent supplier of pickled pike bait), spent four
months pondering that question, from the moment Ted sent him
Enter Rumour in July 1983. He knew it mattered, knew how much
water had always meant in Ted's poems, how much more than fish
water had always held. In November Keith attempted to bring
scholarly order to the lines where Ted set to exploring the first of
those pools, that run, felt 'a superabundance of spirit'. Prompted
perhaps with what that ram's skull had become, 'magnified – a
Medusa', Keith followed his scholarly nose, looked for sources.
Dug about in books, found Burnet's *Early Greek Philosophy*

(1892). Grasped and lifted, triumphant – I know that moment of excitement – a sentence from it about the Milesian school's own belief in water as origin of earth and body that seemed to explain this bracing whole-body embrace of bogland river. But wrapped it in a qualified suggestion. Presumed that was the explanation. Offered it up, respectfully.

Wrong, said Ted. Centuries out, and two whole compass points.

Keith clearly hadn't then heard him read the poem in public, as he would when *River* was published. Ted's script begins, 'The Milesians were the fabulous race of early Celts, responsible for the more incredible kind of early Irish saga'. At least then Keith would have looked, as Ted told put it, 'not Greekwards but Irishwards'. He'd also have heard the third and last of Ted's brief hints. This one you need if you're a folktale novice, if you are to have any chance of seeing what happens to the river when it seizes Ted's heart-nerve and crashes. Suddenly it's not just a salmon lie. It's something even more incredible. It's the site of a brief wrenching encounter with one each of those other inhabitants of the valley, 'Gruagachs and Glaistigs and Boggarts … who speak Gaelic'. And if Keith had heard all this, he'd also have noted whether or not Ted gave that last word a short 'ă' or a long 'ay': Scots Gallic or Irish Gaelic.

But even that hint might not have been enough. Keith would have needed to know more of Ted's sources than he was ever likely to share with an audience. Too much prose eclipses the poem. And where would he have begun? Two legendary royal brothers had wandered as far as Egypt then come back to Spain, sailed north. These Spanish soldiers (Miles Espanie …) became Irish kings, fought off all comers, northern gods and dark invaders, call them Fomorians or Vikings. And the convergence of the twain, Hughes-wise: Ted was a boy when he had encountered these stories, a teenager in Mexborough, and began to record them. There's a Gruagach right at the start of the notebook where he kept them. It's before his writing settled into the shapes and loops I've come to regard as Ted's hand, and just before he turned, in that notebook, to 'Irish'.

And, of course, Keith could never have known how recently all that word-hoard had been renewed, topped up, over that boozy lunch at, and then under, Borris House. Andrew's family now comes clean about their lineage. Here's their website, or at least as it read in 2017. The McMurrough Kavanaghs of Borris House are the lost royal family of Ireland; the Kavanaghs can trace their pedigree:

> to the dawn of Irish history. Tradition, indeed, carries it far beyond that limit – to the legendary Feniusa of Scythia, coeval with the Tower of Babel, whose descendants, having wandered into Egypt, found their way back again to Scythia, and thence to Spain, from which country Heber and Heremon, the 2 sons of Gallamhy or Milesius, crossed over to Ireland, reduced it to subjection and divided it between them. From them sprang lines of Kings ruling over the 5 monarchies into which the island was split up.

Things get even fishier. Cousins of the Sligachan salmon run the mountain stream to spawn on the flanks of Mount Leinster; may join their Skye clan somewhere out in the Eastern Atlantic.

What Ted knew went beyond the Borris House website. Descendants of tall and bold and fleet heroes of the sagas came from Ireland to these western isles, brought stories of their wisdom and valour with them, left them imprinted on the hills. Like the Cuillin, themselves in all their skeletal immensity an echo of Cuchulain, the hound of Ulster: was it his vertebrae Ted saw when he looked up from his foil-wrapped salmon that August day?

Ted knew, in short, as the most learned and lucky of fishermen, the possessor of myriad keys to the lore of men and fish, how much these tribes of heroes shared with the Atlantic salmon of this bogland river. He felt it, too. How infinitely, achingly desirable those Sligachan salmon must have been to a fisherman as open to dreams as Ted was, who'd woken in his sleep sixteen years ago to the leap of writhing salmon surging up wild mountain streams to spawn. This went beyond a flight of poetic fancy, a tall story. It went deeper, too, to the fishy heart of him.

Ten years later, some of this emerged. Ted wrote of his wonder at the heroism common to 'different tribes' of salmon, each responding opportunistically to each fall of rain in the summer months to surge upriver. He was thinking, then, of West Country fish, responding to a Devon deluge after months of drought; recalling an eighteenth-century diarist's account of having his horse terrified by huge numbers of salmon desperate to spawn pushing desperately up the Tamar at a ford he was about to cross. Ted himself had seen a shoal of baby salmon, each two inches long, four months out of the egg, leaping at some trickle in the wall of a weir, battering themselves in infant heroism against the stones.

That drive is what had made salmon 'such sensitive glands in the dishevelled body of nature'; behaviour that it was possible to think of as moody, mysterious, unpredictable was actually 'attuned, with the urgency of survival, to every slightest hint of the weather', 'every moment-by-moment microchange as the moving air and shifting light manipulate the electronics of water molecules'.

That day on and almost in the Sligachan, Ted responded to it as salmon and their hunters did. 'One of the rewards of having been at some point in your life an obsessive salmon fisher', he'd write, is that 'salmon remain installed in some depth of your awareness, like a great network of private meteorological stations, one in every pool you know, in every river you ever fished, in that primitive otherworld, inside this one, where memory carries on "as if real". You can receive a report from any of these stations unexpectedly, at any moment.'

The scholar in me wants but doesn't need to know when Ted wrote his poem. But I'm pretty sure that whenever it was, he had just received a report from that ear-shaped pool on the Sligachan. He saw in that peat-filtered water what, on the Torridge, by Concrete Pool, silt suspended from quarries upstream meant he'd only been able to imagine: those eyes of the salmon, 'so like mine', straining to zero; and with their whole bodies bent into their own union just as ecstatically as those honeymooners, down in a rather warmer bed two miles downstream.

Ted took all that, slipped it into the poem he wrote for his friend Simon and his son Rupert. Smuggled more than is quite proper into the Blundell's School magazine. He shared with its readers the excitement of apprehension, the delights of fishing as foreplay. He roused that 'pondering amber' with that fluttering extension of the self, 'Tiny Toby', that lure, to tickle, stroke, lick, a pool whose ear he really had. And then he roused its inhabitants from where he could see they should be lying, and shared the moment when the station in his awareness brought him that report, and the river thrust itself at him in that 'travelling bulge' of water, and the river, and fisherman, both came to a weird, heightened consummation in an encounter too extraordinary quite to be believed.

All hell broke loose then, or at least that otherworld, and the fairies of that valley, and Irish valleys before them, rose and fell, from cracks in the rock, but also 'out of the skull', and became again, or for the first time, what even that brief rather sketchy diary had failed to catch. Not him, or it, but the real thing:

Only a little salmon.
Salmo salar
The loveliest, left-behind, most-longed-for ogress
Of the Palaeolithic

As well as changing sex, she'd lost weight in her passage from diary to poem: four pounds now, not five. The only time in the history of fishing literature that has happened? Well, Nick and Barrie knew he had a history of optimism.

There's no doubting her, though. Ted knows she is watching him, then and still, in her 'time-warped eye-glass' in Skye's ruined castle 'As I faded from the light of reality'.

*

My own journey into Skye and then beyond really started, as Ted's had, in Devon, months before a long drive north. And like Ted's it began with Simon Day, though my eventual destination owed more to the fellows and chaps he first encountered on quaysides and sundecks the far side of the Sligachan.

Over coffee one August morning in his beautiful house near Ivybridge, above a weir pool on the Erme where summer sea-trout shoal, Simon – now Sir Simon, for his services to Devon – confirmed what I'd gathered from Ted's diaries. He had a business proposition to which, when stated in a letter, Ted had entirely failed to rise. So he changed his angle of attack, cast the same fly in different conditions, at a dinner Anne and Conrad Voss Bark were glad to host for the purpose in May 1980. I've seen the seating plan. Simon – Tory councillor, gentleman farmer, networker supreme, and in due course a key figure behind the construction of Roadford Lake, the reservoir that unburdened Dartmoor of its responsibilities of supplying drinking water to the south-west – was heading a syndicate bidding for the region's TV broadcasting rights. Simon wanted a cultural heavyweight on board, and aimed high: Ted.

His lure?

An open invitation to fish some prime salmon and sea-trout water, rights to which he'd acquired in the late sixties: three miles of the Dart between the bridges at Dartmeet and Holne where its gorge was at its deepest, and the half-mile of the West Dart above its confluence there with the East Dart. Whether it was hunger or just that old curiosity, instinct, it was irresistible. 'Is this how it begins', Ted wondered about that dinner.

When we met that morning near Ivybridge, Simon extended just the same invitation to me. I had no idea then what awaited me, or what extraordinary use Ted had made of it, with rod or either kind of line. But in 1985 Ted described the river below Dartmeet, in a poem I think he wrote for Prince Charles but copied out for another fishing friend, as 'the prettiest and wildest fishing in the West', and he told the fine fishing journalist and Conrad Voss Bark's successor as angling correspondent on *The Times*, Brian Clarke, that one Dart salmon was worth fifty in Alaska. Soon Ted caught two in a single morning: lugging them up out of the gorge he melted all over again.

*

I met Simon a fortnight before my day beside, and in, the Mole with John Martin. Ted wrote of 'the wonderful river Mole, which … according to the salmon and sea-trout brings in the best water' in the south-west, off Exmoor. He'd met those fish, taken their word for it, at Watertown, with John and his brother Michael, the Westcountry Rivers Trust's first president; though John has now died and Michael's fishing days are over, the beat is still in the family. Carol Hughes had suggested I write to them both; in his reply, John had suggested that we might talk as we fished.

I confess I had only half an ear to all he was telling me: not just about Ted's idea of a picnic, but about the guests Ted brought to Watertown. I do remember him mentioning Diana Rigg, who needed a casting lesson; and you know, John said, to learn effectively, nothing beats the instructor's hand guiding the learner's rod. Only when I'd landed my salmon, killed it, admired its astonishing silver-lavender scales, did I really begin listening to John, as I watched him fish down the pool above, and heard him tell that, really, he'd spent much more time in Ted's company up in Scotland, first on the Tweed, and then, above all, again and again, at the Grimster. I must visit one day, he said. There's nowhere like it. I'd love to, I replied, my heart and eyes still on my salmon.

That night, Rose Ward of Parsonage Farm, just above the Torridge at Iddesleigh, froze my fish, guts and all – better that way if I wanted it smoked, John had said. And the next morning I took my prize proudly south, to within a mile of Powderham Castle, across the Exe from Exeter, and met John's old friend and Ted's Bill Tucker, a small, self-contained fellow, gently spoken.

Bill was happy to take the salmon and arrange for smoking – Jacksons of Newton Abbot would trust his account of its provenance as they would never trust mine, a stranger's. Never has fish tasted more delicious than those ten packets of sliced salmon we ate that winter, though I did pause for a moment at the colour of it. The dark pink of wild salmon is carotin-rich, from the krill on their feeding grounds off Greenland or the Faroe Islands. Don't be fooled by the cheery brightness of the farmed stuff: it would be grey if it weren't for the dye the multinationals who own the farms choose from a chemical engineer's palette to add to the pellets.

But what Bill really wanted to do was talk of Ted. Of how he'd met him, on the quayside at Uig one August afternoon, some years before they'd first fished together at the Grimster. Bill thought that was probably with John. Which was, from memory, Bill thought, sometime in the early eighties. Thereafter they'd shared the drive up from Devon together for years in Bill's toffee-coloured Rolls-Royce, more often than not in long companionable silences. In 1992, from Bristol to Carlisle, Ted gave Bill a lecture on his latest book, *Shakespeare and the Goddess of Complete Being*. Four hours of it: 'Of course, I didn't take notes. But it was utterly brilliant.' Then silence again.

Imagining it filled my own long drive home that night.

*

And then in December, out of the dark, John Martin wrote me a letter with an offer I could not refuse. Would I join him for a few days as his guest at Grimersta on Lewis next July?

I left Cambridge at first light. It was the day after the 2013 Wimbledon final: 'Welcome to Murraydonia', a sign read as I crossed the border after lunch into what had been Scotland. By four I was in rich Kelso; I had an appointment at the Factor's Office at Lower Floors Castle, just upstream on the Tweed. There I received directions down an estate track to the river, which glittered in the sun. I wanted to see, if I could, where Ted had first fished with John; he and Bill had stayed there in May 1985, part of a grand Devon party. It was all stately magnificence, and I knew that from a poem he wrote as Laureate on the Duke and Duchess of York's marriage in July 1986, the salmon of the Tweed cavorting – presumably in pleasure – over the Garden Wall of Lower Floors, where, Ted must have known, Andrew and Sarah Ferguson first met at a ball. The descendants of those fish were keeping their snouts down today: do salmonids inherit embarrassment, or was it just the heat of that afternoon? Under the shade of a bankside oak I did come across a family of dancing stoats, watched them for four minutes, got within six feet of them at play, before they slipped into the long grass. But the pool or, in this low water, the river I was looking for both eluded me. And that made me doubt my chances of finding what I wanted further north.

I didn't, that night, or the next, sleep rough in the car. Generous friends spared me that, and one of them, David Profumo, who fished with Ted, even guided me to a trout, after the first leg of my long journey north, then west, then north again. So I was at Mallaig bright and early, and caught the day's first ferry to Skye in brilliant sunshine, watched clouds chafing dark peaks as Armadale loomed. At the Sligachan Hotel, no matter that reception was unstaffed: I already knew that it no longer controlled the fishing – day tickets lay in Portree, twelve miles further north, and back, and I had no time for that. But a page of the fishing book was open on a great month, August 1922. I read of the river's famed clarity, even in spate – a property it shares, along with peat moors doing the filtering, with the Dart – and of a guest who had claimed to catch his wife from the river. Then I grabbed boots, and camera, and *River*, from the car, and headed upstream.

*

I thought I'd learned my lesson from Ted. Went up the west bank, avoiding those two side streams. And followed the path walkers had worn into the heather. But that fizzled out within a few hundred yards. Soon I was daddy-long-legsing myself, slithering and leaping and marvelling and cursing by turns at the bog cotton and the bog, and then melting as the vastness of this valley swallowed me.

The sun burned through the wispy clouds that had masked the peaks on either side. I kept checking my watch. At 11.30, came to a drain I stood not a chance of leaping. Damn. I seemed to have drifted twenty or thirty yards from the river. And, of course, I had come without a map. I could at least gain height and a sense of where I might be by climbing away.

Two minutes later, I was on the real track. Gasping. And then almost run down: a mountain biker with a point to prove charged past. I looked round. Mountain biker's gentler partner was approaching. 'Sorry!' she said. 'Hi,' I said, weakly. And then: 'Can I borrow your map?' I asked. It was on her handlebars. Triangulating meander against peak beyond, I found the drain I'd just followed, traced it back to the river – and saw a giant ear.

I spent as long as I dared beside the water. Reading the poem. Imagining where, on that far bank, Ted stood to cast.

I can report that the gravel of the meandering Sligachan is still a luminous pink. Weeds still twitch their tails under the flow of that water. Which still runs astonishingly clear. I teetered on the sprung moss of the high bank. I peered. Then found a place to wade. I felt cleansed, undercut.

But for all I tried I couldn't, that day, be sure of Ted's last pool, and what he saw in it, and why. Couldn't swear to have seen that:

> broad, coiling whorl, a deep ear
> Of pondering amber,
> Greenish

which had always fascinated me in his poem. Or, for all the Irish improbability of Ted's encounter there, to know why it was 'greenish' at all, that ten-foot depth of 'whisky'. From where I stood, I didn't see a ram's skull, that Medusa. Perhaps a spate had dislodged it. No lamp shone from out of that water. Perhaps it was too low. Or perhaps it held mysteries I was still too green, myself, to identify. Three more years would pass before I came close to solving them.

I had to go. I had a boat to catch.

On the quay at Uig I met Bill Tucker. He had decided to join me and John for what he knew would be his own last visit to Grimersta. He wouldn't be fishing, he told me. It was to be a purer pilgrimage, back into memories our conversation last August had revived.

Our caravan had only two cars. Bill led me north from Tarbert past the turnoff to Amhuinnsuidhe. So I've never seen that fairytale castle, those views, or the lochs in the North Harris hills – Voshmid, Scourst – where Ted thrilled at salmon coming to his muddler lure from out of the face of a wave. He returned there at least twice, in 1983 and then in 1991, when Graham Swift came, too. Ted still broke all the rules, still took salmon on spinning gear from the sea pool, where Graham found him first thing, grateful for the rare chance to be with him. Otherwise the

rhythm of the day, the week, the enforced conviviality, ghillies
and packed lunches and boozy dinners with those rich enough
to take all this splendour in their stride, Graham found hard to
take. Ted loved the fishing at least, and was completely absorbed
in its routines – one letter to Leonard Baskin he began on castle
notepaper he finished, apologetically, a month later at home,
pleading piscatorial commitments.

By the time we turned off the Lewis moorland road down the
unmade track to the Victorian lodge by the sea at Loch Roag
which Ted called 'the last outpost of the Raj' (Bill had told me
this on the viewing deck of the ferry across the Minch, along
with many other tales of the ghosts and glories of the place)
I was ready, or even braced, for whatever lay at that track's end.
I'd read a book John had also sent me on the history and culture
of the estate, the lodge built by Lord Leverhulme and now
managed by the syndicate of twenty-five members who own its
17,000 acres, its four lochs and the river that links them. I knew
that most of the fishing happens in boats, two anglers in the
stern, taking their turn to cast while a ghillie controls a drift.
I had my own laminated map of the beats, between which rods
rotate each day, with the end of one day coming with pre-dinner
drinks, the next beginning with the two hours after dinner: last
cast, 11.30 sharp.

I'd also read Ted's Grimersta diaries. At least half a dozen
of them, from 1986 to his last summer, 1998. He came to love
Grimersta. For all he doubted it, on his first visit, as 'the pampered
playground of the elite', he came to know, and understand, its shape
and economy. He came to know that the privileged can sometimes
make use of their fortune: on his first visit, the renowned surgeon
Stanley Rivlin, who had done Margaret Thatcher's varicose veins,
spotted that the young manager of one of the first salmon smolt
farms had a goitre on his neck that had evidently not been treated
well. Rivlin went back to the lodge, rang some friends in London,
paid for the young man's treatment there.

The lodge itself was, and is, more intimate than imposing.
Ted always found time to withdraw into his room and himself,
to write and read. He signed books for the fisheries manager;

wrote a poem for the housekeeper Debbie's birthday. It was easier to feel comfortable. No fairytale castle here; just a Victorian lodge, much extended since, along the shore of an inlet of Loch Roag.

Far more important were the river, the water, the fish. That was the reality that kept bringing him back. A clear vision of abundance that, down in the West Country, netsmen and pollution had reduced to a memory. Grimersta's Sea Pool caught his eye first, as Amhuinnsuidhe's had. Thinking it 'too shallow, too curtained with weed?' Ted soon saw it was 'supercharged' with fish waiting for high tide to swim upriver; the estuary below, just opposite the lodge, was all 'crash + flash' with shoals 'electrified' by the scent of fresh water. He watched as a netsman's boat came in, unloaded its harvest: 273 fish, in shocking glory on two tables. 'We were amazed, + disturbed. The layered loafed fish, and the netsmen, alarmed with what they had done, hushed, culprits.'

But Ted never forgot his own complicity in this, as an angler. His own desire undimmed, he imagined the fish out in the bay, holding their exact position as they waited for the tide, 'moving towards the precise moment in which we will meet'. And 'pressing towards – being killed, one by one by us. Strange thought. The details of the meeting still to be arranged.' He crawled out onto the old road bridge, peered down into the tumult of Bridge Pool, and caught the urgency of it, his diary turning to verse:

Festooned under the boil, big shapes,
Greyish-green, a dozen here …
Half a dozen there, concentrated intent,
Waving and plying their limber lengths
Big fish, in the endless work + hurry of the river.

And then he recorded the meeting itself. After a day and a half of shimmering and fishless heat and calm up the lochs, Ted decided to resolve the dilemma facing any member of a fishing party: 'Partnership or solitude.' Beat One at Grimersta begins at the mouth of the loch nearest the sea and takes in the mile or so of tumbling river down that shallow valley. Ted explored it alone: dibbling, or letting a fly skate and dance as he drew it across the surface of the river, in the hope of drawing salmon up from the depths. I have a whole tub of Ted's muddlers, with buoyant heads tied from hollow deer's hair, and bodies with a gold tinsel rib to catch the light as well as fisherman's and fish's attention. He used one now. And a fish did come to him, within feet of where he stood. 'That surprising explosion at my feet, then a fish all over the river – in memory, more fish than river.' But its reality left no room for those other realities, on the borders of this and that and the other, that he had spun from that other brief encounter on the Sligachan. 'That effort – that cornered + desperately contriving savage attempt to escape, that focus of craving for life – might stop me fishing some day. Bad day it will be.'

That bad day never came. In an album at the lodge at Grimersta is a picture of Ted and Bill Tucker waiting to board a boat, each dragging silver carcasses of salmon. I envied them queasily. His last Grimersta diary dates from July 1998, three months before he died. The summer before, on the Thurso, Bill Tucker had first noticed the effects of his cancer – Ted had murmured that this might be his last visit to the river on the north coast of the mainland, and Bill guessed why.

That same trip, they'd stayed at the Grimersta, and Stanley Rivlin, noticing what Bill had seen, asked some direct questions, made sure that Ted, too, found the best treatment in London. When Stanley, a keen shot, dropped dead himself at New Year, while out shooting, Ted wrote a poem as a memorial; then was the last to join the congregation, slipping quietly into the back of the church, and the first to leave. Stanley's daughter Anne told me this.

Now in his last summer, Ted noted Bill's kindness in giving him space while offering a discreetly helping hand. Sharing Beat One, Bill told Ted not to worry about a net: he would run down from the Bridge Pool if a fish took.

Near the end of writing this book, I learned something else about the depth and quiet power of Ted's friendship with Bill Tucker and John Martin, something neither of them mentioned in the boats we shared or at the curious but to me familiar fellowship of Grimersta lodge's table. At a lunch in 1991, down in Devon, Ted spoke of the need to ensure that primary school children, even those in rural schools, had at least a chance to learn about the natural world. He deplored the fact that, when he'd read his poems at a whole school assembly, not one of the pupils could tell the difference between a swift and a swallow. The Kingfisher Award Scheme still runs across the south-west, from Wiltshire to Cornwall. Bill and Carol continue to support it; John did until his death in April 2020.

*

My first morning at Grimersta was an early one. At 5.00 a.m. I walked out into the dewy stillness and up, along what my laminated map confirmed were the Sea Pool and Kelt Pool, and watched the river at its work, the coils and plunges and eddies and broadenings-out and only wondered, hoped: are they here, these fish? Late that evening, I knew they were: a touch and a loss – only a little salmon! – to a cast from a croy at the mouth of Loch One. That made short work of my night's sleep, woke me to a grey stillness – 3.30 a.m. No rules prohibit fishing before breakfast. So I slipped out through the lodge, back up the road, and was soon casting across and out and down and into an extraordinary sky. Stillness. Enormity. Peace. And then, not quite. At about four, another vehicle on the road – too early, surely, even for a farmer? It turned up the track, bumped its way along, became a Jeep, which pulled up beside my car. A figure went swiftly to the boats moored fifty yards away on Loch Two, before roaring into the hills: a river watcher, of course.

I got back to work. Feeling my fly, imagining it, eyes alert for anything. I made my way down that loop of concrete, gave the fish that had come to me last night every chance. Nothing. At 4.20 a.m., the sky gaining light and colour, mauves and pinks adding themselves to grey-blues by the minute, I was reaching the limit of my cast, even with the long, stiff, fast-actioned Boron rod I was using: Ted's, entrusted to me by his sister Olwyn, on condition I use it. It punched a line. And finally, something grabbed the tip of my heart-nerve, crashed, crashed again, surged, and did not let go. Her scales came off on my hands, like silver gilt, as I laid her beside the rod.

*

It was my last evening, Saturday. Another rod, here for a full week, generously let me have one last chance at the river. High tide was due: if I slipped away before coffee, I might just see fish coming into the Sea Pool off the estuary. In the event, I think I missed it. The throng and slide and rush of the water going over the lip as the light seeped away into grey held me, of course, in its grip, and I cast and cast from the tussocks of grass across and down, covering the water; once I thought I saw a bulge and a slither of a fish easing over that lip, surging into the pool. But in truth I couldn't be sure. And I made no contact. But I do know that, as time passed, and I headed to the Bridge Pool for a last run down it, time was running out – 11.28, 11.29 p.m.

Last cast, last throw. The line went out, and I followed the water for a gleam or a silver shadow towards the lure. Instead, a darkness, not below or through the water but definitely breaking the surface. A head. An otter, inches beyond my fly.

12

'The Flight into Light'

Through several nights and days, the river has been a brown volcano: silt-stained, turbid water has surged up and over the high banks, tearing oak roots and even whole trees from their moorings in the earth; an oozing chocolate lava has smeared the flood plain. The roar of water sounds like fire in some hellish forge; battered branches creak like the hinges of diabolical bellows.

But then the rain stops; the flow loses its wild force, retreats. Some deranged sculptor must be responsible for all this chaos, all these rooms reshaped in the house of the river; he lies down, exhausted by his labours.

And now comes the revelation, the one remarkable true note of pure healing. Listen carefully. 'Now comes the still small voice.' A mould – whether sculptor's or blacksmith's – glows, still hot; what sits within it is essential, pure.

I'm deep in *River*. 'The Mayfly is Frail', a poem Ted didn't add until 1993. And he doesn't need to identify the voice, because he trusts his readers to recognise whose it is. What he has just given is a watery translation, to one of his beloved West Country spate rivers, rough and ready, rain-fed, of the Book of Kings. There it's earthquakes and tempests, here a spate river at its wildest. In both, this is God's calm whisper.

What emerges is no golden angel. Instead, Ted's eyes are fixed on a tiny animal moment that breaks the mould. Literally. A case that has somehow survived the destruction of its world, of the mud and riverbed where it's lain hidden, or clung to a pebble for comfort, over two years, and then this apocalypse, and has somehow risen from the carnage, as if delivered from a wound.

> And the mould splits at a touch of the air.
> A shimmering beast
> Dawns from the river's opened side.

And that's it. It is fleeting and mysterious as the Northern Lights, which shiver at the start of the poem; a trick of the light, or a pattern of electrons under strange charge. But all we get is this glimpse of momentous bestial birth; nothing of the brief life of mounting drama and collapse that it unleashed. To learn more about the mayfly, as well as to discover the real story of the most consuming passion for an insect that Ted, or for that matter any English poet, had ever known, I had to travel into the west, again and again, and back in time. That's what led me to the Murphys that evening at Isham, and unlocked more wild and implausible stories, then and in the years to come. But now I've seen what Ted saw, I've fallen for the mayfly, too.

*

It turns out that the story of Ted's passion itself started in aftermath. It had a false start. It ended in a peculiar piscatorial frustration. But in between it touched the heavens.

On 19 May 1982 Ted was at home, writing late into the small hours, finishing his essay 'Taw and Torridge' for *West Country Fly Fishing*. The next morning he got up early, posted his typescript to his friend and the volume's editor Anne Voss Bark at the Arundell Arms, then foggily assembled his fishing tackle for another trip to Ireland, managing, in the process, to forget his favourite rod; the one he did pack, a ten-foot-long Bruce and Walker, had evidently had its handle broken in the car door, so he brought it to mend. He had only just finished 'The Great Irish Pike' but this time trout would be his quarry. He would be joining Barrie and some friends during the most exciting fortnight of the Irish trout fisherman's year, when great numbers of *Ephemera danica*, the largest and oldest member of the order

Ephemeroptera, emerge from the great limestone loughs of the west to provide fish with a ready meal and fishermen with sport. They'd be meeting where they had set up camp in a farmer's field beside Lough Key, on the borders of Co. Roscommon and Co. Sligo. Ted knew the place: during that wild autumn half-term of pike fishing, this was the lough where in fifteen minutes he and Barrie had been drenched, double-rainbowed, transfixed, 'Keystruck'.

But his route there was even more involved than the usual drive up the M5 to Holyhead or Liverpool: this time he would zigzag north-east across England before he headed west. And it began badly.

Preoccupation marred the first long leg of the journey out of Devon. He and Carol were visiting Nick in Oxford, who was then in the second year of his undergraduate course in zoology at Queen's College, and meeting their friends Leonard and Lisa Baskin for dinner. But Ted was in no mood for company. Getting 'Taw and Torridge' right had been an agonising, exposing business: he'd already worked too hard at it, put too much of himself into it, then taken a great deal of himself out. He fretted at a copy of what he'd just sent off all the way up to Oxford, wrestling with yet more cuts and corrections as Carol drove. In researching his essay Ted had encountered horrifying detail, some of which he'd already shared with Tom Rawling, about the pollution blighting his two home rivers – 'they used to be the best, and now they're the worst, and still sinking', he told his editor at Faber, Craig Raine – and there was, he knew, a strong argument, now he'd uncovered 'the neglect, the statistics, the outrages', to 'spill the beans' on the causes and institutions responsible for the damage. But this wasn't the place for it. Outraged green polemic would have struck too gloomy and too stridently self-righteous a note in a book designed to lure fishermen, and hotel guests, to Devon's rivers. Besides, instinct and experience told him that it was bad for his prose, obstructing the sparer, clearer flow he craved in the river of his writing self: 'it is clear how the unsuspecting rioting of this weed has caused me in the past much trouble.'

That afternoon Nick took him and Carol punting on the upper Cherwell, above Magdalen Bridge: 'a green river among green willows. Pea-soupy.' Another odd coincidence: I was a student at Magdalen in the mid-1980s; Sarah and I had spent our first summer evenings together walking beside the Cherwell. But I knew nothing, it seems. In all my punting up that same stretch, I never had eyes for the harvest Nick shook from the overhanging branches: 'a big crop of Mayflies, both green drake + spent.' That night, Ted did register, briefly, what Nick, student turned tutor for the hour, was telling him about these relatively unfamiliar names and the insect's life cycle, evidently to prepare his father for his Irish trip. The river couldn't be too polluted, from the number of spent and discarded shucks on the surface, even if he did catch a whiff of sewage.

After the punting, Ted was 'for some reason in a stupor of exhaustion'. 'Could hardly speak.' This wasn't the speechlessness that came from fishing in solitude, concentratedly, alone, contact with the self and the spirit deeper than language. It was, in fact, quite the opposite. This weariness was, he reflected, 'just the desire to be doing something else altogether ... Anything to be free of friends, for a while.'

*

These notes break off after a dismal lunch the next day, en route to Cambridge. I mean break off: someone has torn the page in half. They resume, after a missing page and a half, in a completely different folder in the British Library. I can only guess why. It took me days to piece them together.

Now it's five or six days later, and Ted's wish should have been granted. He's in Ireland, and the thick of something else entirely. In the company of Barrie and his fellow anglers, all of whom he's met before – Paul Cullen, in whose cottage above Lough Arrow he and Nick and Barrie had stayed in 1979; Roderick and Caroline, whom he'd last seen at that lunch at Borris House – he has been plunged into a consuming round of fishing and fish-focused talking. Most of the talk is of tactics, different methods, their comparative success; some is about fly patterns, the hardness of fish's mouths, the best hooks and the best materials for artificial flies. It's all evidence of extraordinary devotion to a very particular art. And trout have been 'raised', attracted to the surface by bunches of natural flies impaled on hooks and then 'dapped', from long rods held high in the wind, with thick floss line that swells like a miniature spinnaker in the breeze and makes the poor insects dip alluringly onto the surface. Locals are catching big trout by that means – three or four pounds. Caroline raises five or six fish a day, but has caught none. Roderick caught one smaller fish on a wet fly, a 'Green Peter'; another new pattern for Ted.

Ted himself has caught nothing. It's tantalising, and frustrating. The frustration continues wherever they fish: on the River Unshin, which flows out of Lough Arrow, and then at a place they discovered after reconnaissance, and promised more. This is Saint's Island, where with Paul he fished one evening 'a great spreading calm' on the other side of the promontory on which, in March 1978, Nick and Ted 'were almost wrecked'. It's on the east shore of Lough Ree, an hour and a half west of Dublin, not much less south of Arrow; if you stuck a pin in a map of Ireland you'd choose Ree to see the map hang straight. Locals they meet there rave about Saint's Island as the site of the very best mayfly fishing.

Yet here, too, they catch nothing. And it's not just the fussiness of the fish or the weather that is to blame. Sitting in a hot car on the quayside at Dun Laoghaire on 31 May, waiting for his ferry home, and choosing, as he often does in his diaries, what to 'Remember', it doesn't take him long to identify his oldest fishing friend as the real source of the trouble. It's an odd Barrie-shaped echo of what beset Ted that day in Oxford. Barrie's refusal to dap; his 'terrier snarl' to Roderick, who remains loyal despite all provocations; 'Barrie's nearly complete lack of ready adaptability to circumstances: his fixity, for instance, in what Paul calls his dry fly snobbery, which nearly ruined this trip.'

Nearly.

There were consolations. Ted makes himself remember, too, the cry of the godwits, 'like a stone bouncing on ice', perfectly choreographed to their spasm flight; a total ruin in a wood he discovered after a lunch with Roderick and Caroline. And that reminds him how remote ancient and even just old Ireland, both once so recent, is now becoming. A wave of modern building will turn Ireland into a version of Sweden.

But best of all there are the mayflies themselves, in both of the forms Nick had first shown him on the Cherwell. Now they have seized hold of him:

> Memory of the beautiful spents – or moulted greens – hanging under all the leaves, marvellous magical living fruit. Very fascinating that. The whole process of these insects – emerging green – writhing little dragons – sitting on the water, flying up, hanging in the leaves, dancing above + between the trees, flying out onto the water, coupled sometimes crashing like dud helicopters. Flying sometimes far out over the lake.

How could those lines not catch any reader's eye? Even if you didn't know, as I've come to, what 'writhing' always meant for Ted, from that dream of salmon high on the dream Taw to the python pike of Lough Gur guaranteeing a life-releasing surge of twisting energy, wouldn't you be piqued to know more about 'the whole process of these insects', from green emergence to 'living fruit' to their flight up and their dancing and their final flight out? Who wouldn't want to see what was hanging there in Ted's memory?

*

My own first glimpse of this world came the afternoon I left Barrie's house on the ridge above Lough Arrow on 19 May 2012, drove round to the jetty at Ballinafad at the eastern end of the lough and stared mournfully into the glass-clear waters. My smuggler fly rod was in my carry-on suitcase, which I'd packed in the fantasy that Barrie would take me fishing, and which sat in the footwell of the hire car ready for the flight home that evening. I did the odd furtive shadow cast. But then a van drew up, and its driver, Ollie, a retired prison officer, took me out in his boat, for four glorious hours of fish hunting. We didn't catch anything.

But an astonishingly beautiful creature – a Green Drake, Ollie confirmed – landed lightly on my palm. An inch-long Irish mantis but with full schooner sails for wings, here was a miniature dragon who posed, unruffled except by the breeze, for a picture.

But then, in a bay below an old, white, tree-shrouded house, trout swirled and sipped and one rose within feet of the imitation I cast. I saw a lazy, sure and massive snout, dorsal fin, tail. All the way back east, that trout kept coming at me out of the windscreen. I wanted, but never thought I'd get, more.

*

It seems Ted was haunted, too. So he returned to his diary. He didn't just rely on his memory, fascinating though it was. He set about recovering the 'whole process', turning rough notes into a narrative, 'Mayflies in Ireland 1982'. He knows it's a challenge: 'See if I can tell you the true story of my trip to Ireland, to catch fish on the imitation of the Mayfly, Green Drake and Spent.' Those capital letters boast of new confidence with those fishermen's names for the different stages of the fly's development. With Ireland behind him, he used his experiences there to revisit that hour's tutorial from Nick in the punt and establish its place as a necessary prelude for what was to follow.

The Cherwell is still 'pea-soupy'. But much more now shines clear; so much he 'did not appreciate' at the time. For one thing, Irish hindsight has sharpened his sense of what Nick had told and showed him; for another, he's fallen for the business of entomological identification, so crucial for any fly fisherman in matching his artificial fly to the natural insects he sees on and above the water. But Ted isn't any fly fisherman. And he's got all the equipment he needs to make this personal. Nick's description of the natural history of *Ephemera danica*, 'the ancient of ancients' in evolutionary terms, the archetype of the survivor, becomes a score to a dance. As Nick talked, 'the insects began to distinguish themselves, performing on the water and in the air', and the details of their bodies Ted observed, first through the magnifying glass on his Swiss Army knife, then through the much more powerful naturalist's headglass Nick gave him that day, help lift him out of that first torpor. I see it happening on the page: his own prose breaks into vivid poetry, enters the world and way of seeing I recognise from Ted's response to other shape-shifting, element-breaking creatures of the river. There is the newly hatched dun, or sub-imago, or Green Drake, 'quivering in a vibrant halo of rings' on the surface, but then lifting the sails that gave their name a 'piercing accuracy' and trying again to clear the water, 'survive + live some purposeful life'. Torn between admiring the engineering of their physical structure and a sense of their sheer beauty, he notices the semi-translucent green and amber of the armoured casing of the Drake's thorax and abdomen that would itself split apart, releasing another slender adult. That's the imago, its one purpose to rise again into the air, dance, find a partner, mate, and then – spent, sated, exhausted, doomed – deposit fertilised eggs on the surface of the water, allowing them to drop to the riverbed, where two years will pass before May's warmth and light triggers their rise to the surface. He catches the black lace of wings, and – just as sensual – the 'silken mascara darkness' as the spent tumble, eddying, back to the water in their dying fall. This is Shakespeare crossed with an even older, wilder ritual. It's the journey of the body and spirit in miniature, of beauty and suffering. Ted isn't just identifying the stages of development. He's identifying *with* them.

Reading all this, my own memories stirred. I began to see in the story Ted was drawing from his diary lines and ideas that had been staring me in the face for months. Literally.

In March 2012, during that glorious sunny week reading *River* above the Tamar, I realised I'd forgotten my copy of *West Country Fly Fishing*. So I returned to the Arundell Arms for the first time in eighteen years, and read 'Taw and Torridge' in the lounge. That was when Anne Voss Bark's stepson, Adam Fox-Edwards, who'd succeeded her as proprietor and inherited her office, handed me the framed manuscript of a Christmas gift from Ted to the Voss Barks in 1983; it had hung on the office wall ever since. 'The Mayfly'. The copy he made me that day, having put the original, frame and all, through his Xerox, is still on my noticeboard above my desk, now beginning to yellow. Every time I look up from my screen, Titania and Oberon step from their Midsummer Night's dream to dress themselves in 'a lace of blackish crystals'. And I see what awaits these 'Poetic atoms', sun worshippers whose faith in a 'fierce religion'

> crucifies them
> Through the sacrament of copulation
> Onto the face of water,
> Where Heaven shudders.

But I had still to see the whole process, in its proper place.

*

Late that first bibulous evening with the Murphys at Isham, after I'd read 'River Barrow', we were all beginning to relax. Caroline startled me with unexpected intimacy. Ted's. One morning over breakfast in 1982, in the caravan whose table doubled up as Barrie's fly-tying laboratory, Ted told her he had just dreamed of an enamelled maybush, with bejewelled and filigree mayflies hanging from it. I already knew Caroline was an artist – her first flame, another friend of Barrie's, has since told me she worked as a jeweller in central Dublin – but without knowing her as well as I now do, wondered whose artistic licence she was bringing to what she told me. I shouldn't have doubted her: Ted's story confirms it. He had come to know the spent as 'a creature of unique properties or characteristics – I had it photographed in an X-ray of excitement. As my sleeps began to prove, it had entered my dream world – microscopically seen, gigantic, delicate, intricately knotted.'

For his part, Roderick seemed, that first visit, to stick to the business in hand. Out in the boat the three of us shared, drifting Carra's luminous shell-bedded green waters in generally vain search for flies or trout, he switched in an instant from affable anecdote to hunter's roar. 'Fish!' Before I twitched, he had cast at it right across my own slow line. 'You're as bad as Ted,' he muttered: meaning, too slow. In one of Barrie's letters to Seamus Heaney, Barrie complains that Ted was both too impatient for the

'Lurking and Pouncing' involved in fishing the spent gnat, and too slow. A few days later, on the phone from Lough Ree, Paul Cullen would echo that, complaining that 'Ted's rod was too big and too stiff'. It really was: remember that diary of bleary packing after too late a night at his desk. Ted had brought the wrong rod, a heavy ten-footer rather than the lighter nine-foot rods needed to keep pace with cruising trout. Later I confirmed this, too: I found it in one of the rod-boxes in my Cambridge study, which Ted's sister Olwyn had entrusted to my care along with Barrie's battered stuffed trout. Inspecting it, I saw that its cork handle had been deftly fixed, perhaps during that holiday, with Araldite.

Ever the purist, Roderick also affected astonishment that a Cambridge scholar – my occupation as well as my nationality has, not unreasonably, taken a bit of knocking in fishing boats in recent years – had not read, and learned by heart, J. R. Harris's *An Angler's Entomology* (1952). It's a wonderful book, full of its own fine photographs of flies, and a bracingly crisp prose that urges fishermen to make the most of their unique opportunity to study mayflies close to, whether as Green Drakes or – the rarely seen plural of imago – as '*imagines*'. Try pronouncing that word. See how classification begins to split, Latin noun releasing English verb: poetic atoms. Once more, it's not just the book that counts. It's whom its author knew, and served. Harris ran a Dublin tackle shop, too, when he wasn't lecturing in entomology at Trinity, and not just any Dublin tackle shop. The very best. Garnett and Keegan's, on Parliament Street. It had been Harris who, two years after publishing his book, had directed a young Barrie out to the Fergus in search of the best trout fishing in Ireland. In March 1981 Ted had bought a reel off him, and owned a copy of *An Angler's Entomology*. Shamed by Roderick, and admitted to its secrets, so do I.

But Roderick also let me borrow another even more precious book, which showed me what, in 'The Mayfly', had obviously not come from that tutorial on an English river. This volume of the Murphy family fishing diaries contains entries from the mid-1980s. One, in their son Justin's hand, from 1987, shows that Ted was not the only one to identify with mayflies.

I hatched from my pupal bag when breakfast was called. After dressing (2nd stage of development), I left my shuck (ie boxer shorts) behind as proof of my existence and entered the feeding stage which took place in the glorified tent. Two spents and one green were also feeding although the spents looked as if they didn't really need it.

At once I saw where my favourite line in 'The Mayfly' had come from: emerging means 'haul[ing] its green dragonish torso / Out of its sleeping bag'.

Or: almost. But where exactly?

*

I was to find out the following May. Perhaps out of pity for my failure that first trip, perhaps in the hope that fishlessness wasn't a character flaw, the Murphys invited me to join them again. But on Lough Arrow this time, where they were renting a house as close as they could to the site they had identified, back in the mid-1980s, a year or two after Ted's trip, as the perfect spot for their caravan during the Mayfly fortnight. It was on the Annaghloy peninsula, halfway along the north-east shore, and I worked out I could spare a flying visit, via Knock Ireland West, the pilgrim's airport, seeking a fishy miracle, or at least a long weekend away from university exams.

By then I'd taken Ted's story properly to heart. It filled in the gaps left in those first rough notes, and told of his own arrival at Brick Bay, just below a new caravan park where I would be staying, for the start of that trip in May 1982. He described his own ritual change of clothes into angling gear, and then driving to meet Barrie and the Murphys and Paul Cullen at Monaghan's field, five miles away at Lough Key. He described a huge cloud of mayflies dancing about the Murphys' caravan, and the sense of promise that represented for all of them. One evening Roderick drove me there, returning for the first time, he told me, since 1982. He waited, eyes suddenly bright, moist, up at the gate while I walked down to where they'd parked the caravan, pitched their tents, leisurely tackled up.

Ted also described the 'long vigil' that unfolded in the next days, when the flies declined to reappear: first on Key, then, over three days, on Arrow. They'd launched their boat from the jetty at Ballinafad, where I'd had my first afternoon on the lough two years before. We, too, did our time on the watch that weekend: hour after hour of drifting, searching, peering hard and generally in vain, through binoculars or my zoom lens, for flies dancing above the trees. Just as they had in 1982, we had minutes of boiling excitement, as big trout surged through rolling waves to take Green Drakes. When he wasn't casting, Ted watched, through his headglass, as newly hatched flies slid mysteriously back under the surface, while his companions denied it could be so. When I wasn't casting, I read my transcriptions of Ted's diaries. 'Barrie's to-fro agitation of disappointment + bafflement were a trial', which, back then, Roderick only echoed and amplified. 'The skin began to peel off my palms.' Now Roderick was my guide. I listened to him and Caroline argue, asking me to adjudicate. That bay or this headland?

Eventually they had all had enough, struck camp and relocated to Lough Ree, where Ted joined Paul, and loved the change in company. There Ted 'moved closer', to what he felt was the best fishing and the best local knowledge. He explored the low expanse of Saint's Island, and discovered where the Green Drakes tended to gather, in the low hedges and bushes around the ruined sixth-century monastery that gives the place its name and atmosphere: he gathered a boxful. The spents, by contrast, favoured trees nearer the lake, and he used this knowledge to position himself in a boat, spinning and then dapping as he waited, both to no avail, but properly prepared this time, with imitations tied on just the right hooks, ready for the moment when the dance left the treetops and came out over the lake. 'I anticipated some sport alone.' But it never happened. So he turned again to the flies he'd found under those leaves, and now still in his spirit. This time, he knew, they were much more than a consolation prize. 'Something about searching for living things under leaves that engages the soul. Every detail + feeling is unforgettable + fascinating. The way the spents hang, like a spectral sort of spirit under the leaves.'

One afternoon in mid-July 2014, at a safe remove from my own growing intoxication with the mayfly, and en route to another appointment in Connemara, I made it out through the dark fields piled with drying peats and along the causeway linking the mainland with Saint's Island, then walked the north-east shore and heard, in a silence that teemed with flies when you really listened, the cry of birds – could they have been godwits? A gang skittered off along the shore. I saw, too, descendants of the gulls Ted noted seeing: they were picking among the ancient limestone walls he noticed, ancient field boundaries down into the water. A blur at my feet in the grass revealed, in the image I'd captured, a young damselfly: it had not yet taken on the vivid colour of maturity. And I saw a line of regular sandstone blocks, the beginnings of an abandoned jetty perhaps, or an act of homage to those old walls. Inscribed in the face of the block furthest from the water, was: 1982. Ancient history.

*

But it wasn't until I went back to Lough Arrow one more time, in May 2015, that I finally felt I was fishing in Ted's footsteps, seeing what he saw. Roderick and Caroline took me to Lyttle's Island on Lough Arrow.

Paul Cullen bought it the year after Ted first visited, and when Ted returned in 1984 for another fishless visit, but one in which, perhaps because he brought his own distinctive orange and white boat, he also seemed to relax, to divide his time, too, between casting to rises he heard and reading in warm sunlight, Ted described this island as Paul's kingdom. It's a wonderful place: 500 yards long by a 100 wide, dense green woodland right down to its stone shores, with a castle hidden somewhere, and a neat old cottage, still without mains electricity, just up from the landing stage. 'Yours whenever you want it', Paul offered Ted. Paul and Lyttle's Island starred in and narrated *The Irish Mayfly*, David Shaw-Smith's atmospheric 1988 documentary of the craft, or art, and all-consuming culture of mayfly fishing, in all its forms. I peered through the cobwebbed window, saw where, on camera, Paul had tied one of the deadly Copydex spent patterns Barrie had invented for use in oily calms; it would sit in the surface film, its buoyant glue body around fibres of pheasant tail permitting the tiny light wire double hook that – those conversations in the Murphys' caravan – gave them a better chance of connecting with Key's hard-mouthed monster trout.

On Lyttle's Island I saw them at last: clouds of dancing flies under warm clouds pregnant with rain, tumbling, some coupling above the trees, some falling into the grasses, and hundreds more hanging under the hawthorn leaves. I found Green Drakes, spent and, just once or twice, those marvellous living and spectral fruit of his diaries, or in the most tenderly poignant twist he gave them, 'Spooky fruit'. That split pellicle, the wing husk, the empty scabbard, the cast shell of a body, beside the new frail life that had stepped, or fallen, from it, and hung beside it now, waiting for the moment of its own nuptial flight. It didn't matter, then, that I didn't catch fish that weekend, or that, in some weird and vexing parody of piscatorial propriety one evening, when light and wind and warmth all seemed for once in danger of giving us our best chance, Roderick took a mobile phone call from his younger son, Humphrey, who had just found a bay full of rising fish, but declined his offer to let us join him. I still felt that I was moving closer, as I did when I left the Murphys, fanatical fishers all, at lunchtime on the last day of my visit. I'd just played them *The Irish Mayfly*, and read them the poem in which I found those 'Spooky fruit'. 'Saint's Island'. You won't find it in *River*, simply because it's a great lough of a poem, but it's the one poem he ever dedicated to Barrie, and its waters run as deep as its eye fastens on every detail of the whole process of the mayfly. And as Justin Murphy said, in the silence that followed my reading: 'It is right, absolutely accurate, but nobody but fishermen would know this.'

I drove south-east, for an hour and a half. I picked Green Drakes off the hawthorn bushes at Saint's Island, putting them in a paper cup with a mesh top I'd kept from Ryanair – designed for coffee grounds, it was perfect for my captive dragons – then took another twenty minutes threading my way around the shore to the closest bed and breakfast with a boat for hire in that quarter of the vast lake. I headed out, bumped my way across two miles of ridgy lough, landed, waited for the dusk, and for the wind to drop. It was, for half an hour, an evening of perfect promise, and complete peace.

But then the wind didn't drop, and the temperature fell. When it didn't, I dapped, raising rod and arm high into the wind, and hating myself for impaling those three beautiful flies at just the amber spot on their thorax that Ted's diary had specified, however many thousands of them clung in the hedges. And then I waited, watching, as Ted and his friends had done, for conditions to be right: understood at last how, better equipped than I was, and with others to compare notes with – wind direction, cloud or sun, whatever fluctuations they spotted and checked again with their thermometers and barometers – the fishermen tracked the flies when they saw them above the trees, and agonised when they did not. 'A reel, unending and Irish', Ted called it in 'Saint's Island': the mayflies' dance, and the humans' pursuit of it. And I found myself quoting their questions: 'What time will they come out? Will they come out?'

They didn't, of course. The wind kept up; the temperature continued to fall. The one other boat waiting for fish off Saint's Island saw sense hours before I did. In darkness, I turned my boat back towards Inny Bay and the one faint light at the jetty.

At least I was in good company. Ted's second fortnight shared one obvious connection with the first. He never caught a single Irish trout on the mayfly. I heard this from Barrie in 2012, and didn't quite believe it; that competitiveness still had its barb after thirty years, and was there in all its gleeful spite in a photograph one of the company took of Barrie rubbing a large trout against the windscreen of Ted's car. He'd see that fish print on the long drive home.

But that makes 'Saint's Island' all the more wonderfully tender. Ted chose not to answer back. Instead, he brought all his resources, all his rough workings, all his storied insights, to a poem that really does get the whole process of the mayfly right, bringing all the frustrations of Key and Arrow, and all the quiet beauty and promise of Ree. You might be tempted to call it a flight of fancy. Instead, his words, not Nick's, now supply the melody, accompanying flies which are, themselves, 'The Lough's words to the world'. They're

> the closest it comes
> To consciousness and the flight into light.

What could be more serious than this dance? It's both consuming and a consummation. The ephemera become 'like Dervishes' in their religious frenzy. And Ted's caught in that uplift, carried with them: 'truly they are … / Touched by God'; 'casting themselves away', 'they soar out of themselves'.

The same continues to be true for the younger of Ted and Barrie's Irish friends, the spent purists, and their families. In 2017, with eightieth birthdays approaching, Roderick and Caroline concluded, as Barrie had done, that they needed to lay down their rods, but their sons' addiction continues to grow. Every year they return to these waters, still describe the same infuriating but beguiling journeys, binoculars to hand, around those bays, eyes glued on the depression between treetops, for the chance of the cloud that danced that day above the caravan on Monaghan's field. And when you see that pulsing dance, I know, it is magical. It could happen, given the right air and warmth and cloud cover, just the right atmosphere, soft weather, this afternoon, as I'm writing this, in mid-May, or any afternoon or evening for the fortnight to come. That's why I brought Sarah and Ben to Arrow in the days after I'd helped Roderick hitch his boat to his trailer for the last time. And I know I'll do all I can to be out on Arrow, describing my own long vigil. I want to be there, if only for a long weekend, every year. Because I managed it: at last, on my eighth day of trying, fooled one canny three-pounder, and brought it to the net, to Caroline and Roderick's absolutely genuine delight.

The day after my fish, Roderick and I drifted down the edge of a windlane on the lee of Lyttle's Island. We lurked, talking, Roderick casting the whole of his life away that afternoon, sharing story after story. Our friendship deepened, or soared, quietly. We took turns at the oar, holding the boat back then occasionally stirring it into a little life, giving it the nudge it needed. At last we saw a trout that was not a oncer, but following its own steady course upwind, taking spent. And, having learned from Roderick not to keep casting, but to hold my imitation in my hand and rod cocked, line ready, until the time was right, I pounced. But that golden gleam ended suddenly after a minute of tussle right under my boat, ten feet down. And the following afternoon, off a point dense with hawthorn and alder and oak, waiting for fish, we saw the other fanatics, the ones with whom Ted and Barrie and their extraordinary, educated company, including Roderick, of course, continued to identify. It was real enough, that sense of admission, elation. For twenty minutes we were surrounded by those dancing beauties, and though not a fish rose within range, to be floating within that halo felt like plenty.

13

The Dry-Fly Purist?

Every river has them. Whorls after whorls. Some rock, or twig below the surface, some obstacle, interrupts the edge of live water, sets a curl in motion. It catches your eye. It spins, deepens, but is itself pressed downstream.

Since reading Ted, and thinking of Barrie, I'm lost in water: whenever I can, I spend minutes watching, wondering how fast those whorls, turning on themselves, draw in some flotsam on the surface, or form a mobile dotted line for feet, sometimes for yards, a flashing morse code of distress or celebration. Then they slacken and are gone. That leaf you'd seen gyrating is still there, but on serene, smooth water, mid-pool. What has become of them? No telling. But upstream, in the rough and tumble of the pool's throat, it is beginning again. That twig, that sunk boulder, provoking another involvement, an involution, a whorl, a spin. This mystery folds itself in, then relaxes, melts.

Following this as intently as you need you could be anywhere in the world. Yesterday I was in Suffolk, looking for otters, but found this instead. The water playing with itself, and me. This evening I'll walk down to the mill pool at the end of our road and will for once not search for the pike that lurk there, the roach. I'll look down over the rails of the footbridge over the bypass channel and let my eyes rest, or dance, on the rushing twisting surface.

So it could be anywhere. And you don't need to be a fisherman to watch them.

But if you are, a biological dynamo drives your eye: at least, that's what Ted told Brian Clarke, another fishing writer, who told me. Ted Hughes was a fisherman, and whatever Barrie added to it the fascination of water took deepest hold of Ted on the Dart, on that half-mile of the West Dart, its 'spicy torrent that seems to be water / Which is spirit and blood' above Dartmeet, and the three-mile stretch of the main river between Dartmeet and Holne Bridge which Simon Day had opened to him in 1980. He'd admired the self-wrestlings and callisthenics of Concrete Pool, but that took heart, head, will, imagination, experience to fathom. The Dart was simply, clearly, drop-dead gorgeous. It was in his first hymn to the dangerous music of the Dart gorge, 'In the Dark Violin of the Valley', that he first let the river in that gorge's 'dark skull' sound in his head, too, first heard its water 'Searching the bones, engraving / On the glassy limits of ghost / In an entanglement of stars'.

It sounds impossibly romantic. But I've spent a midsummer night there in June 2014, with Gerald Spiers and his friend John Dennis, another sea-trout specialist. I've looked heavenwards and seen the black marks of oak branches and leaves score and diminish what those gliding pools and the constellations hold in their surface. They seem much deeper. It was just that play of surface and depths, the life water lent them, that fascinated Ted.

At night he had to rely on the music of the river for his sense that this 'quick moor-water', gathered upstream, could not just melt granite, as it had on the West Dart, but then career to and fro down the gorge, 'cutting the bedrock deeper', filling his head. So did its music.

But by day, even when he wasn't looking down with his polaroids, cutting through the glare of leaf-dappled light to spot the waving tail of a salmon below a rock, feet down in that clear water, below one of those rocks the water was still wearing down and smooth, he added shape and detail to that sound. And discovered a dancer, and danger, in it.

Ted knew this secret stretch of the river drew others in: a path leads down the opposite east bank from the car park at Dartmeet. He knew he might find a birdwatcher sitting on the brambled bank; easy to imagine wrens alighting on him. Swimmers, too: at least once he came round a bend in the river and found a costumed bather taking it all in from a rock. What must she have thought of him? Kayakers nowadays, too, bobbing down rapids, risking all. There's a Dartmoor saying: the Dart claims a heart a year.

But to be a real 'Riverwatcher', not those like the one I saw in that grey light at Grimersta, whom estates pay to prowl the banks by night, keep poachers off pools visiting anglers have paid good money for, Ted knew you needed to keep all your wits on the water itself. For once, in *River*, Peter Keen's photograph of the Dart matches the poem. Fishermen-photographers know they need to read the levels of a river's life. Know how to recognise all the winged fish food they can – not just *E. danica* – if they're to have a chance of capturing trout during the rest of the season. And on tumbling spate rivers, with stone rather than mud bottoms, upended then swept clean by spates, the caddis or sedge fly is one of the ones to watch out for. Especially important in these parts; as Dermot Wilson, doyen of dry-fly fishing, wrote in his contribution to *West Country Fly Fishing*, 'Sedges ... are more common in relation to ephemerids than they are on chalk streams. So are midges and stoneflies.' The Hugheses knew all this, of course: at seventeen, Nick had an aquarium dedicated to caddisfly larvae. So Ted knew 'Caddis', too, so intimately that he wrote a poem for it and then, for Nick's Morrigu Press, if not for *River*, supplied the illustrations of larvae and adult. He knew that its 'struggledrudge' larva always finds a way to cast off its armour of twigs or gravel, swim up through the water, and at twilight come into itself, its distinctive tented wings, mate up in the leaves, then rest on the surface, casting its eggs.

And then, as fisherman, Ted knew, first, how to concoct a serviceable imitation: tie in hollow fibres of elk hair for buoyancy, trapping a bunch near the eye of the hook for a wing, but only when you've first spun hare's ear round your thread to trap air along its body, then added a rib of gold tinsel to catch a trout's eye.

Then there was the business of getting this thumbnail-sized confection over the fish: he knew how to send fly line and finer, all but invisible, monofilament nylon leader out over this whirling water to give his artificial long enough to float down those fast

and narrow necks of pools where these lean trout have more
chance of intercepting a meal on the food lane, less time to be
wary and spot a glitch in the tying. To trick one you need to cast
gently not too far upstream of the likely spot, and you need by
the right shake of the rod to insert a bit of slack line. If you don't,
those twisting, diving currents will catch your line, drag the fly
downstream or up after it, and it will skitter, drag, scare the fish.
But you also have to draw your line back towards you at just the
speed of the current: too slow, and if a fish does take it you won't
set the hook before it realises its mistake, spits out elk and hair
and steel, too quick and it will leave a wake that will also scare
the fish. And after that ten-foot drift, perhaps controlled while
you're crouching behind or on a boulder, feeling one foot slide
from you, tipping you off balance, be sure to lift it off gently –
too quick a movement makes the fly pull down under the surface,
pop, spook the fish you haven't seen downstream, or up. Then
you cast again: if you think of this paragraph as a pool, you could
have had a dozen drifts in the time it's taken you to read it.

It's tricky, this, the rough and tumble 'dry' fly fishing of the
valleys. Even on the Dart, which Dermot Wilson knew is the
clearest of all Devon's spate rivers, you are often not fishing for
individual rising fish, as he was on the alkaline, mineral-rich
waters of the chalk streams of Hampshire he had fished since a
boy. Here you are 'fishing the river'. Wilson again: 'Delicacy is at
a premium … since clumsiness usually spells disaster. A splashily
presented fly in a confined space normally acts as a danger signal
not only for the trout you are casting to, but quite possibly for
several others as well.'

Disaster? Well, only in terms of lost fish, you might think. But
Ted magnifies the risk, or shrinks the fisherman. Ups the stakes.
Keep your wits about you, your mind clearer even than this water,
your eye on the signs the other debris in the water's skin give you.

Cling to the gnat, the dead leaf
In the riding whorls
That loosen and melt
Into the bellies of pools.

And if you don't? There's the dancer in the river, of the river. Just upstream. She'll spin you in, draw you down. A liquid form, and as alluring as she can be fatal, there: 'Where a body loves to be', consumed, enraptured, snatched away, and down.

I know all this. Richard and I spent two days fishing the Dart the month after I met Simon Day. Simon invited us for the first of them. Forty-eight hours of torrential rain had left some Devon roads impassable, and below Rose Cottage the Tamar was 'out', the colour of milky coffee. But the swollen Dart still ran as clear as Dermot Wilson said it did. We were expecting to spend one day, but Simon reminded me: it's yours, whenever you like, so we came back. We caught nothing, saw not a sign of a salmon, but each of us lost our footing on the smooth rocks, and lost our hearts to it, and lived more fully in the roar of those rapids, the glides of the pools, those two days than in a week on another river. It was just as Ted had written: 'The prettiest and wildest fishing in the West.'

But the Dart was also a lifeline when he needed it most.

*

The hot summer of 1983 made that enthralling moment early that May morning on Island Run or Concrete Ramp a distant memory. The Torridge was in a terrible state: a 'sick sad slimy river', he called it that July, Yew Tree Pool at Beam 'a sick sewer'. On his return from Kenya that September, where he'd caught a 104-pound Nile perch on the last drift of the three weeks he spent on Lake Victoria with Nicholas, *River* was published at last. He fished the Torridge, twice, with his new friends Peter and Terry Norton-Smith, on their beat at Little Warham below Beaford, fishing he'd only discovered researching his essay for 'Taw and Torridge'. On the 18th the river was 'café au lait thick', and within half an hour 'became unfishable'. On 21 September, he caught his one Torridge salmon of the year, a grilse of four pounds.

On the 22nd, he went to the Dart. Reading his diary entry makes me see what he fished the river for. He '<u>saw an otter in one pool</u>', underlined it. He also caught four salmon, and kept three of them, then, realising he'd never make the climb back out of the gorge with 30 pounds of fish dangling round his neck, strung them on a long hazel pole and dragged them. In one of his 'exhausted breaks', he turned and looked down to watch the owner of the fishing on the east bank teaching a woman how to cast. She hooked her first fish, 'in the Pulpit': one of the pools. 'River very alive.'

And then, two days later, wanting more of that strange, surging life, more even than the Dart could provide, Ted headed north. A mere 540 miles this time, to join another of Simon Day's parties for a prime autumn week at Islamouth on the mighty Tay, one of Scotland's largest and finest salmon rivers. Beside Simon and Hilary there were Lord and Lady Clinton and their son, significant land and riparian owners on the Torridge, Bill Tucker, and Bill's guest – Gregor MacGregor, a name in the diary I'd first heard at Grimersta, where they'd met. He was a Scots Guardsman who had seen service in Borneo and Malaya, and was living it still: he insisted that a hooked salmon was not to be played, but fought. And he was a baronet and twenty-third Clan Chief of Clan Gregor, to boot. According to Ted's diary, he had gold reels, and an 'extraordinary wife'. Yet he caught nothing; at the end of the week, Bill gave him a consolation prize of a side of smoked salmon. Scottish salmon fishing could be just as competitive as the pursuit of Irish trout.

But mostly Ted's eyes were on the Tay. On the first morning, he found a 'Great dark pool of whorls, very exciting'. By that evening, from bank and boat, they had taken twenty salmon; and though in terms of fish caught nothing quite matched that sense of shared good luck – 'We were all thinking the same thing: "My God, at last we've hit it!"' – the week brought more discoveries. Comparing notes with Bill, helping him land fish, and talking to their ghillie Ronnie Mann, Ted came to understand the river, its channels and pots and 'hot spots', the arc of a current beyond a 'dead lake' of inert water he had to cast beyond to find fish. One morning he got up early and met them at seven. 'Never saw such salmon activity as was going on opposite the Croy. Hardly a moment without a salmon in the air.' Returning after breakfast, he thought he knew why: now the river was rising after rain upstream, and fish were 'arrowing at surface – running hard I imagine. Was that earlier activity the excitement of getting ready to go?'

They 'smoked everything' until the Wednesday evening, then went on catching. Though this meant sending the salmon to O'Connor's in Dunkeld, the effect was still intoxicating: the sight of the racked sides of their thirty-six fish united them – 'we felt dizzy with the exultation of plunder', Ted notes, though I wonder whether others called it plunder. The drink consumed, the bill, may have accounted for some of the giddiness.

But for Ted at least there was another factor, an element of the 'stunning impression' this 'immense, gripping river, mesmerizing plenty of performing fish' left in his head that none of the party could share. It reminded him of the Gulkana, the river he and Nick had fished two years before on their second visit to Alaska. He'd worked hard at the poem he'd written about that ghostly encounter not just with the fish but with the sense that he had encountered, beside that pre-Columbian wilderness river, his own prehistoric doppelganger. Here, despite the pretty path, the beautiful avenue of trees, the sense of privilege few could afford – 'this must be sport worth any money' – and for all that the rest of the week never matched its beginning – 'the only real time was the first morning' – he turned back to the language he'd used in his poem. 'Definitely, the slight lovesick feeling leaving it – not so strong as Alaska, but the same thing.'

*

Back in Devon, love and sickness surged and slept in different beds. The 1984 season took Ted back to the Dart, where there were more fish than for a decade. The Torridge was sick. At Little Warham, where he spent two of the first three days of March, and downstream on the tidal water at Beam, fishing had to compete for his time with 'talking sewage', pollution: who was responsible, and how bad was it for fish? Colonel Graham, a Beam regular, was aghast; several times that spring Ted lost the best hour of the day discussing the plight of the river. Ted did catch fish – a 'celt', as he spelt it first, and then more 'kelts' – salmon and sea-trout that had survived spawning but, recovering, still resembled strange, thin ghosts of their former heroic selves, snake fish. One, whom Ted christened Horace, he caught three times from the 'taking place' Peter Norton-Smith had pointed out to him below the historic stilted fishing hut at Little Warham, its pitch-pine plank ceiling reproaching them with the past. Like a wooden Lascaux, it's inscribed with a huge salmon in charcoal. Thirty-three pounds it weighed, caught in Madeira Pool, one of six fish caught before lunch on 13 April 1917: 107 pounds all told.

But at least there seemed to be more fish than had spawned for years, and that gave some hope for the future, if not the current season. But only if the water in the river did not kill the parr, or the smolts they'd grow into. In April he noticed a grey sootiness on the stones at Little Warham he'd never seen before, a flocculent darkness. He knew the causes: an abbatoir and a creamery at Torrington, water abstraction massively reducing the river flow, and further up at the headwaters, farm pollution, runoff from silage and slurry, about which Ted had written powerfully in a paragraph he eventually cut from 'Taw and Torridge'. Then there was the problem of Bideford sewage, which the tide brought up to the weir. One old resident of Weare Giffard in that tidal stretch had told Colonel Graham, who told Ted, that fish wanting to run turned back out to sea rather than put up with the toxins. An Action Group was being put together. An early council of water, that March, attributed responsibility, guilt: the South West Water Authority. But also identified sources of advice: the Salmon and Trout Association, of which Ted had long been a member.

Some time that year, Ted began corresponding with Dermot Wilson. Or Dermot with him. Dermot's widow Renée thought it was that way round. Whether or not they had met at the launch party for *West Country Fly Fishing* at the Arundell Arms that Anne and Conrad Voss Bark held in 1983, Ted's own appointment as Poet Laureate in December 1984 gave one distinguished contributor every excuse to write to another. Particularly, as Renée pointed out to me when we met in August 2012, if you already had his address on file.

Carol Hughes had put me in touch with Renée Wilson. We met at her thatched cottage, its garden running down to the

Ebble, in a village south of Salisbury, one afternoon. A lovely place, in its way, but she was frank about it: she missed Nether Wallop Mill. It is a name fly fishermen still cherish. The Wilsons made it famous. It was there they established Britain's first mail-order fly-fishing business, specialising in bringing to the British market high-quality tackle, much of it American. The service was personal, efficient, the catalogues were works of art, and the service terrific: when you ordered flies from Dermot Wilson, they arrived the next day. The secret? Dermot had assembled a team of friends from his wartime service in the Green Jackets who did not stand on ceremony, but who were happy to be led – he'd won a Military Cross for his part in leading a patrol behind enemy lines in occupied northern Europe: 'I didn't deserve it,' he observed, 'I just got lost.' He clearly brought his own brilliance to the business, having demonstrated it in the City: despite topping the list of candidates at the Foreign Office entrance exams, the thought of foreign postings, separating him from the chalk streams he'd learned to fish as a boy at Winchester, was too much to bear, and he instead pursued a career in advertising, rising to a directorship of J. Walter Thompson.

But that afternoon by the Ebble I had a real sense that Nether Wallop Mill was a family business, a labour of love for Renée as well as Dermot. Fishing had brought them together, she knew, and told me, a spark in her eye. Nothing like standing close behind your pupil to show her how to hold the handle of a fly rod, so, how to lift, so, flick, so, rest, flick forward, so – beside an idyllic river, so much depending on feel, of hand on cork, of hand on hand on cork. And he wrote of her skills as an angler in his first book, *Dry-Fly Beginnings* (1957), the basis for his classic *Fishing the Dry Fly*. Already well connected – he was a member of the Flyfishers' Club – the business connected him even more intimately to his customers. After all, he knew where they all lived.

Renée couldn't find all Ted's letters to Dermot that afternoon, but to judge from the earliest she showed me, from February 1985, it was activism and water quality that got the correspondence going. When he'd sold his mail order business, four years earlier, to Orvis, Dermot Wilson became a founder member of the Salmon and Trout Association Water Resources Group; Ted, as Laureate, and as long-standing member of the Atlantic Salmon Trust, had himself just written a poem, 'The Best Worker in Europe', the manuscript to be auctioned in March to raise money for their cause. The Queen Mother, whom he would later describe as 'godmother to the salmon' for her work as patron of the Salmon and Trout Association, donated a carriage clock, Prince Charles a snuff box. This was also the month in which Ted first visited the Queen Mother, spending the weekend at her invitation at Royal Lodge in Windsor Great Park. (As he would later tell Leonard Baskin, you did not decline invitations from the Queen Mother – 'an invitation is a command'; nor, though, did he ever find a way of admitting to his artistic friends how seriously he took, or how much he enjoyed, this privileged obligation of the Laureate. Fishing the Dee as a member of her party for the second week in May at Birkhall, on the Balmoral estate, would soon become a fixture.)

Now Ted was thanking Dermot for sending relevant extracts from a number of scientific reports and fishing writers about water quality and its effect on fish populations. The problem was ubiquitous, and lay just below the surface, but nowhere fully substantiated by evidence. As he assembled arguments in advance of the public inquiry into proposals for the fine screening sewage plant being proposed for the Taw estuary, at which he would speak that September, Ted needed clinching proof that salmon and sea-trout smolts, at the moment of utmost vulnerability, two years old, as they adapted from the fresh water in which they'd grown as parr to salt on their way out to sea, were affected by sewage and the chemicals that attended it. In the meantime, a recent article in *World Wildlife Magazine* had confirmed his own diagnosis of the Torridge's suffering: abstraction, sewage works and the abbatoir and creamery at Torrington. The article's authors bewailed the 'dramatic' consequences of all this for the river's aquatic life. Ted longed for more of this drama's detail, and supplied a lot of it himself: he apologised for rehearsing a tune that tended to hold him until he reached its final note. And – sending Dermot a relevant report from the Atlantic Salmon Trust – Ted responded warmly to his suggestion that the Torridge Action Group would benefit from having a member of Dermot's own Salmon and Trout Association on board; only two nights before, Peter Norton-Smith had asked him to join. Ted was happy to contemplate bringing both groups together.

But when they did meet, that spring, it was a world away from such troubles. And on waters that could not have been more different from the sick Torridge's.

*

Ted was just back – perhaps not fresh – from his latest Scottish trip. He'd spent a week on the Tweed fishing Lower Floors, arriving in the green light of a spring Borders evening, staying, as fishermen were required to, at the hotel (then the Sunlawes, until very recently the Roxburgh) which the Duke of Roxburgh still ran just downstream, outside Kelso. Then he'd headed north, for a night as the guest of Sebastian and Henrietta Thewes at Strathgarry House near Blair Atholl, followed by a week on the Spey at Craigellachie, with Peter Norton-Smith and his son. Though it was a remarkable fortnight, it wasn't for the fish he caught: three on the River Tweed, a brace on the Spey.

This time it was the people that caught his eye, and pen. Bill Tucker was there, but in company new to Ted: this was his first encounter with John Martin, whom he pronounced 'quite a find', partly because his endless public-school banter, ribbing and friendly insults brought out a sharper and less deferential geniality in Bill. They immediately got on: Ted and John fished together all week. Then there were Bill's friends and near neighbours the Courtenays, Earl and Duchess of Devon, who were up from Powderham Castle. Later in the week, John's brother Michael arrived, with Conrad Voss Bark.

One evening, Dianna Courtenay's in-laws came to the hotel for dinner. She was ready to celebrate: she had just caught her first salmon, on a Munro Killer from the Ferry Pool. Ted records this with a 'poem for Diana' (*sic*), and an accompanying note, in which the Rhymer (which is what comes with being Laureate, I guess), the Brewer (Bill), the Farmer (John) and the Landlord (Hugh) all are 'glad to be alive'.

He liked Dianna. She questioned grand claims, boorish jokes. And above all, he liked what he heard her telling her sister about playing that salmon: 'It's exactly like horse-riding – you have to keep in touch, whatever happens.'

Nothing that followed was as vivid, either on the Tweed or the Spey. Ted did realise what a wonderful sea-trout river it was, but too late in the week to do much about it. He detected Peter Norton-Smith's disappointment at not having been included in that first week's party when Conrad had; Ted's own offer to let Peter fish on his ticket led to more embarrassment back at the hotel about who should claim the salmon.

The three days that awaited Ted on his return south from the Spey – he called in at the Sunlawes to check how many fish that next week had brought – should have been simpler. They were certainly more vivid, and at least one of those he'd told in Scotland about what lay ahead, the mother of the gardener at Strathgarry, had urged him to write a poem about it. But they didn't warrant a mention in Ted's leather-bound journal, and the poem, or lines, took years to emerge from his notebooks. And by then he'd been caught in the act.

Public evidence that this trip took place is provided by the memorable photographs that Dermot Wilson, always with an eye for a catch, took of Ted actually fishing. Ted with a heron's eye, crouching into a fish, mid-stream; Ted handling a net. In fact, Dermot even got Ted to do a bit of advertising, modelling a particular kind of folding net; a picture of the Laureate featured in the next edition of *Fishing the Dry Fly* in 1987, long before Ted did anything about making his own use of the trip. Did he mind? Hard to tell, though even if he did, I suspect he wouldn't say so. It was a small price to pay. To be able to fish with the leading exponent of fishing the dry fly, on his choice of waters as clear as gin and twice as expensive, and to target rising fish which dwarfed the lean moorland trout of the Dart, was to learn the alternative to 'fishing the river'. And afterwards, in thanking him for that 'jewel of a three days', Ted knew how lucky he'd been.

Dermot had arranged successive days, during the height of the mayfly season, on English rivers famed for the richness of their fly life and their place in fly-fishing history. Trout fishing doesn't get any better, or more iconic, than this. First the Itchen, the river of Dermot's youth, and where Dermot had access to the beats on the upper river which Viscount Grey had fished, and then hymned, in his *Fly Fishing*. (I've fished Chilland, too: visiting the Flyfishers' Club in London to seek advice from its secretary on how to display the college's collection of Ted's flies – it really was a research visit, I promise – I was sat next to Nick Measham at lunch, who is both a committed Hughesian and now chief executive at Salmon & Trout Conservation. Once, thanks to his great generosity, I've even had the evening river to myself, one of the most glorious and exciting half-hours I've had anywhere.)

Then the Avon, home of the famed Piscatorial Society – they visited the Society's fishing hut and Museum at Lake – whose rules encourage the use of the upstream dry fly, frown on nymphing and prohibit altogether the use of a weighted fly. Their third and final day was on the Test, the river on which, in the late nineteenth century, Frederic Halford had married entomology to imitation and pioneered the art of dry-fly fishing that succeeding generations of wealthy gentlemen had turned into a cult, a religion. This was initiation. It felt, wrote Ted, like 'performing in an old English mystery play'.

But it was also, at least to begin with, a comedy of errors. The stage was lit as well as set, in weather which would have left 'my Irish fishing companions' despairing. They needed a cloud. As it was, Dermot had set things up perfectly; had even set Ted up. The Itchen was ' "difficult", in the way I'd been led to expect'. Ted, clearly bringing with him a selection of flies Dermot had recommended in his piece in *West Country Fly Fishing*, had tried a Beacon Beige, but that 'felt like a W.D. helicopter, my casting like a lion-tamer breaking in a new whip' – W.D. means war department; Ted was casting a line to appeal to Dermot's own military past – 'and me like a water-buffalo dragging a rice-plough (I expect that's what it looks like on the photographs.)'. Which must have compounded the sense of having to perform: Ted generally had an aversion to photographs.

By the second day, he was getting the hang of it, and self-consciousness began to give way to delight, not least because of the sheer number and enthusiasm of the rises he saw and heard. But beside the Avon's hallowed waters he also realised 'how <u>ill-dressed</u> I was for the part'. He lacked the right robes; he even lacked what Dermot, master of state-of-the-art tackle as well as what to do with it, would have called a fishing rod. At least, Ted reflected ruefully, the casting stick he did wield (was it greenheart? it was certainly old) left him 'more authentically equipped than most' for his role in a drama that had long been the preserve of the most exclusive of English societies: the Piscatorial Society, the Houghton Club. Perhaps this ancient composite was a wand.

Most embarrassing of all, though, was his net. He'd clearly come straight from Scotland; his was the large round Gye, twenty-four inches in diameter, built for salmon, and worn over one's shoulder via a leather sling until the time came for the net to be deployed when you slid it down the long shaft. 'I feel it wasn't far off a bound pack of dynamite.' Still, though, all this kit served: in several of those pictures Ted is wielding it effectively enough, a silver S of a decent trout in the net bag. And at least, too, he'd got his acclimatising done on days one and two; without those preliminaries, he would still have been 'crusted with Salmonising monotonous deep-wader's trance & waiting for a pull, in a waste of fishlessness, Spey-style'.

As it was, Ted told Dermot, by the time the Test came he knew he'd passed it, was ready to 'slip into it so intensely'. 'It was one of the most delightful days of fishing I've ever had', and a week later 'every second of that magic day' was present to him. He'd learned to calibrate weapon against opponent, even when it didn't lead to victory: 'I shan't ever forget the siege of that fish under the reeds on the far side, that would neither take nor stop rising – with its aides fore & aft, to draw the fire.' Talk flowed, too. Ted had registered the Green Jackets.

He wondered how he could ever thank Dermot and Renée for this treat. But he ended his letter with the beginnings of an answer – some verses, intended for the American with whom Dermot was himself about to stay in Montana, which Ted also thought applied to the owner of the fishing they'd just enjoyed on the Test, one Piggy Spooner: a rhymer's hymn to the luck of the roving fishermen, enjoying glorious waters without needing to attend to their upkeep. But deft as this was, this wasn't really him being anything more than the Rhymer. And even then the way he worked at them suggests he struggled to find the right balance between different kinds of passion, for river, for flies, for trout and for the other obvious subject of unreconstructed masculine humour he thought the Wilsons, or at least Dermot, would appreciate:

> A man can match
> The hatch and catch
> The time of his life
> In fish, and in wife,
> But live forever
> He will never
> Land the river

After several more verses, some cancelled, about flies, wives and fishermen – variants on *River*'s own oft-repeated refrain of copulation and death at low water, in which mayflies become the fly-fishers' souls – Ted concludes:

> If this theology
> Is too fine
> Now let Dermot
> Mend my line.

Dermot would have appreciated that nice pun, if he'd ever been given the chance to read it. He was famous for casting as lightly as he wrote. He knew exactly how to put wriggles into his line to offset the current and give his dry fly the few more seconds of drag-free drift it needed to reach its target trout. But these lines stayed in Ted's notebooks, now in the British Library: an admission, perhaps, that, compared to the transcendence he'd found himself rising to with those Irish mayflies, among fanatics who cast themselves away, this refined English version – a him, not a hymn – still fell short.

And then, seven years later, he realised that he could mend his own line, and land something more remarkable than any river.

※

In 1992, Ted was revising *River* as he prepared *Three Books*. Adding new poems, and some old ones, from other May mornings. Discarding others. Tweaking a few. In April Ted sent his new editor, Christopher Reid, and no fisherman, two he'd changed his mind about, decided to rework rather than drop. One of them, 'Be a Dry-Fly Purist', looks familiar, once you get past its title: its body keeps the lines he'd used in 'Riverwatcher', a long lingering parenthesis to imagine the swirl and mad dance of the current of the plunging Dart as a dancer whirling herself into religious ecstasy. But it has a new opening to go with its new title, and the urgent commands of the first version seem closer, now, to a particular kind of casting instructor's light touch: 'Barely prick the meniscus. Lightly caress / The last gleam on the river'.

By then Ted had read, and told Dermot how much he'd admired, his own fully revised edition of *Fishing the Dry Fly*, for its spicily stylish river of language, its current drawing the reader's eye from one seductive pool of a paragraph to the next. (Wisely, perhaps, he passes no comment on the picture of him and the folding net he really should have been using.) By then, too, subsequent visits to the chalk streams, at least once with Dermot's friend the great Shakespearean actor and Piscatorial Society friend Michael Hordern, had convinced him of the real charms both of Dermot's book and of the method he described. Real, yes, but also limited. 'Dry Fly Fishing', he told Reid, was 'the English Art'; but only if you accepted that England meant Hampshire, and the only rivers were the 'elite trout streams', and the only fish worth catching were their elite trout. And only if you were the kind of fisherman who brought an 'attitude of detachment' to the river, were satisfied in 'making slight adjustments at the surface in the hope of interesting the organic mysteries and terrors in the depth' and could thereby delight in the one 'psychologically determined activity' you could reconcile with 'a basic reluctance to get involved'. Respect the rules; accept what is '<u>not done</u>'. All this made 'this regime of the Dry Fly' remind him of 'typical attitudes to poetic form'. 'On the other hand,' he conceded, 'when it works it can be the most fun. For trout it is definitely more fun.'

'Fun' is one thing. But for Ted it was only ever a diversion. Which is why he told Reid he wanted the qualified ironies of 'Be a Dry-Fly Purist' to be put between 'High Water' and 'Stealing Trout on a May Morning', and it's also why he couldn't wait for those poems to make his point, say what real danger, what excitement, what risk, what revelation, lay as it always had within those loosening whorls, in the bellies of pools on the Dart, of the Tay, or – if you were lucky enough to contact your first salmon there – on Tweed.

And that's where he ends his poem: with the risk that you'll 'be lost', and what that loss might mean. In other hands it might be just: if you don't keep your head, keep to the surface, you will be persona non grata among the purists for ever. In Ted's hands, it turns out to be something much deeper and stranger: that you'll really lose yourself, and discover – what? Well, what he'd heard Dianna Courtenay tell her sister that evening in the Sunlawes Hotel. But something has happened to the words of his diary entry. They've been spun, whirled; he's reached beyond them to where he has no right to go, where no amount of old-school ex-military masculinity will take you. Certainly beyond what Ted the Rhymer could have done. The speaker's breathless. And suddenly it's something

nobody ever told I had never
Known anything not
Riding over jumps all I could think it
Was like having my first baby ...

The poem's opened in on itself, just as Ted told Christopher Reid he wanted it to. The whorl has taken us in. And in his letter to Reid, Ted tries to admit his non-fishing editor to the mysterious forces involved. What Dianna Courtenay said, or what, years after that evening in that Tweedside hotel, he heard her say, wanted her to have said, was the last word, not just on hooking a salmon but on what it takes to hook the obsessive angler. Men have other ways of saying it, but the fish is what counts. Except that it isn't a fish: it's an infant you've delivered from that mysterious deep, prematurely. You can feel its fury. It's been hauled from the waters of the womb. It's one of those monsters, those terrors. But this child is also divine.

I paraphrase. I have to: Reid felt unable to include these lines in his selection of Ted's letters. I can understand why. It's as curiously intense a claim for the whole-body experience of fishing as any I've ever read. But to the obsessive fisherman it rings true. In 2015 Gerald sent me a photograph from Devon. He'd just heard Ted's 'magical' voice on Radio 4, and then went fishing for trout on the lower Tamar, using weighted nymphs on a long leader and three-pound line. But a salmon took. It took him 500 yards of genuinely dangerous slither down towards the sea through tidal mud. But there Gerald Spiers is, soaked, beaming, crouching in the cloudy water below the bank where they finally met. And there's a stunned pride in his eyes as he holds the fish, the freshest monster, thirteen pounds of power, ready for release, deliverance.

*

In May 2015 I sent David Profumo a photograph of my wild Lough Arrow three-pounder, and almost regretted it: he replied with a silver Trevally ten times that size he'd just caught in Tahiti, with Marlon Brando's son for a guide. David's next assignment, he said breezily, was rather closer to home: a day on the Test with Sir Tom Stoppard.

The least he could do, my fingers spluttered into my keyboard, was to find me the home of Piggy Spooner.

Incredibly, he obliged. At lunch at the fishing hut on Bransbury Common, between beats, David had bumped into a once-familiar face: John. They'd boarded together at Eton. But home for John had been Gavelacre House, half a mile upstream. He'd had the run of the river. Now a car dealer in London, and the house and fishing rights in other hands, he retains a rod one day a month. That was the day. John's surname? Spooner. Piggy's son.

Two months later, I was John's guest. Which is why I know that when Ted knelt to demonstrate the state of the art in folding trout nets, he did so on Piggy Spooner's water.

It's an idyllic place, and it was moving to see it with John; once a month, he revisits his boyhood, knows and loves every inch of the river. Though just off the A303, the wind obligingly blew traffic noise away, though not so strongly as to make casting impossible. Swallows made sorties up and downstream, low over the water, enjoying what fly life had made it up through the water as nymphs and survived their drift downriver. Showers helped it all feel almost wild, particularly where it edges the ancient expanse of Bransbury Common. Remarkably, I can say the same for its elite brown trout. One of them, at four butter-smooth pounds, rose elegantly to intercept my dry fly, and became, a couple of minutes later, the largest brownie I have ever drawn over my own folding net, on one of the most delightfully improbable days' fishing I've ever had. A jewel of a day.

But that fish wasn't really wild. I still preferred the smaller Arrow beauty.

And I knew I still had work to do back in the west.

14

May Salmon

Friday 20 May 1977. The middle day of the Devon County Show. Ted woke at five in an ocean of birdsong. Through the still mistiness he drove to the Torridge, under cloudy skies and into a blue dawn. The wind had dropped, he noticed, since yesterday. There was mist over the surface of the water, which looked milky, even though low: fish-wise, the river looked distinctly possible, he thought. But it 'proved impossible'. He looked in vain for signs of flies and minnows, and then registered redness in the sky to the north-east, over Brimblecombe Brake. As the sun lifted clear of the line of hills between the river and Iddesleigh, a heron plotted its way down, a jumbo jet on final approach, only just missing Ted's line and the 'total conversion to din + disaster' that would have followed – before coiling back when it saw him, rearing high again, dashing away in escape through the tunnel of the trees.

His poem 'Whiteness' opens on one such dawn, this month, and on the Torridge, its 'whorls clotted with petals'. Its heron, too,

Tumbles up into strong sky
Banks precariously.

The hole in the page adds to that awkward drama. But the great bird manages it: flight.

Ted had no such escape. Herons don't have 'bad thoughts of London'; his had been with him since waking. *Gaudete* had been published on Wednesday, and the first hostile review – in the *Guardian* – had followed yesterday. True, there were 'careless strokes of genius on most pages, all at the level of rendering sensation'. But 'sex and violence give way to nothing else, and so don't liberate [...] *Gaudete*, simply, is a fantasy that has enslaved its creator.'

That must have stung. Because London also meant: guilty as charged. London meant Jill Barber, the Australian literary journalist he'd met the year before in Adelaide. The magazine she edited, *Mars*, had published an advance instalment of *Gaudete*, that extraordinary scene in which one Lumb rises naked from the water of a lake ringed by mountains to wrestle with his double, fishing. A fisherman of Barrie's generation I met in Ireland claimed he'd seen Ted and Jill together in Co. Sligo; I decided not to pursue this. Had they gone to Connemara, to that lake's original at Aughrisburg? Could he have told her why if they did? And Emma Tennant: their liaison had begun, messily, only the month before.

Looking forward didn't help. He was due in San Francisco in three weeks, which was likely to mean more vilification, heckling. Should he go on or give in? He was trapped in, and by, his strength. That review again: 'Strong but blind, Samson got nowhere, till the last time, when he pulled the house down on his own head.'

The *Guardian*'s books page turned the screw. The environmentalist Robin Page had spent a year trying out blood sports. The result was *The Hunter and the Hunted*: how could that title, and the review, not catch Ted's eye? His conclusions were damning. Otter hunting was gratuitous, but mercifully inefficient. Hare-coursing's slaughter was appalling. But

> angling is the cruellest sport. The terrain is littered with snobbery, postures and double standards; it is easier to look a gaffed pike in the eye than a foundered stag, and Saint Hubert himself, having long renounced hunting after a miraculous vision, was drowned fishing in the Meuse.

No wonder hope ebbed from Ted as he fished that morning; those thoughts 'intensifying + totally destroying my concentration, preoccupying me in anger + pain'. Nowhere else in his fishing diaries is there this kind of pollution, the more toxic because he brought it with him.

But even now he didn't retreat, or emulate Saint Hubert. He just went on downstream. And at Stump Pool, at the lower limit of the Nethercott beat, found unlikely solace and more reliable company: as though he'd become an otter, he found the jagged edged ridge of rock that sticks out more than a human body's length into the river there. He knew that in its protection, under the flow of the water and a little further into mid-stream, the salmon would be there. And he fell asleep, then in his drowsiness felt the sun rise into his face, as though it, too, were seeking out the shade he'd found beneath the fringe of leaves of the ashtree that overhung Stump Pool.

That May sun went on rising. The river was ablaze with reflected light: as the air warmed, flies moved up from the surface, 'though not midges as on Taw'. But today the flies weren't the point. Nor were the perky daisies and the dandelions' spent clocks, puffed away in the wind. Instead he found baptism, communion, release. 'Delicious self immersion in river presence.' The water coming over the pool rim mimed the sound of a weir, and then became 'dream distortions' – of horses galloping, 'shouting of a mob, + so on'. But 'interesting', now, not threatening. Who needed the Devon County Show? This was the river healing. As far as he could get from the world, as close as he could get to the surface of the river, on that granite ridge under the ash where, 'further out + under flow, the salmon collect'.

Reading this – in London, on the Euston Road – I thought of 'Go Fishing', still four years into the future. I remembered what Ted had told Aoine in one of those half-terms she spent in Devon: 'fishing is my way of breathing'. And I thought: I need to find that rocky ridge, in May.

*

Ted was forty-six. Near the end of his life he would tell Nick that he only became a serious salmon fisherman at forty-eight. This was before Irish pike, before Scotland, before the Dart, nine years before he'd tell Gerald he was 'knit together with knots' to Simon

Day and other wealthy fishing pals, types Robin Page would call posturing snobs. I knew now that was unfair. I knew what came first, and after. Private communion with the fish he'd been dreaming of for years, felt close to them; ever since that November high on Dartmoor, before Ireland, he'd fused their fertility with his. He'd spent whole seasons searching them, giving all he had for a touch of *their* wealth. Praying with a lure. But now he began to go further, deeper, a planned campaign.

*

It's mid-April 1979, and he's back at Stump Pool. And this time the flies were the point. As they rose, they seemed to become the river. Drafting 'Taw and Torridge' three years later, he could still remember it all. The water was warming; a pair of buzzards circled mewing over Brimblecombe, and now the current seemed 'electrified – with that mid-April elated gauzy feeling, when everything seems to be struggling softly into life. At those times, the river almost reminds me of a nymph gurgling out of its shuck and riding down over the currents with wings lifted.' Remembering a tip from Lemon Gray's *Torridge Fishery*, about a local doctor Gray had helped to a salmon in Stump Pool over twenty years before, Ted fished a tiny spinner, a whirling French Mepps with an oval copper wing that whirred and fluttered through the water, 'brought across just under the surface like a fly'. 'And at eleven a.m. exactly' a salmon – 'eleven pounds, fresh from the sea, sea-lice still on him' – 'flung himself across the surface like a goalie'.

Ted caught more than that fish. And this was more than a game. The moment that made it happen made it into *River*, twice. 'Stump Pool in April' stays true to it; the oxygen boiling at the throat of the pool, the 'river [...] trying to rise out of the river', in all its gauzy limb twitchings, the flight into wedlock, the shadow of that April hill-wood, in its 'bridal veil'. And it provides at least one of those 'Salmon-Taking Times', which he published that December. There it is 'a religious moment'.

Another came two or three days later – remembering it for 'Taw and Torridge', he couldn't be sure. But everything else about that memory was precise. It was colder, and a cold east wind had brought more rain. Ted walked up and then over the steep little hill that lay between Meeth and the river, 'looked out over mid-Devon ... green, magical hobbit-land – and let myself down among those marvellous female curves of the coombes that close in on the Torridge at this point', 'trying to persuade myself that that brown-looking snake away there below was still fishable'. Or even alive: it looked inert, dead. The water was higher, four degrees cooler; despite its volume, the aspect was depressing. But he was confident that the fish would be there.

He had only two hours. So he walked upstream from where the path descended to the river at Stump Pool, and 'decided to investigate the concrete "Buttress" in depth. This is the deep little coiling pool' below what remains of the bridge that Lemon Gray 'describes building magnificently' in *Torridge Fishery* – 'an inadvertent but perfect piece of pool making, since it is the best holding and taking pool for a mile or more, either way'. The collapsed stanchions of the cable bridge, and then, fifteen yards downstream, the buttress itself, nosing out from the east bank to ensure a deep, scouring, twisting current, between gravel Gray had bulldozed from the island just upstream: here that snake of a river coiled, lived, swept the bedrock ten feet below as clear as it was beneath that granite ridge in the shade of the ash tree. Here, too, the salmon would be lying just above the rock.

Ted fished all this 'as deeply as I dared', first with that little Mepps, which he'd doctored to give him confidence, tying bucktail fibres around and between its treble hooks. But the rain came down harder. Hope wilted. Had the fish dashed on upriver in this flood after all? 'I revived myself' with a second thought: 'No doubt the salmon were asleep – and in that hungerless edge-of-life coma which must surely be quite pleasant, not to be lightly broken.' Remembering the example of a teacher in a local school who once fished this bit of water, and his dogged persistence – 'once he'd located a fish, he stuck at it + badgered it with everything he had' – Ted now followed suit. A dog in the pool could sometimes, he knew, stir fish, agitate them, wake them up: this was a legitimate 'part of the "deep investigative" technique'. Several times he sent the fisherman's equivalent of the dog crashing and splashing: heavy metal, a much larger lure, a big Toby. 'In such a small pool, it takes nerve to fish such a monster, but I relied on the thickish colour to muffle the fireworks, + alert those eyes down there.'

And then, after standing back for five minutes, in which he 'renovated my tufted Mepps', he knew it was time. As he resumed his fishing, 'I saw the sign that has always seemed to me one of the surest indications that "this is the moment".' Despite the heavy clouds, the rain turning to sleet, 'that deadly East wind', salmon parr were rising, taking March browns, all across the pool tail as it slid towards the Frothpot below. So he cast upriver, into the backwater and what he guessed were the deep upstream currents around the point of the concrete buttress, bringing his little lure 'back downstream as deeply as I could'. It was intuitive, subtle fishing. 'I could feel by the pressure on the mepps that I must be right about the undercurrent, very deep.' He took two fish from it, a dozen casts apart. Twelve and eight pounds. 'Enough, I thought. It was 2.30 + my fingers were almost too stiff to tie another knot.'

But he wasn't too cold to think. Lugging those fish back up the coombe, he reflected on his 'attitude, throughout the successful operation', then drew a box around those reflections in his drafts for that essay. Something wasn't right. 'The excitement + satisfaction of it, I found, was tainted with shame. Catching fish … is as obsessive a passion, for me, as for some other fishermen, but I have evidently been at it long enough to begin to feel another impulse – to protect the fish.'

He wrote this three years later – as he worked on 'Taw and Torridge' – and was still wrestling with the dilemma. 'How can I do this, without stopping fishing – and if English law stopped me fishing, it seems [to] me I would emigrate.' This was the spring of 1982. Soon he'd be in Ireland again, see those mayflies. Emigration was a real possibility. But so was restraint. He knew what he had done, tricking those fish out of that self-denying coma, 'was way too easy'. This was 'a river that needed its fish more than I did'. And long before he wrote these lines, boxed them, then decided to include none of them in the published version of his essay, he'd acted on them.

*

It's 24 December 1979. A research trip, with Peter Keen and Nick and a David I thought I recognised, into what was still relatively unfamiliar territory for a man of the two rivers. 'To Lifton to Tamar', he notes, 'to see the Salmon stripped'. If you didn't know better, you might think it some alternative to stripping the willow, a merry old dance indeed. But in the verse diary he wrote of that day Ted knew better – and worse.

The salmon needed help, and the Fishery men who bumped past them along the frost-hard track in a Land Rover knew how. They were bound for the Lyd's weir-trap, the only one that still worked in the West Country, and two miles above the Lyd's confluence with the main river. It was an odd, exclusively masculine midwifery. All you needed was a net, a determined grip on the tail, rough hands, an armpit in which to clamp the head, practised fingers to work the belly and polythene bowls to catch and swirl what spilled from it.

David Pilkington knows the Lyd and its fish as well as any man alive. He once gave Ted a salmon fly-casting lesson, on a pool David introduced to me when I was seventeen, Mar Lodge, a mile or so downstream. That pool itself has a more famous original on a Scottish river; that's clearly why Ted was here, arming himself for those trips north. I'm guessing 1981. David's was the advice that I needed to trust when I first edged out across the lip of that weir one August night in 1983 on that course, cast into the stillness for sea-trout in the stillness that lay above it, without ever really thinking of how they'd got there. Teenage excitement, and dread, left little room for sympathy. In 2016 I asked David whether he was with Ted and Nick and Peter that morning by the Lyd. No, he told me, he wasn't there, but those men were from the Cornish Water Authority. To help secure the future of the Tamar system's salmon, they wanted to collect and fertilise 80,000 eggs that day, which they'd then take down to the Endsleigh hatchery to grow on before releasing the parr – many more, they trusted, than would have survived the fury of winter spates, and predation from the fish and insect larvae that eggs would have encountered in the gravel of the redds – into the spring river. The mature fish that were to provide these eggs and milt were near the end of their long journey back from their shrimp-rich feeding grounds far out to sea in the North Atlantic.

And they'd just climbed what Ted saw that day for the first time, 'Five tiers of salmon ladder up across / The weir face, under the weir-lip'. For some it was their final act. For this weir to 'work', to be 'worked', there was 'a wire cage / To catch their last curving leap'; and the first fish that came out of that cage when they lifted it were dead. Out they were swung, 'rigid in the net, / Scabbed with fungus, irreplaceable ingots / Eggs rotten in them, milt rotten'. Ted watched helpless, weighed the 'one in five thousand' luck of a female making it back to 'her birth-pools' against this fate: 'dead / Within days of marriage'. He counted the dead. He weighed the sharp-edged beauty of this bright morning – bright frozen mud held a footprint, 'the moment of a fox': I love that 'moment', have come to know that some people, as some creatures, leave their imprints in particular places – against the damage done to these salmon by a week of frost. It had 'ripened them, but / Killed five with sudden death-bloom'. He saw the four stripped fish, 'nearly certainly doomed', 'flung back / Below the weir, corpse-careless'. One was kicked back into the river. And he also recorded a detail he kept out of the poem he drew from this, 'The Morning Before Christmas': 'the five corpses' he'd counted now 'collected + dumped' in the depth of a gorse thicket, far from 'the easily-appalled eyes of walkers'.

Ted saw above all, amidst and after all this, the eggs collecting in those bowls, the cock fish's 'milk-jet of sperm' ('A little is plenty.') The 'violation' of the cock fish; the stroking, the 'writhe into a real mating', of a female he'd thought had no more eggs to yield. Now he's voyeur, not spectator, of this manipulated intimacy. But he also saw the unexpected tenderness to the aftermath. 'Gently', in the diary, 'lovingly', in the poem, the rinsing, the washings and rewashings, 'the lavings'. A priestly liturgy.

He felt all this, too. Brought it to the poem. The frost-embellished 'beauty' of what the diary calls the hen's 'helpless face', the poem 'her helpless, noble mask' as Peter angles his camera to catch the moment eggs come spurting into the bowl; the horror of the lost, which no photograph could do justice to either:

Nothing
So raggy dead offal as a dead
Salmon in its wedding finery.

These are warriors in warpaint, red and black. They're human. He counts costs and benefits. The 40,000 eggs, only half what they'd hoped for, they did collect.

He also looked upstream, into the future, his and the salmon's. Six of the fish weren't ripe yet, and produced no eggs, to those massaging hands. They were free to go, released into the still water above the weir; they 'dissolve / Under the working, smoking, whorled, sliding / Flat above the pool above'. The image of its flint-olive waters is the one Peter chose for *River*. Ted reckons how,

With luck
In natural times, those six, with luck,
In five years, with great luck, might make nine.

But knows how deeply this has marked him.

That morning
Dazzle-stamped every cell in my body
With its melting edge, its lime-bitter brightness.

*

Every other poem Ted ever published about salmon carries that whole-body conviction. He loved them. He followed them through the months of the season, the year. And saw more of himself in them, in their driven return to their home waters after wanderings, their story of bruising leaps, surges, trapped contemplation, than he did in any other creature, except perhaps the sea-trout. Is that one reason why *River* watches them so closely? 'An August Salmon', 'September Salmon' are pools he looks into and sees himself. I'm sure they're pools in Devon, almost certainly on the Taw and Torridge, where you need luck and the right angle of sunlight and water conditions even to see them, months before the destiny he'd already witnessed at Hartley Weir.

They're both male, these salmon: trapped, waiting, somewhere between holed-up gangster and priest and 'a god on earth for the first time', discovering the dazzlestamp of mortality Ted knew with every cell in his body. Now he saw it, sounded it, in that fish: 'Features deforming with deferment.' Both man and fish waiting, watching, the salmon in the 'wedding cell' of a sunlit pool, months after his last food, months before death. No great Irish 'pike in his cell'. By September, Ted sounds sure of the salmon's purpose. 'Famously home from the sea', he's back in the present for more than his future. 'He serves his descendants.' And not by monogamy, but by serving any hen fish he could find, when he and she and the time were ripe. But not now, not yet. These months of mid- and late summer, the predator's moodiness can come on him. At the end of a hot day, that August salmon can smash his glass ceiling, the watching fisherman's surface; in September, a month wiser, he can rise as though he were a parr again and give that same sliding glass, now 'a molten palate', the faintest 'daub', an artist perfecting himself in middle age. The seven ages of fish.

*

But Ted doesn't only see himself. Now he watches with a son's helplessness.

It had been coming. Willie Hughes, Ted's father, had been living in North Tawton for years. Miles from his own roots, a widower since 1969, he'd carried older traumas with him: from Gallipoli, and the Great War. In one of Ted's 'Orts', leftovers, he'd guessed what Willie saw when he turned the 'T.V. off' and heard restless trees outside, 'leaves swatting the glass'. For 'a day and a night and a day' he'd lain, 'Golden-haired', in a no man's land he'd never left, beside a friend with a bullet hole in his brow, who 'ripened black'. Ted saw Willie in his sitting room, staring into the fire, 'like a late fish, face clothed with fungus, / Keeping its mouth upstream'.

In mid-May 1980, while Barrie and Sonja were staying with them – Sonja's first visit – Willie fell and broke his hip in the care home where he lived in North Tawton. In the main hospital in Exeter, he may have suffered a stroke under anaesthetic. On the way to or from one of his visits in the months that followed, where he'd sit in silence beside his father's bed, Ted stopped by the town bridge, walked back, stood on the arch and looked upstream into the long pool beside the disused town mill. The Taw's water that October was as clear as when I saw it one April; almost too clear. And Ted's searching eye and the light combined to reveal that late fish: a single cock salmon, of about six pounds.

In 1961, the one autumn he and Sylvia had shared in North Tawton, that same pool had held a hundred salmon. Eighteen months after Connemara, in 1967, the year that ulcerative dermal necrosis (UDN) first blighted salmon, as a species and individuals, eating away the protective mucus that sustained them in their heroic leaps upriver and then leaving open sores – ulcers – and fungoid growths in place of lavender-silver and black scales, there were still almost fifty in the pool. Five years ago, when Nicholas was thirteen, this was where he'd found that salmon carcass right under this same bridge, lifted it, and found eggs spilling from it and the redd, the spawning gravel, it lay on. The stuff of poetry, dreams. But then that guillotine of a remark from Nicholas's teacher, reading the poem he took from it and confusing the urban confines of his own experiences with this country boy's.

Now just this one small fish, 'lying in poor water'. UDN had returned with a vengeance this year. He'd made it up and over the weirs, survived those odds. Had he spawned? Had he found a mate to spawn with? It's his 'graveyard pool'. In 'the October light' 'he hangs in the flow', 'patched with leper-cloths' – the uniform of the carcasses at Hartley Weir. He's another 'death-patched hero'.

But more, and more cruel: 'a dinosaur of senility'. He's become 'his own spectre'. Nothing for it but to accept that role, and suffer it, 'His living body become death's puppet'.

But there is more. Ted looks back, out to sea, into the past. To his one winter at sea. The flash and surge of freedom, the glitter of his 'sea-metals', 'the eye of ravenous joy', 'Body simply the armature of energy', 'The salt mouthful of actual existence / With strength like light'.

And then further back still. He was born in this pool; 'this was the only mother he ever had, this uneasy channel of minnows / under the mill-wall' strewn now with rubbish. Boys – boys who know no better – will kill him if they can. But the current's caress never stops giving him 'The epic poise / That holds him so steady in his wounds'.

Hearing Ted read 'October Salmon', in a recording he made in December 1982, in a tiny studio in Greenwich, is to know this is not just for his father. It's a murmured elegy for himself.

*

By then, sometime that same autumn, in 1982, Ted had settled on an order for the poems in *River*. But it wasn't yet 'October Salmon' that rounded things off, even if it would eventually settle there when he came to revisit his collection and enlarge it. It was instead the poem he'd been trying to write ever since he'd seen Barrie's pictures of those 'vital' objects, fish, women, ever since he'd seen that Kilnaboy Venus overlooking the River Fergus twenty years before. 'Salmon Eggs'. He'd definitely finished it a fortnight after his father fell, in May 1981, because that was when he sent it off to an old American friend and editor with the letter I'd read to Barrie when I'd seen that Sheela in his bedroom.

It must have been that January, walking by the Torridge – below Nethercott, I guess. He leaned on a tree, till the cold seeped into his bones, and knew what he'd just missed: salmon, coming together deep in the turbid river, just below where he was standing. Already drifting downstream to their deaths.

But still he feels them, intimately, in their intimacy: 'Shedding themselves for each other'. He takes his time, listening to the water, watches it 'Till my eyes forget me', and then the river takes him as well as the salmon and makes them and all the rest of the life clinging onto its banks – catkins, spiders – a part of a larger process, a more mysterious story going on under the surface:

> More vital than death ...
> More grave than life

And now it's his job to work out what it is, pass it on. He hears 'this telling – these tidings of plasm', before he knows exactly what they're saying. He makes out, in and beyond the ceaseless, wordless movement of the river, what it's done over time, what it's swallowed, what it's absorbed, how it can heal. Who better than Ted for this task, this seasoned riverwatcher, alone on his river? Perhaps those collapsed buttresses of Lemon Gray's bridge were really 'the sunk foundations / Of dislocated crypts'. But if that's true, and if the altar at which he's watched his September salmon worshipping has itself been shaped and then split by time and that unstoppable flow, then perhaps the lesson of Kilnaboy old church and its ancient little Sheela opening herself over the Fergus, perhaps the lesson of the Morrigu and the Dagda and the Unshin, is there in the waters of the Torridge, too. That's what Ted sees, that January.

> Perpetual mass
> Of the waters
> Wells from the cleft.

And then he hears it, too:

> Only birth matters
> Say the river's whorls.

*

River was done, at least for now. Ted's passion for the salmon and their water was not. Their luck had run out, and the river needed them even more than he did. They needed him.

In December 1984 he published his first poem as Laureate, on the baptism of Prince Harry. But this royal child was just the occasion. Ted's 'Rain-Charm for the Duchy' was about water, lots of it, pouring in a livid thunderstorm from the skies over Exeter and drenching the dry moors of Devon, bringing rivers back to life after a four-month drought. Ted named those rivers in his spell. And then, from the Cathedral Close, he 'thought of those other, different lightnings, the patient, thirsting ones',

> The salmon, deep in the thunder, lit
> And again lit, with glimpses of quenchings,
> Twisting their glints in the suspense,
> Biting at the stir, beginning to move.

Three months later he wrote and auctioned his poem for the Atlantic Salmon Trust. This was Ted the rhymer, and he broadcast an extract from his 'ditty', 'The Best Worker in Europe', to stir bids. 'The cause of the salmon is very close to my heart', he told an interviewer. 'Everything in the North Atlantic and in European Society seems to be against it – has been against it.' The fish, tireless, an extraordinarily efficient converter of energy to flesh, meat, did not deserve this. He gave that worker a human voice, speech as plain as the water he needed. But angry, too:

> My respiration, my circulation,
> Compulsory-purchased by the Nation,
> Are now Sewers of your Civilisation.

Human policy and practice and good ideas at the time – the nets, the early salmon farms – had already made this smolt a slave, 'owned by everyone'.

That September Ted spoke out again, at the public inquiry at Bideford against the fine screening sewage works. Wrote a savage ballad he never published, 'The Ballad of Bideford Browns'. This wasn't a hymn to trout; that would have been a much more delicate, tentative affair, like the poem he'd written out for Nick in that wonderful Christmas present of his *Animal Poems*, with

fish, 'A Trout?' Later he'd give the gift again, dedicating it to the
Scottish poet and lover of Assynt trout lochs Norman MacCaig.
No, these browns were the human sewage afloat on the Torridge.

But he kept the faith as well as anger, with friends who shared
the cause. That Christmas he gave Terry and Peter Norton-Smith,
who, with Colonel Graham of Beam, were the only salmon fishers
to join him at the inquiry, a copy of 'The Best Worker', inscribed
with a verse Terry showed me in her kitchen at Little Warham.
'When it happens', it dared to imagine; when salmon run again up
every one of the river's arteries 'like a reversal of the blood'. Ted
knew every cell in their own bodies would thrill with it.

And until they did, friendship sustained them. On 28 February
1986 the North Devon branch of the Salmon and Trout Association
held its AGM just up the hill from Little Warham. Dermot Wilson
was there; Sir Michael Hordern spoke memorably of playing
King Lear and catching gravid Swedish sea-trout someone had
attached to his line for a promotional film for Abu, the fishing-
tackle manufacturer.

Ted was listening. The next morning, the first of the season, ice
in the river, snow on the banks, Sir Michael was tricked into netting
a salmon Ted had taken from his freezer for the purpose, flung out
into Boat Pool. The player played. Ted as fool, as well as rhymer,
in a poem he called 'The Torridge Tragedy'; he set it on Little
Warham's answer to the blasted heath. But beneath the practical
joke, the consolation of bonhomie, a deeper bleakness: these

<blockquote>
shadows of the stage
    That God could hardly see
Shattered the ice and waded deeper
        Into tragedy,
    Like herons in an afterlife
        Where not a fish could be.
</blockquote>

He didn't need to say why. His fears for the future of the Torridge
salmon were as real as his faith in them.

One June Sunday in 2014, when I'd returned to the house with
my largest ever wild river trout – no monster, but a stunning

brownie of a pound and a half – Terry Norton-Smith couldn't contain her delight: 'The first fish of the year from Willow Tree Run!' Then she added: 'Ted and Peter were watching you, I think.' That was the day she let me copy her photographs of that icy day. Square little polaroids the years have darkened. But it was still like looking down from the gods on the Gods at play.

Ted found stages. Or they found him. That year he accepted an invitation no loyal subject could refuse: and after he became a regular member of the Queen Mother's salmon-fishing party at Birkhall on the Dee in the second week in May, he wrote a 'Little Salmon Hymn' for her. But it was really to celebrate the salmon itself: what he called 'the totem of the sexual creation, the weaver at the source'. It was the burden of 'Salmon Eggs', and he kept finding every way of getting as close to it as he could. In 1990, in the long public poem he wrote for the Queen Mother, and her century, on her ninetieth birthday, he still put her and its great turning points in their place. He threaded through them slender lines, about

> a drama
> None has revised
> Since it rehearsed
> The first scene first.

It was still playing in dozens of Highland headwaters. Its cast was modest: 'a mother of heather, / A gravelly burn'. Its one prop

> Her cradle where turns
> A salmon beneath
> A breathing shawl
> Of bubbles.

And it played, too, on another 'stage', the shadow of a white stone in a pool on the North Esk. Watching the salmon it sheltered was, I used to think for a long time, the closest his poetry ever came to showing how close to his heart the cause of the salmon really was.

A moment ago
It slid into place
A sliver of ocean,
Barbed, fletched, notched –
So strange, so near,
So like love's touch,
Almost a fear –
Now, while you watch it,
This moment, and this,
It rests there.

*

In July 2015, my elder brother Chris and I drove west. We'd booked in, months before, for three nights at the Half Moon Inn at Sheepwash, to try for Torridge sea-trout. But I think we both knew we were fishing for something else, something – four years before those old family photographs emerged, when we had summoned up courage to ask – neither of us was in the habit of putting into words. Well before we reached Devon we'd both realised that this was as long, already, as we'd spent in each other's uninterrupted company in our adult lives. The age gap between us, of eleven years, was only just wider than the difference in our sensibilities – Chris is a commercial lawyer. We talked about that, and about my work: parallel lives. Then, perhaps in the hope of encouraging something similar, I told him Bill's story of the long companionable silences in the toffee-coloured Rolls on the way up to Lewis. I had my own Ted talks ready, too; we listened to recordings – 'Learning to Think', 'Stealing Trout'. Still, though, sometimes the car felt much too narrow.

But we needed to do this. We had both talked fishing for years, at family Christmases or weddings; it was a fiction, a fantasy, we shared, that we'd always fish together, so it was important that we were trying it. And life had just given us another reason to test the strength of our knots. Dad, eighty-six, who had retired twenty years before to Topsham on the Exe estuary, had been admitted to hospital. He was in the Royal Devon and Exeter. All the wards were named for Devon rivers; his was a stream I hadn't heard of, the Lowman, a tributary of the Exe that runs through Tiverton.

We spent an hour with Dad on our second afternoon. The visit wasn't silent. Dad's mind was sound, his mood gentle. But his skin was smoother than I'd ever known. He was fading, a man brought low, and we all knew it.

That evening, to restore us before our last evening on the Torridge, our night on the beat Charles Inniss rents at Okement Foot, I took Chris to Iddesleigh. While I was ordering at the bar at the Duke of York, Chris fell swiftly and deep into conversation with a complete stranger, a local, started blowing my cover, revealing too much about his eccentric brother's research.

I needn't have worried. Of course he'd heard of Ted Hughes. But he hadn't read him. No, he wasn't a fisherman. But he was involved in the hatchery, the one not far from here, on the Okement. I knew it had been opened in 1981. Would he mind if I showed him something? I reached into my bag, read him 'The Morning Before Christmas'. There was a long, wondering pause. 'He's got it exactly right. Exactly right.'

*

The following morning, I took Chris downriver to Beam. We knew there should be sea-trout in the river; I had not been expecting to see a huge two-foot-long lamprey wafting lazily upstream, as I had the year before on the Taw at Umberleigh. These survivors of prehistory are anadromous, too, come miles upriver from the salt. In the glide above the neck of the long wall pool, right below the Bideford road, I was convinced I'd actually seen three sea-trout, only to be gently but firmly corrected by Charles Inniss when I reported back: grey mullet. Here we weren't so far above the tide. And anyway, sea-trout don't show themselves easily in daylight. Funny what desperate desire can make you forget.

In early afternoon, I had led the way wading up Elm Tree Run, trying to see if sea-trout in that long pool could be interested in a flicked dry fly or nymph. An occasional fish showed, always just out of reach, and almost certainly a trout. But it was wonderful just to wade, waist-deep in clear, green-grey water, on smooth stones, and let the line go out, and be caressed by that flow, and know, or guess, or imagine, the fish you might be sharing this glorious river with, for a moment.

And then, barely a rod length away from me, in mid-stream, I saw it: a salmon. A big one: ten pounds, I guessed. I saw it because of those badges, leprous, fungal. All over its head, and down its body. I watched it hang there, its tail frond under the trees holding it steady against the flow. I took a very gentle step towards it. It moved, equally gently, away from me, then hung there again. Of course it was not interested in the fly I let drift over its sliding sky. And even if I'd remembered what Ted had done one morning in April 1984, fishing fifty yards upstream from here with Roy Davids, when they'd seen a diseased fish – reach for the spinning rod, foul-hook it with a treble, dispatch it, save it from months of pain – I'm not sure I could have done the same. It was immensely, slowly, patient, the way it hung there, slowly moving, dignity undimmed by the tell-tale blight. Instead, I caught it, but only on video, to show to Charles Inniss at the Half Moon. Unusually early for such damage, he said that evening. Could have been an encounter with a seal, or a boat, or a rock, downriver. Following me ten minutes later Chris saw it, too. We guessed this fish would not make it upstream, to October. Perhaps we underestimated its heroism. That is: his, or hers. We couldn't be sure.

*

Dad carried on fading. In early September I knew the time was coming. I left Cambridge at dawn, was by his bedside at ten. In the afternoon, during normal visiting hours, he'd been tired, confused, sometimes wandering, my stepmother Pam and youngest brother Peter had said. But I surprised him; we had a lucid pool of an hour together, confirming memories, renewing things, closing things, saying what needed to be said without saying much; we never had. That cricket match Dad had umpired when I was eleven. And that course at the Arundell Arms. I said goodbye, and kissed his forehead.

When, ten days later, I was down on the Torridge again, for two more nights at the Half Moon, I visited Pam and Peter at home in Topsham, to talk about the funeral.

Days of rain had brought the river up. But, they told me in the bar at the Half Moon, it was dropping, might just be OK the next morning. I reached Beam in grey light, at about six, for two hours before breakfast. I had in my head a sketch Ted had drawn of Weir Pool for Graham Swift, of where to stand to cast a fly up into the swirl below it; the point from which he cast, twenty yards or so below the fish ladder to the right, was awash with water, so I tried flicking a fly round in the current of the outflow from the ladder that led to the point and beyond. On my sixth or seventh cast, a take, firm, serious, deep. No trout, that. Then nothing. I fished as the clouds brightened and the sun pushed through. I worked my way down. Worked my way through. Three-quarters of the way down the pool, another firm, steady pull, to which I could not respond. But that contact was enough, and even right. I knew salmon were there, and would be there when I returned. That was enough, for then. It was the right place to be, to think of Dad, and me without him, to say nothing, speak to nobody, but to be within sight of the heron on Beam Weir, and let the words that I would speak, on the first day of October, at his cremation in Exeter, begin to come together.

Words from 'That Morning', Ted's Alaskan rhapsody of fishing in July 1980 with Nick, bears fishing nearby in transfiguring light, swim into my head. 'So we found the end of our journey'? Hardly. Or: perhaps just that one.

We become 'creatures of light' for rare moments, if we are lucky, for rare days: as sons, as readers, as fishermen. There was, and always will be, unfinished business. Always another reason to go fishing. Or just to go where Ted fished, and when. However long you have to wait for the chance.

I work, too far from the right kind of tumbling rivers, alongside fishing sceptics. Cambridge can be a dry, flat world, full of words. I've learned who I can share my obsession with, and who will regard it as only a hobby, or an indulgence, or escape. And, yes, sometimes, as an idea for the next trip begins to twitch, wriggles to the surface of your life, emerges, rests there, unnoticed by everyone else in the meeting, while wings dry, before taking flight – yes, it can feel like an escape – from the pressures of all that. From family troubles, too: mostly our adopted sons, young men now. While I've been following Ted, they've been growing into a world they've found harder to read than their younger brother. More than once they've found themselves deep in trouble when I'm by a Devon river, and I've emerged from a cleft in the hills that has had no mobile signal and picked up Sarah's message, and the guilt has been as hard to bear, then, as the long drive home to help.

But much more often, going fishing has been not an escape from but into. Another dimension. Another world. Into water, yes. Into the life of the fish you have to trust it holds. But while you're searching for that fish – and no other pursuit I know comes close to the concentration it demands of hand, body, eye, balance, will, confidence, care, faith – while you're reading that water for signs of where the fish may be holding themselves in the current (in the shadow of that rock? In the dappled shade of that alder? Close against the gravel of the riverbed where the flow is swift?) it's reading you. Putting you in your place. You feel your way. You deepen. You remake yourself. You become, for as long as you can make it last, a part of the river's life. A young kingfisher stares and stares from its perch an inch or two above the water only thirty feet away and lets you be. And you rest while its gaze holds you, and then press upstream, gently, gently. A decent fish shows, and, who knows, it might show again, to the fly you've offered it. And if you control the excitement, lift into it, you feel that fish; the line thrums and jags and, with luck, in a few seconds, a minute, two, five, who knows – what has happened to time? – this extraordinary beauty glides to you across the water.

In those last moments, of weariness, those flanks are always more dazzling, the shawl of water more miraculous, than you could possibly have imagined. What have you done? Now you are responsible. You wanted this, the hunter in you wanted this. But you also have to be protector. So you moisten your hands, everything under water if you can, ease the fly from the gristle of that gulping jaw, return it to its element, cradle that fish, working until the body flexes and it's away upstream again, into the stream, gone. Taking something of you, too. Humbled, but recovering. Recharged. Healed. All this before words come back. The first call home. Or at the hospital bed.

I return home having broken through. And Sarah can tell, Ben can tell, the friends who know me well can tell. It can last, this feeling, for weeks, months. I make do, through the winter, with walking by our local lode. And when that doesn't work, or my concentration wanders, I read Ted's poem 'Go Fishing'. Discover it yourself. That never fails.

*

It's 18 May 2017. The Friday of the Devon County Show. But also the day after I first followed the course of the Taw to near its source, found Ted's memorial stone. Already today I've driven back to the Taw, stolen a trout on a minnow. Now, mid-morning, I park at Meeth, where Ted had told Tom Rawling to park, and, a copy of his map in hand, follow it: down the track, up and over that steep coombe, then down the fence. The snake of the Torridge below me. The farming country of Devon beyond. Not hobbit land, but Hughes country.

At Stump Pool, I clambered and slithered down to the river, using the roots of the ash tree high water had licked clear of the high banks as handholds. I found that granite ridge. Found, in fact, two. Tried the downstream one first, but then thought: no, the one near the pool throat, under the ash, must be the one. I sat there. Then the sun broke through high cloud. Light played on the ash leaves and keys above me. Flies danced above water brown with silt. And out beyond me, as I found a way of fitting my body to the rock, I looked out and into the water, and upstream to the lip of the pool, where the river was still raising its voices; then looked down again, at the mending whorling turning currents less than a rod's length from me.

I had no rod. I wasn't here to fish. The gentlest of inquiries via the appropriate channels to the owner of the fishing rights on the Nethercott beat had gone unanswered. I just took Ted's word for the depth, and for the salmon I hoped might still be collecting there.

*

It took me another year, another fifty-three weeks and two days, to be precise, to make it back to Island Run. I'd needed it to be the right time, as well as the right place. But I also needed to be suitably equipped. Now I was. I had found Ted's missing salmon.

For years after that marvellous moment when Ted's struggle with the salmon at Island Run, or Concrete Ramp, or Concrete, had left its mark on my index finger, I'd been wondering. Why did he never write a poem about that salmon, that month, that pool? *River* needed it. The pool with the concrete buttress and its salmon were there, deep down, in that March watercolour. There was 'Stump Pool in April', the poems of high Alaskan midsummer, 'Gulkana' and 'That Morning'; there was 'An August Salmon', 'September Salmon', 'October Salmon'. Reading those poems made me see the fish, Ted in them. But why no May, apart from that dawn heron, and that one supercharged parenthesis of Dianna Courtenay up on the rich Tweed?

At first I thought that May dawn had simply come too late, in the history of Ted's battle to save the river; the only story that needed telling now was the story to save the river and the salmon from the real Torridge Tragedy. But then I'd flown west, and in that high library tower in Emory discovered those restlessly worked and withheld drafts of 'Taw and Torridge'. I knew how closely he'd fished it, and how subtly, and for how long; how close he'd come to sharing that with the world, before deciding not. I knew, too, that a decade later he was still sharing it with friends who understood, Graham Swift and David Profumo; Ted showing them, and their writing about it, had made me write to them, launched our own friendship.

Near the end of my week in Atlanta I found it. Seven untitled pages of fair copy manuscript, not a smudge in sight. Untitled, not quite complete. One hundred and seventy-two lines long and still not quite yet long enough. A cataloguer has called it '?May Salmon?' If Ted had included it in *River*, in *Three Books*, it would have dwarfed the longest of its poems, 'The Gulkana', about Alaskan salmon and the selves that river surfaced in him.

But I can see why it's not in *River*. I think again of what Ted had told Keith Sagar in 1980, when he thought he was two years closer to finishing the book than he was: that while he was in the material he wanted to write another book 'not intended for readers'. But I also know what he told Leonard Baskin in 1984, long after *River* was on people's coffee tables, long after reviewers had failed to wonder why on earth he was so often beside these rivers at dawn or dusk. The fact that very rarely was tackle mentioned, and only in 'Stealing Trout' was a fish caught, may have fooled these non-fishing townsfolk. And it was also long enough after *River* for him to have begun to wonder about its future. What it would look like, how it might look without photographs. He didn't think it needed to be so different. But, he ruminated: 'Somehow, the central poem for the River book is not yet in it. Will it ever be? There's a kind of poem which is the golden egg, + the kind of poem which is the goose that lays it.'

Whenever he wrote it, '?May Salmon?' might just be that goose. It's not a fishing poem, not a self-haunting, not even the great salmon hymn he could have sung. Just a wondering, lingering, precise anatomy of a cock salmon, fresh from the sea, the little purses of sea lice still on him, getting used to the coil and ebb of water just out from that buttress, on the east bank of the Torridge.

Ted can't see him: the laws of opacity, reflection, refraction, and the ten-foot depth of the Torridge's flow, ensure that. But all fourteen pounds of him – the size, I note, of his Dromore salmon, the most beautiful Barrie had ever seen – have still made it into his mind's eye. But because 'You can't even be sure it's there', 'you have to imagine it here'. And so Ted does, with the eye of a scientist and an artist. 'Only a mental act can grasp him', only 'a deep-sunk thought'.

Ted sets to it.

Imagining: The whorl + whirl + twirl of clear water
    Just aft of his tail fringe.

Barrie would have liked those whorls.

The lacquered tail itself. The vent of the anus, closed now for months, now he's no longer eating, and as the milt-pods begin their ripening. The belly resting on the smooth bedrock. Does he know it's chafing, feel pain? The pectorals, working like the fingers of a pianist listening, rapt, to the fugue that's holding him. The amazing pearlescent rainbows of the gill covers; the gills themselves, forcing the new toxic water, unfamiliar fresh after years of salt, to surrender its oxygen. 'A chemical masterpiece'.

And finally the head, engineered like a helmet but with a rare familiar intelligence: the eyes, that work, as Ted's do, 'for every cell of the body'. The mouth, analysing the water, working at it, like a babe at a mother's nipple. But wiser, more accepting, than a Hamlet: 'Unable not to be'. This is one who 'understands freedom', 'Becomes the sexual urge', 'the compendium of senses', 'learns + performs death'. Accepts his destiny, to mate and die. Even to think all this, to see it in his own mind's eye, is to realise: 'ocean I eat', and 'river I eat'. Is to see how ungainly, inadequate, by comparison, it is to be a man. That is 'Being two legged + mammal, + a teetering weight'.

He's 'a living nerve'.

But none of this is enough.
None of this draws the steely thread
Of magical being out his body.

It ends there.

*

On the last Sunday in May, over two years ago now, and two years after I first thought this book was finished, I leave the Duke of York at Iddesleigh at 4.30 a.m. The night before had been all thunder and lightning, and I spent the evening filling the endpapers of my battered copy of *River* with all I need. The diary that had left its mark on me first, and then, after the appendix, '?May Salmon?', in all its length; it only just fits.

At the tunnel of trees on the lane at Nethercott House a bat, on one of its last forays of the night, shows the way, just above my head, to a thrush, on its first dawn flight. I'm at Okement junction by 5.10, where I disturb a red deer. It bounces off across a hay meadow in seconds. I try going through the narrow fisherman's gate between the field-edge wire and the bank, but no one has been there before me. I retreat, pass the cow drink at Sprackmann's Pit. By 5.30 I'm at Island Run. The sky is on the boil; another thunderstorm's forecast for early morning. I lose track of time. The river murmurs to itself. It wears its brown, ignorant face; no one who didn't know would give it a second glance. But I see it: the concrete ramp, or the remains of it, the buttress, and more concrete along the water's edge just below.

And now I add a voice: my mouth, Ted's words. I read Ted's diary entry by the pool that inspired it, thirty-five years before. And then read '?May Salmon?' in its place. I watch the brown snake of the Torridge twist round the concrete buttress, which now has its own ash tree growing from its nose, watch the whorls of may blossom on the surface, white on the silt-stained brown, loosen, twist towards the near bank, the east, eddy. If a fish is there, it will be alert; the rain will have excited it. But I don't need to know. One day, as Ted must have known, sending it to Atlanta, people who care about the salmon will read it in full, even if by that point there are, God forbid, no wild salmon left for them to care about, except when they look back for signs of the glory and heroism of a nature that at last fell to human greed. In the meantime, it is enough to know this 'secret blood stuff' of the salmon, and the man who loved it, here.

15

Wildest Expectations: A Connemara Loop

One summer, perhaps, I'll travel to Alaska, find the junction of the Moose and the Copper River, watch king salmon surge upstream. I'd better make it soon: though one of the world's natural wonders, humanity's industrial exploitation of the planet's wild waters and their extraordinary inhabitants means that we can take none of the salmon runs for granted. And with luck I'll find myself in British Columbia, beside the Dean River, and fish for steelhead as Ted did and watch a bear ride a log down a flooded river from under a tarp. I have an invitation from a friend, and the unlikely and probably unpalatable promise of Ted's waders, twenty-something years after they last saw action.

But until then, I have Connemara.

*

It's July 2014. Two mornings after a long, long weekend at Doonreagan, the grand old house in Cashel that Richard Murphy had found for Ted to rent, where he and Assia and the children had spent six weeks in 1966.

Now it's just staged the second of its Ted Hughes Weekends. I'd come to the first, a year before: that was the appointment I had to keep when I left Roderick and Caroline Murphy at Isham and drove through the wild mountain country that rises around Maum Cross and keeps on rising all the way into the Connemara Bens, then falls towards that straggly Atlantic coast, and Richard's own High Island beyond. I'd returned to lecture, to listen, and – thanks to the implausible generosity of our host, Robert Jocelyn, who bought the place in the late sixties, and with his wife Ann Henning, a playwright, have made it even grander – to fish.

I arrived a day early, in time for my first thin Irish sea-trout – as white, in that dark water, as it was silver – to lunge at my fly from a pool beneath the opulence of Ballynahinch Castle, once owned by a cricketing Maharajah. And then, somewhat nervously, I stood at the lectern in the library converted from Doonreagan's old cowshed and dared to talk Irish pike to an Irish audience. But I needn't have worried. Conversations overflowed the room, spilt out between sessions onto the gravel, where local knowledge came to meet my presumption. There were fishermen there, poets, novelists, as well as dry-footed scholars. A generous company. Confessions and hints and directions came my way. And all this under skies that started bright then darkened and then released mist, drizzle, the odd brief downpour, then eased again. The river was low, needed much more rain than this if the day Robert had fixed for me on the Upper Ballynahinch water on the day of my flight home was to give me a real chance of a salmon. In fact, it needed to pour.

But I couldn't breathe a word of that wish. My friend Terry Gifford, a climber as well as a scholar, and a fine poet to boot, needed fine weather to climb the famous Carrot Ridge somewhere high in the Connemara Bens, as he'd longed to for years. And he was in luck. Though Robert and I did some desultory reconnaissance of Upper Ballynahinch that Sunday afternoon – two or three salmon heaved themselves out, well out of range, but only to wake themselves from a boredom we couldn't touch – we knew that same glittering light gave us little chance. Not until Terry and his climbing partner Lesley had joined us at the pub, exhilarated, in mid-evening, and the World Cup final was inching its way towards penalties, did we slip back to the river. Fishing started as the bats took to the wing in thick clouds of Irish midge. And three more little silver sea-trout came to me, thrilling the line and then the hand in a flurry of action just before midnight under the main Clifden road bridge.

On the Monday morning I'd woken too early. I blamed those mocking salmon, the darting pull of those fish still vivid on the fingers of my line hand, then dozed till it was time to wake. And I still had a day to kill before fishing again. At breakfast I suggested to Terry that I take him and our other friends, Neil Roberts, another distinguished Hughesian, and his wife Christine, who had only the morning to spare before heading home, on a tour of Connemara: the mountain road, then the twist west to the coast, then back. Bleak grandeur guaranteed.

We went north. I led. At Lough Inagh Lodge, one of the great fishing hotels, I persuaded Terry we needed coffee. We had to dash from the car. The teenager who served us told us it had been raining here all night. There were boats out on the Lough, in the rain. Heavy rain. Hopes stirred. The streams on the mountain flanks were white scars.

Back on the road immediately, and it was still raining hard. Soon I was stopping, joining a German photographer to wonder, and catch, the tumbling fury of a torrent tearing under the road. The bridge could barely contain it. But the water was pure, Guinness-dark, and where it foamed and then reformed itself a whiskey soda. Clear, though, clear. Good news.

Then we were turning left up a farm track, through a gate, and it was pouring; farm dogs out on the loose, bristling round the car as they rushed, anti-clockwise. And what Terry had wanted us to see – as rain eased, stopped for a minute, and allowed us all out of our cars: six standing stones, aligned on a mound to shadow-draw the line of the sun as it came over the mountain at winter solstice, bless its slopes for a sacred moment, clouds permitting, and move the year on, clockwise, towards a slow brightening. Beyond that, the vastness of the valley whose steep walls he'd scaled yesterday, and then as a door in the cloud swung open for a minute Carrot Ridge emerged, its wet marble gleaming. This time yesterday he'd traversed it. Trying that today would be madness, suicide.

North, to join the Lenane–Clifden road. And then west, along the wild Atlantic way, on the Connemara loop, to Cleggan farm, and the ramshackle roomful of silence across the bay from Cleggan where Ted found more peace, more of the freedom and flow he'd discovered at Doonreagan. Terry and Neil, who've been friends as long as they've been studying Ted's work, almost forty years now, stood and posed for me in the doorway where Ted had once posed for Jane Bown of the *Observer*. Unused to being in his footsteps, they seemed meek, even bewildered. I was moved to be showing them this place, which I'd discovered on my first visit here the year before. Five minutes later, across the bay, we went to Cleggan pier, where that same spring day in 1966 Bown had found another poet in his own world: Richard Murphy on the quay with the Galway hooker. And then I led them along the straggly coast road where otters rise from the sea lough, to Aughrisburg, where Ted and Nick fished together for the first time, and where a naked man rose from the water to fight his changeling as he cast for trout. Did I tell Neil this? Probably not. I was a long way off feeling ready to share my secret. We parted, anyway: Neil and Christine turned east for their ferry home.

And Terry? 'In your hands, Mark. Really.' Really?

I looked inland, east. Beyond Neil and Christine's shrinking car the peaks of the Connemara Bens were still lost in rain-heavy cloud. My thoughts turned back to that torrent under the road, and from there to another river, the Erriff, which I guessed had caught the same rain to the west and north of the Bens. The waterfalls at Aasleagh had been magnificent on the afternoon I'd seen them the previous May. But that had been in low water. How would they look now, I wondered?

As we drove, I told Terry what I knew about Aasleagh and the Erriff. Back in 1952, as a student poet home from Oxford, Richard Murphy had spent a summer as a riverwatcher, sleeping in an old cottage by day, and by night keeping poachers off the best pools. Robert had put me in touch with Richard, who sent me passages from the meticulous diary notebooks he always kept. He told me over email that in 1984 he turned poacher's friend, telling Ted of Dead Man's Pool, which lay out of sight of the road; and Paul Cullen, who was with Ted and Barrie when they tried it, said that on the day they were there it lived ... well ... up to its name. Hopeless. No life at all in the water. But that was where Ted had caught a salmon on a worm he cast into a reed-thronged backwater. Paul told me it defied logic. But logic's no rival for informed instinct, or hunter's magic. That same trip, after a wonderful day catching sea-trout from Doolough, the three friends had considered making an offer for Delphi Lodge, which sits in all its magnificence now, a disordered squat then, under a mountain at the head of the Bundorragha River.

By the time we got to Aasleagh the sun was out; we could hear the roar of the water from the bridge. We followed the path up the left bank, and gazed a while at the foaming wall of water a hundred yards away. Other walkers were crowding on this bank, but we retraced our steps, crossed the bridge over the road and went through the iron wicket gate and headed upstream through rhododendrons, to where a fish ladder ran up the weir close to the fisherman's path. Aasleagh Lodge was just above us at the crown of the pine-crowded knoll. Last May I'd wandered in, sneaked a picture of the beat map, drove upriver, found Dead Man's Pool, wandered to it through knee-high grass.

In trying this bank under the Lodge I wasn't just avoiding crowds. I thought I knew better, wondered if there might be some activity in the fish ladder right under the lodge. I was wrong. The water foamed over the lowest step impressively enough, but five minutes brought not a fish. Still, we were close enough – some ten yards away perhaps – from the main frontage of the falls to feel their power, so we stood there watching that. And almost at once my eye caught on a blur near the far bank, a flash, just above the surface of the water. Twenty-five seconds later, another. And then again.

Fish.

Salmon.

In mid-air.

I have a wobbly video of the minute that followed. My commentary ruins it. 'For God's sake … For *God's* sake … For God's *sake* …' But, of course, it wasn't for anyone's sake but their own. These fish had no choice but to take their chance, to respond to the teeming, bubbling energy of that freshly fallen downpour and press upstream from the sea. Only once had I seen a salmon leap before, at a weir on the Tanat, a tributary of the Severn, between Christmas and New Year, when I was nine or ten. Almost half a century later this baffling beauty of *Salmo salar*, salmo the leaper, seized me again.

Dead Man's Pool lay miles upstream; I knew the fish would pass, and guessed that eventually they'd learn their lesson and come east to the ladder, perhaps when the water had eased, or if, somewhere, those furies of water over natural rocks on the far side permitted them passage.

And now we realised why that crowd of other watchers were where they were, much closer to the salmon crashing – for God's sake, no! – into a wall of white water four times, at least, the height of their greatest leap. The further the fall, the fresher the water. How could the fish resist that excitement, at least at first? We hurried back downstream, crossed the bridge, did what we should have done in the first place: joined that crowd. But when it thinned, we stayed.

Terry had little choice. I was obsessed. It was simply, unutterably, overwhelmingly moving. I found a rock to which I could leap from the shore just under an overhanging hawthorn, where the fall was comparatively short – five feet or so, but still far too far for the fish that were, I now saw, in the teeming pool below me. Grey snouts kept showing every five or six seconds, as if they were extensions of the waves, but made flesh. Were they gauging the distance, preparing, summoning courage? And three or four times every minute, but never more predictably than that, a whole silver body shot writhing completely clear of the water. Some were finnock, harling, school peal – or, in Irish, the white trout; whatever you call them, here were sea-trout joining the salmon in the intoxication of the challenge above them. I began to understand why the gutsy fish I'd caught the night before were as thin, lean, gaunt in their ghostly silver as they were. Others were grilse, of four or five pounds in weight, doing this for the first time. There was the occasional larger salmon. I managed one shot of such a beast, my lens struggling to focus on it, catch it, in the spray. But then I found a way of stopping movement, choosing a shutter speed of one five-hundredth of a second in the bright sun, and tried and tried again to catch these smaller even more heroically selfless leapers in the act.

I got close. I saw, in the process, and again that night, when I reviewed what I'd caught, how the foaming water could be tricked from constant movement into rectilinear chambers of air; how much of that oxygen was reaching the fish below, spurring them to one more effort, and then another, and then another. Two fish I saw misjudge the direction of their leap, land on bare black rock, writhe forward, slip back down. How long could they take these defeats? How often would they try? Would they succeed? Or would a group mind take hold, the intercommunication devices Ted detected in sea-trout in the pool under Beam Weir on the Torridge, and lead some or all of these fish eventually across the main wall of the falls to the fish ladder and their onward journey?

I stayed there crouched for as long as my limbs would let me; an hour, Terry reckoned. I will never forget that hour.

And on most days that would have been more than enough. But it was barely lunchtime: a day already so implausibly full of the literary and the wildness of land and sky and people and fish was barely half done. So I thought back to one of the tips I'd received after my talk. The novelist Deirdre Madden had suggested we call at Oscar Wilde's fishing lodge. Terry and I had no idea he had one. Oh yes, Deirdre said. On Lough Fee, I think she'd said. At least, it sounded like 'Fee'. And it worked, when we asked for directions at an oyster shack above the Killary Fjord.

Ten minutes later and we were beside the lough, on a lonely road. A wooded promontory loomed to our left. Between the dense rhododendrons that overhung the water I glimpsed the stern of a fishing boat, but otherwise it looked like one forbidding, tangled bush. And when we found a lay-by to stop in and walked towards it, the rusted double gates we came to had a chain looped across them. But we lifted it clear, found a way. Ted would have done, we reckoned. And we were soon in a clearing, an imposing house to the right of its yard. Steps led up to a glazed door, and I remembered Deirdre's particular advice to peer through it. The lough glinted, and a slipway, through matching glazed windows beyond a staircase that rose from a narrow hallway. But then I saw the rod-racks, and rods in them, pointing up the stairs; and, getting used to the gloom, picked out an ornate Italianate frieze painted over the archway through to the lough room, bright cherubs disporting themselves with creatures that looked much closer to dolphins than trout. 'Tight lines', I read.

I took it all in, took a step back, gazed up; a sash window in a bedroom was three inches open. It was as if we'd missed the occupants – by a minute, not by more than 140 years. Oscar, Bosie, friends down here for the summer. It felt too good to be true. Could this really be an original frieze? Could this really be the right house? Our trespass had been too easy.

The door knocker answered me.

A verdigris fish, its pouting mouth the hinge, its body arching fully away from the door, the wrist of its tail the knocker, and the tail itself a cunning variation of the lacquered hand Ted imagined. Here it was split into a W, but with an O snug in the first wedge.

*

That day held other wonders. The rough little quayside at Rosroe, where Richard Murphy had first tried out the life of a poet, two years after Ludwig Wittgenstein had abandoned the dry courts of Cambridge to spend his own wild time there, thinking, writing, making friends with the birds. Then Roundstone, too, the village tucked into a fold of the southern coast. The great mapper of Connemara Tim Robinson lived here, I knew. But it will always be for me where, the year before, I'd spent an hour on the phone in the car listening to Paul Cullen, genius fisherman, while he was on his boat on Ree. That was when he'd told me about Ted and the Erriff, and that salmon in Dead Man's Pool, and their mad Delphi scheme. We had dinner in a pub on Roundstone's sea front, full of its own charms: a water scooter unzipping the sound as we pulled in and walked along the seafront; two dinghies full of sailors heading over to the village from their yachts moored a hundred yards out. I stared through them. I was back at Aasleagh, within touching distance of those driven fish; then peering again through that glazed door. Tight lines. What was it about this wild, magical place, where land leapt into mountains and crept down to gaze on water and wave, that had brought so many minds, in forms of escape, to kinds of discovery? So much more, clearly, than we had stumbled on in the course of a single day. Space. Peace. The farm at Cleggan. Ted's roomful of silence. And dedication, each of them, to drawing words from it, from deep in the body, or out of the air, onto paper, undisturbed, at least for an hour, or a twelve-hour day, and then another, and weeks, and months, of a life that needed to be simple, elemental. We knew we were just scratching that surface. Tourists. But humbled by what we'd seen.

*

We headed back. It was gone 10.00 p.m., but this was an Irish summer. Dusk was only now beginning to thicken. And my appetite for revelations was still sharp. So – Deirdre's recommendation having turned out so marvellously – I now recalled what her husband the poet Harry Clifton had told me. On their way to Doonreagan, they'd said, they'd stopped to watch a netsman at his surreptitious work, but seen an otter waiting, just beyond the net, for any fish he missed. That was at dusk, too, at high tide. So having crossed the humped bridge over the Owenmore at Toombeola, I pulled into the disused petrol station forecourt above the river as it eased out into its own small bay.

We walked back onto the bridge. Looked upstream. The river widened, and in fifty yards or so made a leisurely bend inland; across it flexed what I first thought was the net, but realised was instead a length of black polythene pipe. The lower boundary of the Ballynahinch Castle fishing, I guessed.

And then Terry pointed, hissed. 'Mark, an otter!'

He pointed down, just below the parapet. That's what Harry had told us to look for. And, yes, there was a head in the water, then nothing; and then three, four seconds later, a head broke surface ten feet to the left, out in mid-stream. And then, a second after, in by the bank. Could that possibly be the same animal, speed-of-light shape-shifter?

These weren't dark, furred heads, though. That otter in the Bridge Pool at Grimersta, and then that pair on the Tamar; there's no mistaking them. But then, now, again and again, all over the river, within seconds, snouts were breaking the surface, and then

dorsal fins, and backs, and tails, wriggling easily, dark water-grey
flashing silver as they did so. Salmon! A pod, at least a dozen of
them, just in off the tide, which sheer luck had brought us to the
bridge to witness, reacting to their first fresh water since last year
at least. None less than four pounds in weight, I guessed; some
much larger. It was like watching a family on an outing, or – as
I watched them from above, jostling, easing alongside each other,
frisking – like a herd of sleek elephants. Or dolphins. Were they
all feeling this return for the first time, or were some old hands,
leading the way? I was too inexpert, and the light too thick now,
for me to be sure.

By now, the cup of this day was well above the brim: to see
this quiet, murmuring, nudging gentle form of what, at Aasleagh,
we'd seen in all its fury: the working out of a purpose, between
salt and fresh, water and air, sea and river, self and the turning
inward and onward of the urge to reproduce, return home. This
shoal fresh from the tide, skittish, colts, bullocks, but relishing the
fresh water, getting used to it, anadromous. Too little pressure on
their organs, suddenly. The water lighter, less concentrated, after
the sea. And all this within sudden reach.

'It would be a good moment to fish for them,' says Terry.

And, of course, he's right, this resolute champion of the green,
this friendly antagonist, who had written to Ted in 1994 asking
him whether he could justify the pain he caused to fish. It hadn't
entered my head, but – now that I check – there's no sign there, no
private fishing, and if that really is the bottom of the Ballynahinch
fishery …

I take my smuggler from the car boot in a minute, and have
slipped over the parapet of the bridge and between gorse bushes
in another. I slot it together, thread line through the rings, select
a fly, one of Robert's, and the line is looping out gently over
the water, and I'm among them, swirling, moving, yards away.
I'm standing well back, crouching, working line out, twitching
it back and then stripping and wondering at, really wondering,
in wonder not frustration, why they're not taking – it would be
just too easy – but then remembering what I'd at some point in
the day been telling Terry of their diet at sea. So I draw in my

line, snip off Robert's fly, and replace it with a cartoon shrimp. Remember Ted on the Torridge that morning: moisten, try and test the half-blood knot so that it really holds. Then send out line, first inching it, then more firmly, rhythmically, and a touch, a brush, a murmur, and at last one is on! And the fish leaps and I know if I land it I won't kill it. I'm a catch-and-release poacher, a purist, and I play it from the hand not the reel, and loops of line slip from my fingers and the fish comes towards me and it's gone.

Every cast, then, for eight or ten, my line miraculously gentle for a change, the loops I make deft, easy, searching, every cast finds them, brings murmurs and swirls and brief contact in the fading light with a family group now inevitably moving upstream. Whether they've been spooked by what one has just told them, chemically, of the sharp shrimp I can't know but Ted might. And then the puckering and skirls and swirls and fin dark movements cease, my line feels lonely searching an empty river, and Terry, looking up from his notebook, tells me they're gone. I say: 'It's over', and he says, 'No it's not', from the bridge, smiling, gesturing at his pad, his pen, his head, and he's right. It's just changed element, moved into words.

*

One thirty a.m. Immediately wide awake. A still night; no more rain. I lay in the darkness for a while, thinking of those fish. Still moving upstream in the darkness, the night sky awash with silhouettes of leaves, twigs, whatever is brought down above their heads in the new stream, their new water. They'd be leaping the Owenmore's falls and ladders. And now I loaded and looked at the pictures I'd taken from Aasleagh, 350 stills of water and fish and foam in different configurations; and for minutes after I'd closed the lid of the laptop those pictures swirled.

I had a longish drive ahead: to Shannon, that afternoon, for my flight home. I needed sleep.

What to do but write?

For two hours, three, I wrote. Much more than I've left here. The first I'd written since my talk on the Saturday. I hadn't had a

night like it since my last night in Rose Cottage above the Tamar
back at the end of March 2012, when all I'd heard and read and
seen that week of Ted's poems and their places rushed and roared
and needed recording, before I left the valley. Of course I was
weary now, as well as elated; fingers slipped as well as danced.
And so, at some point – no, at 3.25 a.m., saving my words to the
cloud, flipping the cover shut, lying back in teeming darkness,
then at once remembering something I'd left out – my decision
not to push our luck, after that marvel at the waterfall, to keep
Delphi and Doolough to myself – I sat back up, awoke the screen.
And saw this, irrupting into the middle of one of my sentences:

Ireland came up to Nicky's wildest expectations.

Ted, of course: my transcription of a letter to Leonard Baskin in
the British Library. At the last minute on Saturday I'd wondered
about using it for my talk. He mentions the 'friend of mine who'd
set this up'. Barrie, of course. It's October 1977. Ted will get to
Nick's great queen. But first he has his own fantastic tales to tell.
Of rowing himself out into the action in Barrie's armchair-sized
coracle. Of his own first cast, and the fish so deep-throated that it
cut the line above the ten-inch steel wire trace. And then, three or
four hours later, the explosive consequence:

> the surface burst and what looked like a crocodile came
> writhing vertically into the air. It spent the rest of the day
> crashing in and out. It was the pike I'd hooked trying to get
> rid of my hooks in its jaws – probably in its throat. Once or
> twice we got quite near it. It was four feet long.

I'm quite near it too. And not just that big fish. Once more I'm in
the Manuscripts Room, but now on that first afternoon. I'm by
the Torridge, staring down at that smudge on my thumb. Ted's
hooked me again. I feel, in that darkness, completely alive.

At 4.15 a.m. I hear the first birdsong. Another Connemara
loop is about to begin.

What now to do but fish?

The road inland to the pool at Upper Ballynahinch where we'd caught sea-trout is all mine. Ziggurats of cut peat stand in the dew-drenched shadows of the rough moorland tussocks from which they'd been lifted. The sun gilds the cloud-edges above the Bens. Half an hour later, light finds the water as it flows under the bridge of the main Galway–Clifden road where I am casting, and dusts the few flies already dancing in the bright steam. I fish my way down under the bridge, twice, three times, become fascinated by the luminosity of the drumlin beyond the pool caught in the light while, in the shadow of the bridge, I'm still in touch with dark water. Claimed by it.

The water's higher by three or four inches, but perfectly clear; the excitement of that and my fatigue turn my thoughts upstream, under the bridge when the sun comes up, whiteness, to a river amazed at itself. A sandpiper, alarmed at my presence, dances and flits to and fro.

Still nothing. Conditions are as good as they're going to get. Where the channel spreads out beyond a bluff on the near bank into a huge pool, almost a lake, a hundred yards long and fifty wide, there are big fish moving, purposefully. But can I touch them? What I'd give now for a tug, a pull. But by 7.30 I'm yawning. I've given all I have. Back on my station under the drumlin, I slip. Impale my hand on the rock, then, trying to get to a point on the bank where I could cast for those distant fish, misjudge the width of a ditch, or my capacity to clear it, and go in up to my knee. I don't even need a Milesian suck hole to swallow me.

I retreat, for breakfast, and Robert and Ann's old newspapers, to dry my boot. Here, Robert says, try these: Silver Badgers, small but, he assures me, deadly patterns for salmon on the river. Silver tinsel ribs the black body of the fly; you spin their hackle from a single black-cored, white-tipped feather; a blue tag at the tail catches the eye.

One last try. Terry comes back with me. Are you sure, I ask? Few things are more tedious than watching a fisherman. But Terry has his notebook: 'Don't you worry about me.'

Back under the bridge, I work my way down, patient, methodical, covering the water. Fish continue to move, their necks and backs showing like frisking colts. And now almost within range. But oblivious to the charm of the Silver Badgers. I rest the water, move downstream, leaping this time like a breakfasted gazelle. Pick my way back up to the bridge. Twenty minutes to go.

And then I thought: what would Ted do?

I know he never fished this water. It's tantalising. Their weeks at Doonreagan in 1966 though in the wake of that great dream on the high Taw, were in February and March, too early in the year for the main salmon run. In 1985 he and Dermot Wilson talked of visiting – that letter of thanks for his first day on the Test which Renée showed me had ended with the resolve not to forget Ballynahinch: it was a favourite resort, John Spooner told me, of Piggy's. But I knew from Richard Murphy and a couple of other Irish friends that Ted had never returned to read in Connemara, for all their attempts to dress up their invitations with the offer of free fishing.

I think of Ted's fly boxes, in his and now my Cambridge college, on permanent loan from his Westcountry Rivers Trust. Among them, one small plastic tub stuffed full of one pattern. I think of his first Grimersta diary: the one fish of the day came on the river to one of those same flies, a Muddler. Its head, of clipped deerhair, each fibre hollow, is naturally buoyant. Ted 'dibbled' it – raising the rod tip and reducing the line on the water to ensure the fly spent as long as possible dancing alluringly, with a visible wake, in the fast water at the head of a pool. Even if salmon didn't take it, they'd be sufficiently intrigued to turn away and down and take a heavier fly on the point, inches underwater.

I find a Muddler I'd bought specially: though there must be a dozen in that plastic tub in my office, I've never dared use one, in case I lose it, violate the terms of that permanent loan. I steel myself with the lines I'd read to Barrie at Graiguenamanagh, that had held him then, cleared his failing memory:

One moment nothing ...
The next, solid communication
with the prize.

Then flick it out.

Ten yards down, where the flow begins to ease, and pleated currents fill and spread, out in mid-stream, I master the technique. The fly dances, the water split around the head of the lure, and I keep it there in the current. And after 200 casts that morning, 300, nothing, I watch the surface burst and a large snout rise and turn on the Muddler, and I lift, rod and soul, and the river explodes and the line slides sharp and true away and within me.

Contact.

But this time contact's never going to be enough. Just as on the Mole with John Martin and in the glimmering grey of a Grimersta dawn, it hurts too much, the violent pulsing throb in the shoulder I relish still, the lunge and rush of a wild fish, that has proved its strength in returning to the river of its spawning, trying to get free. Days – or hours, maybe, here – of fresh water, of not eating, have not yet dimmed its strength. Now I must contain it. All I have is concentrated in what's needed to bring this silver and dark explosion to the net.

The net!

Where is the net?

Robert had offered me a great dark folding triangle of a net. I'd almost left it behind as embarrassingly too big, tempting fate. But I brought it. It lies ten feet away, behind me, up the bank, out of reach. Is it too soon to look for it, too risky, tempting fate? The salmon has an answer: he leaps, wrenching; I dip the rod; the fish hits the water, the line still taut, the hook set. I draw the fish upstream, still in the body of the current; I see that silver, feel its swirling writhing power, but then his composure in the oxygenated current. He recovers. Downstream he surges again.

But then Terry's at the top of the bluff. 'Do you need this?' Assisting, keen. He hands me the net; with the line caught between the finger of my rod hand and the rod's cork handle, I flick the arms of the net away from its handle, into place. Lay it beside me in the water, then, at the third attempt, bring the salmon over it, lift the net around his body. Done.

Panting, I sink on it, him, it. Stare. At the lithe beauty. The freshness. The machined power.

And I kill that wild fresh salmon.

*

Regrets? Of course. I will never kill another. Writing this book has made that clear to me. The rivers need their salmon more than I do. And the last years and months of writing have brought proof of how much Ted's example, the lesson he learned in caring for the salmon and the water they swim, still needs our attention. Our salmon are still in decline. We must do all we can to understand why.

But that fish wasn't wasted. I took it back to Doonreagan, and with Robert's help and newspaper and a plastic binbag and duct tape made a parcel of it to lie diagonally across my suitcase, which then somehow cleared Shannon Airport's X-rays and came unscathed up Stansted's baggage reclaim chute and into my grateful hands. I got home after midnight: I eased it into clingfilm, slid it, just, into the largest drawer of my freezer. Recalling John Martin's advice that day on the Mole, I didn't gut it. I cleaned it on the day we ate it with my family, out in our Cambridgeshire garden. To my brother-in-law and his wife and our niece and nephew and my son and my wife, and to me, that flesh was delicious. But to me it was also sea, river. And the knowledge of both it brought me. A gift, too. Robert's, of course, and I thank him for it. But Ted's above all.

The catch.

Sources

Ted Hughes's papers in the British Library were made available to the public in 2010, under the call sign Add MS 88198. Most of his fishing diaries are at Add MS 88918/122-5; the leather-bound Victorian ledger in which the 1983 season is described is at Add MS 88918/122/5.

1. CONTACT

p. 1   'in the Green Devon evening light … river': from Ted Hughes's 'Taw and Torridge', in Anne Voss Bark, ed., *West Country Fly Fishing* (London: Robert Hale, 1983; revised paperback edn, 1998), pp. 25–39; p. 30.

2. RIVER

p. 9   'Selections of his letters': Christopher Reid, ed. and selected, *Letters of Ted Hughes* (London: Faber and Faber, 2007; hereafter *LTH*), p. 433. The friend to whom Ted wrote in June 1980 about losing the power of forming words after fishing was his Cambridge contemporary, the academic and founding editor of the *London Review of Books* Karl Miller.

p. 11   'never write anywhere near fishing': the writer to whom he told this was Anne Stevenson in 1986, *LTH*, p. 521.

p. 11 'A Taw flood can look like blood ...': 'Taw and Torridge', p. 31; 'The most enthralling thing ...': 'Taw and Torridge', p. 36.

p. 11 'Night Arrival of Sea-Trout': in *River* (London: Faber and Faber, 1983); reprinted with significant revisions and notes in *Three Books* (London: Faber and Faber, 1993); paperback edition reflecting these revisions and notes, and cited hereafter (London: Faber and Faber, 2011), p. 55.

p. 14 'in the upside-down ...': 'September Salmon', in *River*, p. 43.

p. 14 'Up in the Pools': 'A Milesian Encounter on the Sligachan', in *River*, p. 50.

p. 15 Ted Hughes's letters to Peter Keen are in Peter Keen's papers, also at the British Library, Add MS 88614.

p. 16 'finished more or less ...': letter to the literary critic Keith Sagar, in Sagar's papers at the British Library, Add MS 78759, but also collected in Keith Sagar, ed., *Poet and Critic: The Letters of Ted Hughes and Keith Sagar* (London: The British Library, 2012; hereafter *PC*), p. 91.

p. 16 'the verse text ...': *PC*, p. 96.

p. 17 The copy of *Animal Poems* signed and inscribed for Nicholas is available to the public in the Ted Hughes collection at the Library of Pembroke College, Cambridge; 'alive in the river of light': 'That Morning', in *River*, pp. 73–4.

p. 18 'these pad-clusters': 'Visitation', in *River*, p. 63

p. 21 'Charlie' and 'Peter the corn farmer' are in '1984 on the Tarka Trail', in ibid., pp. 13–4.

p. 21 Within three months of making my own visit, equipped with my own rough transcription, the maps Ted Hughes drew for Peter Keen were published online: <granta.com/dear-peter/>

p. 22 'the most enthralling': BL Add MS 122/5 f14.

p. 22 'Four March Watercolours': *River*, pp. 85–9.

p. 24 The box advertisement appeared in *Trout and Salmon* as follows: March 1982, p. 112; April 1982, p. 114; and May 1982, p. 105.

3. STEALING TROUT

p. 27   'Ted's main dream come true ...' Peter Steinberg and Karen Kukil, eds, *Letters of Sylvia Plath*, Vol. II: 1956–1963 (London: Faber and Faber, 2018; hereafter *LSP*, II), p. 639.
Sylvia's letters are the source of many of the details in the following pages.

p. 27   no thatch: *LSP*, II, p. 637.

pp. 27–8 See 'Error', 'The Lodger', 'The Afterbirth' and 'Suttee', poems from *Birthday Letters*, in Paul Keegan, ed., Ted Hughes, *Collected Poems* (London: Faber and Faber, 2003; hereafter *CP*), pp. 1121–8, 138–9.

p. 30   'just a tug & a thump ...': *LTH*, p. 198. The complete letter, from 9 May 1962, with details of Ted's rod and line, and Sylvia's note, is in the Ted Hughes papers at the Lilly Library, University of Indiana at Bloomington. I am grateful to Peter Steinberg for this information.

p. 31   'Stealing Trout on a May Morning': *River*, pp. 38–41.

p. 32   'the best ever evocation ...': James Driver, 'Catching Pike with the Poet Laureate', *Waterlog* 67, pp. 42–3.

4. 'I FISHED IN STILL WATER ...'

p. 39   The weekend visit of the Wevills is the subject of extensive treatment in Yehuda Koren and Eilat Negev, *A Lover of Unreason: The Life and Tragic Death of Assia Wevill, Ted Hughes's Doomed Lover* (London: Robson, 2006) and in Jonathan Bate, *Ted Hughes: The Unauthorised Life* (London: William Collins, 2015), pp. 185–6.

p. 39   A huge golden serpent: 'The Rag Rug', *CP*, p. 1132.

p. 39   'Had a globed, golden eye': 'Dreamers', *CP*, p. 1146.

p. 40   'No dreams': 'Dream Life', *CP*, p. 1135.

p. 40   'refused to interpret': 'Dreamers', *CP*, p. 1146.

p. 41   'the grandfather pike': *LTH*, p. 96.

p. 41   'Stop this': *PC*, p. 74.

p. 41   'shamelessly plagiarized': Peter K. Steinberg and Karen K. Kukil, eds, *Letters of Sylvia Plath*, Vol. I: 1940–1956 (London: Faber and Faber, 2017), p. 1292. Sylvia's 'terribly humorous little story' is 'The Wishing Box', in *Jonny Panic and the Bible of Dreams*, ed. Ted Hughes (London: Faber and Faber, 1977), pp. 48–55.

pp. 40–52   Sources for these details include Richard Murphy, 'A Memoir of Sylvia Plath and Ted Hughes in Connemara, September 1962', in Anne Stevenson, *Bitter Fame: A Life of Sylvia Plath* (London: Penguin, 1989), pp. 348–54. Barrie Cooke, 'With Ted Hughes', in Nick Gammage, ed., *The Epic Poise: A Celebration of Ted Hughes* (London: Faber and Faber, 1999), pp. 214–15; Barrie Cooke's letters to Jack Sweeney in the Sweeney papers at University College Dublin; a letter from Ted Hughes to Barrie Cooke in the Barrie Cooke archive at Pembroke College, Cambridge, GBR/1058/COO/2/2/1, and Aidan Dunne, *Barrie Cooke* (Dublin: Douglas Hyde Gallery, 1986).

p. 43   'A pond I fished': 'Pike', *CP*, pp. 84–6. A typescript of this poem is in a letter he sent to Gerald in late August 1958. Gerald Hughes papers, Manuscripts and Rare Books Library (hereafter MARBL), Emory University, Box 1 folder 2.

p. 43   'It had grown so directly': Moira Doolan's letters to Ted Hughes are in the BBC written archive, Caversham. The first of his broadcasts, 'Capturing Animals', was transmitted on the BBC Home Service on 6 October 1961.

p. 44   'classified secret': Letter to Terry Gifford, *LTH*, p. 694.

p. 45   David threatened: Bate, *Ted Hughes: The Unauthorised Life*, p. 190.

p. 45   'the virginity of [their] marriage': *LSP*, II, p. 796.

           'a good place': Sylvia Plath, 'Burning the Letters', Sylvia Plath, *Collected Poems* (London: Faber and Faber, 1981), p. 204.

p. 47   'pulling herself wide open': Ted Hughes, *Gaudete* (London: Faber and Faber, 1977), p. 110.

p. 49   'to wash on his paint ...': James White, 'Stimulating Paintings by Barrie Cooke', *Irish Times*, 29 March 1962, p. 5.

p. 49   'God yawns onto the black water': 'Fishing at Dawn', *CP*, p. 126.

p. 49   'you were slim': '18 Rugby Street', *CP*, p. 1048.

p. 49   'the colossal, horrendous Aztec mother': Ted Hughes, 'The Hanged Man and the Dragonfly', in William Scammell, ed., Ted Hughes, *Winter Pollen: Occasional Prose* (London: Faber and Faber, 1994), pp. 90–3.

p. 51   'completely happy': Ted Hughes to Seamus Heaney, 21 October 1992, in Seamus Heaney papers at MARBL, Emory University, Box 40, folder 16.

p. 53   'Thinking is as natural as breathing': This and other quotations from 'Learning to Think', one of Hughes's broadcasts for *Listening and Writing*, republished with slight revisions in *Poetry in the Making* (1967), pp. 56–61. Here I quote his broadcast, from May 1963, included in a double CD, Ted Hughes, *The Spoken Word: Poetry in the Making* (London: British Library, 2008) disc 1, track 13.

p. 56   'a lifeline': Introductory note to 1993 *River*, p. 75.

p. 56   'five inches huge': 'The Canal's Drowning Black', *CP*, p. 477.

p. 56   'as it really happened': *LTH*, pp. 422–3; and 'The Burnt Fox', *Winter Pollen*, pp. 8–9.

5. HEADWATERS

p. 59   'catching big fish': BL Add MS 88918/128/1 f9r.

p. 60   Some of Hughes's book reviews are in *Winter Pollen*. 'Opposing Selves' is from his review of Pushkin's letters, pp. 48–9; 'If, by some spectacular development', p. 55, about T. C. Lethbridge's *Ghost and Divining-Rod* (London: Routledge and Kegan Paul, 1963), p. 51, and 'a technique of moving' from a review of Mircea Eliade's *Shamanism: Archaic Techniques of Ecstasy*, translated from the French by Willard R. Trask (London: Routledge and Kegan Paul, 1964), pp. 57–8.

p. 61   'Ted Hughes introduces': BBC Genome is a useful online source of information for dates and such accompanying descriptions of broadcasts.

p. 61   'a very necessary passion': *The Spoken Word: Poetry in the Making*, disc 1, track 26.

p. 62   'about how poetry', Ted Hughes, letter to Assia Wevill, 31 August 1965, in Bate, *Ted Hughes: The Unauthorised Life*, p. 244.

p. 63   'the life flows unselfconsciously': *LTH*, p. 250.

p. 63   'completely': *LTH*, p. 710; besides Nick Hughes, in this letter, the other person Ted Hughes told was Thomas Pero, 'So Quickly It's Over', *Wild Steelhead & Salmon* 5.2 (Winter 1999), p. 50.

p. 64   'Ireland had fish in it': Frieda Hughes, *Forty-Five: Poems* (New York: HarperCollins, 2006), p. 9.

p. 64   'one of the Plesiosaur type': *LTH*, p. 256.

p. 65   'The lake was like glass': *LTH*, p. 56.

p. 66   Sonja Landweer told me about Connemara in April 2016 at her home, Jerpoint, in Co. Kilkenny. Conversations and email correspondence with both Richard Murphy and Paul Cullen supply other details.

p. 67   'watching father and son': Frieda Hughes, *Forty-Five*, p. 10.

p. 67   'poaching': Ted Hughes papers, MARBL, Emory University, Box 113, folder 20, 'Earlier Days on the Upper Taw', published as 'Trout on the Upper Taw' in *Taw Fisheries Association News Letter* (Summer 1990), p. 6.

p. 67   'with their hopes pre-set': 'Taw and Torridge', pp. 27–8.

p. 67   'fifty yards across': 'Pike', *CP*, p. 85.

p. 68   'basin of black mud': *LTH*, p. 287.

p. 68   'We fished all day': Barrie Cooke to Jack Sweeney, Sweeney papers, University College Dublin.

p. 69   'In the beginning': 'Snow Song', *CP*, p. 266. Hughes's *Crow* drafts are in the Ted Hughes papers at MARBL, Emory University, Box 62, folder 24.

p. 69   Barrie Cooke's letters to Ted Hughes are in the Ted Hughes papers at MARBL, Emory University, Box 2, folders 14 and 15. Letters here in folder 14.

p. 70   Ted dreams: Reported by Ekbert Faas in *Ted Hughes: The Unaccommodated Universe* (Santa Barbara: Black Sparrow Press, 1980), p. 124.

p. 70   'so you can look through the shine on water': *LTH*, p. 312.

p. 70   'flow of good inspiration': Ted's great letter to Nick is in *LTH*, pp. 707–13.

p. 72   'from the warmed blue hills': 'Spring Nature Notes', in *Season Songs*, *CP*, p. 310.

p. 72   'For the angler who lives near the river': Introduction to 'The River in March', *The Spoken Word: Poetry in the Making*, disc 2, track 9.

p. 72   'A salmon, a sow of solid silver': *CP*, p. 308.

p. 72   Barrie's remote encouragement: Ted Hughes papers, MARBL, Emory University, Box 2, folder 14.

p. 73   'lifts his line': *Gaudete*, p. 79; the scene runs from pp. 77 to 83.

p. 74   '<u>real</u> salmon fishing': *LTH*, p. 711.

p. 74   'I go to find salmon': 'December River', *CP*, pp. 339–41.

p. 74   'the Taw near here': Peter Keen papers, BL Add MS 88614.

p. 74   'the fact that they're so scarce now': *The Spoken Word: Poetry in the Making*, disc 2, track 23.

p. 75   'Earth-Numb': *River*, pp. 22–3.

p. 76   'emotion recollected in tranquility': William Wordsworth, 'Preface' to *Lyrical Ballads*, (1798, second edition 1800).

p. 76   'to make an image': BBC Radio 3 broadcast, 17 May
             1980, in Ted Hughes, *The Spoken Word: Poems and
             Stories* (London: British Library, 2008), disc 2, track 20.

p. 76   'I caught 2 salmon': *PC*, p. 55.

p. 77   'the wonderful River Mole': Note to 'Rain-Charm for
             the Duchy', *CP*, p. 1215.

p. 78   'Mink and the cheese factory followed': 'Trout on the
             Upper Taw', BL Add MS 88918/6/12.

p. 80   What Ted had said about the hundred salmon:
             introducing 'October Salmon' on the Faber poetry
             cassette Ted Hughes & Paul Muldoon (London, Faber
             & Faber, 1983).

p. 81   'Don't try to write about things': *PC*, p. 131.

7. STRANGERS

p. 105   'He was fishing for seatrout': Michael Morpurgo,
             Introduction to Henry Williamson, *Salar the Salmon*
             (Stanbridge: Little Toller Books, 2010), p. 12.

p. 105   'The most enthralling moment', 'faded': Fishing diary,
             BL Add MS 88918/122/5, May 1983.

p. 106   'on what was Lemon Gray's own water': 'Taw and
             Torridge', p. 34.

p. 106   'a totally enlivened': Seamus Heaney, in Dennis
             O'Driscoll, *Stepping Stones: Interviews with Seamus
             Heaney* (London: Faber and Faber, 2008), p. 95.

p. 106   'Jerpointing': Seamus Heaney to Ted Hughes, 28
             October 1982, exhibited in 'Listen Now Again',
             Dublin: National Library of Ireland.

p. 107   'you're doomed': Seamus Heaney, 'The Salmon Fisher
             to the Salmon', in *Door into the Dark* (London: Faber
             and Faber, 1969), p. 18.

p. 109   'giant flotilla': Tom Rawling, 'Techniques to induce
             big fish to take', *Trout and Salmon*, June 1970, in
             John Wilshaw, ed., *The Best of Trout and Salmon*
             (London: Virgin, 1994).

p. 109   'you came to my lure': Tom Rawling, 'Fisherman
                to Salmon', in Anne Stevenson, intro., *How
                Hall: Poems and Memories. A Passion for Ennerdale*
                (Lamplugh: Lamplugh and District Heritage Society,
                2009), p. 72.

pp. 109–116 I am grateful to Sue Slater and Jane Rawling for sight
                of their father's correspondence with Ted Hughes,
                and for permission to quote from Tom's letters.
                I do not, of course, quote from any letter from Ted
                Hughes still in private hands.

p. 112   'Night Arrival of Sea-Trout': *River*, p. 55.

p. 115   'After Moonless Midnight': *River*, p. 91.

p. 115   'An August Evening' was subsequently retitled
                'August Evening': *River*, pp. 66–7.

p. 115   'Falkus's dictum: 'Taw and Torridge', p. 36.

p. 115   'the Torridge acquires': 'Taw and Torridge', p. 28.

p. 116   'He'd be a bold man': Hugh Falkus, *Salmo the
                Leaper* (BBC films, 1977).

p. 116   'too immense': 'Pike', *CP*, p. 85.

p. 118   'he had the key to Paradise': BL Add MS 88918/35/37.

p. 119   'The big heavy strangers': BL Add MS 99818/7/4.

p. 120   'There they actually are': 'Strangers', *River*, pp. 59–60.

p. 123   'extraordinary intercommunication system': 'Taw
                and Torridge', p. 35.

p. 124   'the opposition': BL Add MS 88918/122/5 f17r.

8. GREAT IRISH PIKE

p. 129   'a beautiful thirty pounder': Barrie Cooke to Ted
                Hughes, Ted Hughes papers, MARBL, Emory
                University, Box 2, folder 14.

p. 130   'A tragedy': Barrie Cooke to Ted Hughes, ibid.

p. 130   'mania for pike-fishing': Ted Hughes to Gerald
                Hughes, *LTH*, p. 388.

p. 131   'lair theory': Barrie Rickards, 'Hot Spots and the
                Lair Theory, in Barrie Rickards and Ray Webb,

Fishing for Big Pike (London: A & C Black, 1971, second edition, 1976), pp. 144–54.

p. 131   'moderate', 'your chances of': Barrie Rickards, 'Fishing for Big Pike five years on', in *Angling* Special Issue 1976, 'Modern Coarse Fishing Techniques', p. 23.

p. 131   'How complete + final': Ted Hughes wrote two accounts in his journal of this day, BL Add MS 88918/128/2 ff21-30, from which quotations follow over the next pages.

p. 133   'Lough na Cashel's great queen': 'Some Pike for Nicholas', *CP*, pp. 1191–2.

p. 134   'an unusual talent': *LTH*, p. 389.

p. 134   his own first cast: Details of Ted Hughes's own dramatic introduction to Irish pike are in a letter to Leonard Baskin, Baskin–Hughes papers, BL Add MS 83685 f61.

p. 134   new Mark IV carp rods: Ted Hughes letter to Barrie Cooke, in the Cooke archive, Pembroke College, Cambridge. GBR/1058/COO/2/2/11.

p. 134   'terrifying to all pikes', 'second great pike attack': Barrie Cooke to Ted Hughes, 8 February and 16 March (1978), Ted Hughes papers, MARBL, Emory University, Box 2, folder 14.

p. 134   a humbling: Ted Hughes's diary of their March 1978 trip is at BL Add MS 88918/122/2 ff172-181.

p. 135   'summer campaign', Ted Hughes to Barrie Cooke, in the Cooke archive, Pembroke College, Cambridge. GBR/1058/COO/2/2/11.

p. 135   'He persuaded Keith Sagar': *PC*, pp. 66, 68.

p. 135   'Loch Och': Ted Hughes's diary of the autumn 1979 trip to Sligo and Roscommon is at BL Add MS 88918/122/2 ff152-167.

p. 136   one of Barrie's sketchbooks: in the Cooke archive, Pembroke College, Cambridge, GBR/1058/COO/2/3/2.

p. 137   Barrie Cooke's 'Lough Derg Pike, with relics', is in the Crawford Gallery, Cork. I'm most grateful to Dave Hatwell, Fred Buller's archivist, for details of Buller's correspondence with Barrie Cooke.

p. 138   'far warier': BL Add MS 88918/122/2 f157r.

p. 138   'In future': BL Add MS 88918/122/2 f157v.

p. 138   'a memento': Barrie Cooke letter to Ted Hughes, Ted Hughes papers, MARBL, Emory University, Box 2, folder 14.

p. 138   'the perfect lake': Barrie Cooke, interview with Dorothy Cross, in *Barrie Cooke* (Dublin: Irish Museum of Modern Art, 2011), p. 94.

p. 138   'pike-ness', 'It just might be': Barrie Cooke letter to Ted Hughes, Ted Hughes papers, MARBL, Emory University, Box 2, folder 15.

p. 139   Ted Hughes wrote contemporaneous notes and then a diary of the December trip to Gur; the first at Add MS 88918/122/2 f134r-139v, the latter at BL Add MS 88918/128/3 ff55-58.

p. 139   Ted Hughes's diary of the March/April fishing trip to Ireland is at BL Add MS 88918/122/2 f3-f56.

p. 139   'Eighty, and Still Fishing for Salmon': *River*, p. 69.

p. 140   'like a gigantified Charlie Weeks': BL Add MS 88918/122/2 f17.

p. 140   'That Morning': *River*, pp. 73-4.

p. 140   'It's just the most beautiful place': *LTH*, p. 439; the complete letter is in the Cooke archive at Pembroke College, Cambridge, GBR/1058/COO/2/2/12.

p. 141   'Thoughts of how': BL Add MS 88918/122/2 f33-4.

p. 141   'inner émigré': 'Exposure', in Seamus Heaney, *North* (London: Faber & Faber, 1975), p. 73.

p. 141   'this year's visible deterioration': Ted Hughes's record of his and Nick Hughes's April stay at Gur is at BL Add MS 88918/122/2 ff42-50.

p. 144   'my boy, my dream alive': 'Some Pike for Nicholas', *CP*, p. 1192.

p. 144   'The Great Irish Pike': Ibid., pp. 627-8.

p. 144   'Poems and drawings': For a fuller account see my essay ' "The Great Irish Pike": Ted Hughes and the Art of Poetry', in *Anglistik* 25.1 (2014), pp. 129-39.

p. 144   'Jungian analysis': Ted Hughes's account of their last trip to Gur is at BL Add MS 88918/122/2 ff168-172. His bedtime reading was Daryl Sharp, *The Secret Raven: Conflict and Transformation in the Life of Franz Kafka* (Toronto: Inner City Books, 1980).

9. AN ANCIENT THIRST

p. 153   'solid communication': Ted Hughes's verse diary of his trip in February-March 1980 is at BL Add MS 88918/128/3 ff6-14.

p. 154   'the skull tower': 'River Barrow', *River*, pp. 47–8.

p. 155   'summer campaign': Ted Hughes to Barrie Cooke, 1978, Cooke archive, Pembroke College, Cambridge, GBR/1058/COO/2/2/11. Ted Hughes's prose diary of the 1978 summer trip is at BL Add MS 88918/122/2 ff147r-151r; the trip to the Murphys' house and then camping and fishing on the Barrow is described at f148r. A manuscript draft, dated 12 July, torn from the same notebook, is in the Ted Hughes papers, MARBL, Emory University, Box 75, folder 7.

p. 156   'Tiny sedge-flies', 'River Barrow': *River*, pp. 47–8.

p. 162   Barrie was excited in that letter: Barrie Cooke letter to Ted Hughes, Ted Hughes papers, MARBL, Emory University, Box 2, folder 14.

p. 163   'Go Fishing': *River*, pp. 31–2.

p. 165   'I dearly love': to Terence McCaughey, *LTH*, p. 615.

p. 167   'The Dagda meets the Morrigu': Inscription in Barrie Cooke's guest book, in the Cooke archive at Pembroke College, Cambridge, GBR/1058/COO/8/5.

p. 171   'For although both Hughes and Cooke': The blurb, cover and trial image for 'XV Poems' and Barrie Cooke's letters to Liam Miller are in the Dolmen Press archive at Wake Forrest University.

p. 174   'Farmer ferries': BL Add Ms 88918/122/2 f148r.

10. VISITATIONS

p. 177   'lost her insides': The visit to Borris and the Barrow is described at BL Add MS 88918/122/2 ff35-40.

p. 179   Nick's Oxford zoologist friends: email correspondence with Peter Holland.

p. 182   'As kingfishers catch fire': Gerard Manley Hopkins, in *Gerard Manley Hopkins: The Oxford Authors*, ed. Catherine Phillips (Oxford: Oxford University Press, 1986), p. 129.

p. 185   'raggle-taggle tumbledown river': 'The Kingfisher', *River*, p. 61.

p. 186   'Fishermen understand why Christ was said to be a fish': Ted Hughes papers, MARBL, Emory University, Box 56, folder 10.

p. 187   'raised + touched one fish': BL Add MS 88918.122.2 f56.

p. 188   'The otter comes here in the winter': 'The Recluse', *CP*, p. 6.

p. 188   'So the self under the eye': 'An Otter', *CP*, pp. 79–80.

p. 188   'ended up in my childhood dream': The letter is to Mark Hinchliffe. *LTH*, p. 686.

p. 189   '1984 on the Tarka Trail': *River*, pp. 13–14.

p. 189   'A peculiar, thin warbling': *Gaudete*, pp. 173–4.

p. 190   In one old story: The *Buile Suibhne*, translated by Seamus Heaney as *Sweeney Astray* (London: Faber & Faber, 1983) and illustrated by Barrie Cooke in 1984.

p. 191   'one dawn in a year': 'Visitation', in *River*, p. 62.

11. MILESIAN ENCOUNTERS

p. 193   'campinggrounds': Ted Hughes's diary of his fishing trip to Skye and then Harris in August 1981 is at BL Add MS 88912/122/2 ff130r-133v.

p. 196   *Enter Rumour*: Ted Hughes sent Keith Sagar a copy: *PC*, p. 126.

p. 197   'The Sligachan is a river': Introductory notes for *River*, BL Add MS 88918/1/54.

p. 197   'accessible': 'Milesian Encounter on the Sligachan', *River*, pp. 50–2.

p. 199   'The Milesians were the fabulous': Introductory notes for *River*, BL Add MS 88918/1/54.

p. 199   'not Greekwards but Irishwards': *PC*, p. 129.

p. 199   'Gruagachs and Glaistigs': BL Add MS 88918/1/54.

p. 200   'to the dawn of Irish history': <www.borrishouse.ie> accessed June 2018.

p. 200   'different tribes': Introductory note to 'Rain-Charm for the Duchy', *CP*, pp. 1214–6.

p. 203   I've seen the seating plan: With thanks to Nic Voss Bark.

p. 203   'Is this how it begins': BL Add MS 88918/128/3 f7.

p. 203   'The prettiest and wildest fishing in the West': from 'Below Dartmeet, in the champagne stream', poem inscribed in 'The Best Worker in Europe' (Atlantic Salmon Trust, 1985), Roy Davids collection, Pembroke College, Cambridge.

p. 203   one Dart salmon: I am grateful to Brian Clarke for allowing me sight of his correspondence with Ted Hughes. Ted's Dart diaries are at BL Add MS 88918/122/5.

p. 203   'the wonderful river Mole': note to 'Rain-Charm for the Duchy', *CP*, p. 1215.

p. 208   'the pampered playground of the elite': Ted Hughes's first diary at Grimersta is at BL Add MS 88918/122/2 f193r-f207. I am grateful to Simon Scott of Grimersta for supplying notes of his catches from the Grimersta fishing records between 1987 and July 1998.

12. 'THE FLIGHT INTO LIGHT'

p. 213   'Now comes the still small voice': 'The Mayfly is Frail', *River*, p. 44.

p. 215   'they used to be the best': Ted Hughes to Craig Raine, *Areté* 34 (Spring/Summer 2011), p. 17.

p. 215   'the neglect', 'spill the beans': BL Add MS 88918/127/3 f76 – the first part of the first version of Ted Hughes' diary of his journey to Ireland in May 1982 is at BL Add MS 88918/127/3 ff76–78.

p. 217   'raised': BL Add MS 88918/122/1 ff1-12, the second part of that diary.

p. 219   'Mayflies in Ireland 1982': BL Add MS 88918/122/3 ff31-44.

p. 221   'a lace of blackish crystals': 'The Mayfly', *CP*, p. 685.

p. 222   'Lurking and Pouncing': Barrie Cooke letter to Seamus Heaney, 10 May (1984) MARBL, Emory University, Seamus Heaney papers, Box 37, folder 14.

p. 222   'Ted's rod was too big': Paul Cullen telephone conversation, 26 May 2013.

p. 222   '*imagines*': J. R. Harris, *An Angler's Entomology* (London: Collins, 1952), p. 15.

p. 222   Ted had bought a reel: BL Add MS 88918/122/2 f8.

p. 223   'I hatched from my pupal bag': Murphys' fishing diary, loaned May 2013.

p. 225   *The Irish Mayfly* is one of four films in the series *The Angling Experience* directed by David Shaw-Smith.

p. 226   'Spooky fruit': 'Saint's Island', *CP*, pp. 716–9.

13. THE DRY-FLY PURIST?

p. 232   'spicy torrent that seems to be water': 'The West Dart', in *River*, p. 12.

p. 232   'dark skull': 'In the Dark Violin of the Valley', in ibid., p. 58.

p. 233   'Sedges ... are more common': Dermot Wilson, 'Trout of the Valleys', in *West Country Fly Fishing*, pp. 71–83, p. 77.

p. 233   'struggledrudge': 'Caddis', in *River*, p. 24.

p. 234   'Delicacy is at a premium': Wilson, 'Trout of the Valleys', pp. 75–6.

p. 234   'Cling to the gnat': 'Riverwatcher', in *River*, p. 94.

p. 235   'The prettiest and wildest fishing in the West': from 'Below Dartmeet, in the champagne stream', poem inscribed in 'The Best Worker in Europe' (Atlantic Salmon Trust, 1985), Roy Davids collection, Pembroke College, Cambridge.

p. 235   'sick sad slimy river', 'a sick sewer': BL Add MS 88918/122/5 ff19, 18.

p. 235   'café au lait thick': BL Add MS 88918/122/5 f20.

p. 235   <u>saw an otter</u>: BL Add MS 88918/122/5 f21.

p. 236   'extraordinary wife': Ted's diary of his Islamouth week is at Add MS 88918/122/5 ff21v-25r.

p. 237   'talking sewage': Add MS 88918/122/5 f29.

p. 239   'I didn't deserve it': Sidney Vines, Dermot Wilson Obituary, *Independent*, January 1996, <www.independent.co.uk/news/people/obituary-dermot-wilson-1324383.html>

p. 240   'godmother to the salmon': *CP*, p. 1216.

p. 240   'an invitation is a command': BL Add MS 83685 f161.

p. 241   'quite a find': Ted Hughes's diary of his trip to the Tweed and the Spey in May 1985 is at Add MS 88918/122/3 ff2-18;f.3.

p. 241   'poem for Diana': BL Add MS 88918/122/6.

p. 242   'It's exactly like horse-riding': BL Add MS 88918/122/3 f4.

p. 242   'a picture of the Laureate': in Dermot Wilson, *Fishing the Dry Fly* (third edition) (London: Unwin Hyman, 1987), p. 48.

p. 243   'jewel of a three days': *LTH*, p. 499.

p. 245   'A man can match': Ted Hughes's extensive draft verses for Dermot Wilson are at BL Add MS 88918/122/6/3 ff4-6.

p. 246   'Barely prick the meniscus': 'Be a Dry-Fly Purist', *River* p. 18.

p. 246   'the English art': *LTH*, pp. 612–3.

p. 248   David Profumo's story of fishing with Teihotu Brando
          is one of many marvellous tales in *The Lightning
          Thread* (London: Scribner, 2021), pp. 290–1.

14. MAY SALMON

p. 251   'proved impossible': BL Add MS 88918/128/2.

p. 251   'Tumbles up into strong sky': 'Whiteness,' *River*, p. 8.

p. 252   'careless strokes of genius': Martin Dodsworth, 'Return
          of the Iron Man', *Guardian*, 19 May 1977, p. 14.

p. 252   'their liaison': Emma Tennant, *Burnt Diaries*
          (Edinburgh: Canongate, 1999).

p. 252   'angling is the cruellest sport': Christopher
          Wordsworth, 'Lingering Guests', *Guardian*, 19 May
          1977, p. 14.

p. 253   'knit together with knots': *LTH*, p. 526.

p. 254   'electrified': Ted Hughes papers, MARBL, Emory
          University, Box 115, folder 1. The drafts for 'Taw and
          Torridge' are in a folder an inch thick, indicating the
          efforts expended on what became a 14-page essay.

p. 254   'river [...] trying to rise out of the river': 'Stump Pool
          in April', in *River*, p. 7.

p. 254   'a religious moment': 'Salmon-Taking Times', in
          ibid., p. 22.

p. 257   'To Lifton to Tamar': Ted Hughes papers, MARBL,
          Emory University, Box 74, folder 32.

p. 258   'lovingly': 'The Morning before Christmas', in *River*,
          pp. 81–3.

p. 260   'a god on earth for the first time': 'An August Salmon',
          in ibid., pp. 9–10.

p. 260   'pike in his cell': 'The Great Irish Pike', *CP*, p. 628.

p. 260   'Famously home from the sea': 'September Salmon',
          in *River*, p. 43.

p. 260   'T.V. off': *CP*, p. 574.

p. 261   'lying in poor water': 'October Salmon', in *River*,
          pp. 70–2.

p. 262 'Shedding themselves': 'Salmon Eggs', in ibid., pp. 1–2.

p. 264 'thought of those other': 'Rain-Charm for the Duchy', *CP*, pp. 803–5.

p. 264 'The cause of the salmon': *The Spoken Word: Poems and Short Stories*, disc 1, track 15.

p. 264 'My respiration, my circulation': 'The Best Worker in Europe', *CP*, pp. 697–8.

p. 265 'When it happens': poem inscribed in 'The Best Worker in Europe' (Atlantic Salmon Trust, 1985), Roy Davids collection, Pembroke College, Cambridge.

p. 265 'shadows of the stage': 'A Torridge Tragedy', *The Flyfishers* (Summer 1987), pp. 5–8; *The Times*, 29 January 2005, p. 5.

p. 266 'the totem of the sexual creation': *PC*, p. 156.

p. 266 'a drama': 'A Masque for Three Voices', *CP*, pp. 821–31; p. 824.

p. 270 a sketch Ted had drawn: the sketch is in Graham Swift's papers at the British Library, Add MS 88919/104.

p. 270 'So we came ...', 'creatures of light': That Morning', *River*, pp. 73–4.

p. 274 'not intended for readers': *PC*, p. 91.

p. 274 'Somehow, the central poem': BL Add MS 83685 f139.

p. 274 'you can't even be sure it's there': '?May Salmon?', Ted Hughes papers, MARBL, Emory University, Box 74, folder 29.

15. WILDEST EXPECTATIONS: A CONNEMARA LOOP

p. 288 'Ireland came up': BL Add MS 83685 f139 f61.

p. 290 'One moment nothing': BL Add MS 88918/128/3 ff6–14; f.13.

Index

Acknowledgements

My first acknowledgement must be to the inspirational fishing writing of Ted Hughes, in prose and verse. My life as well as this book is forever in its debt. I would urge any reader of this book to buy *River*, his *Collected Poems*, and Christopher Reid's edition of his letters; more details of these, and of Ted Hughes's fishing diaries and other writing made available to the public in archives and libraries are provided in Sources. I am grateful to Faber & Faber and to the Estate of Ted Hughes for permission to quote from his published and unpublished work.

A number of institutions have provided me invaluable support in the many years of researching and writing this book. The Master and Fellow of Pembroke College, Cambridge, and the University of Cambridge's Faculty of English awarded me generous grants to support my research and travel, and even understood that these might legitimately involve fishing. I am grateful, too, for the assistance and advice provided by librarians and archivists at the British Library, the FlyFishers' Club, the Manuscripts and Rare Books Library at Emory University, Atlanta, Cambridge University Library, Pembroke College Cambridge, Emmanuel College Cambridge, University College Dublin, the National Library of Ireland and Wake Forrest University. Particular thanks to Pat Aske, Genny Grim, Lizzy Ennion-Smith, Helen Melody and Kathy Shoemaker.

I wish to record my particular thanks to Roy Davids, Carol Hughes, Olwyn Hughes and the Estate of Olwyn Hughes, Friends of the National Libraries, Art Fund, Arts Council V&A

Purchase Grant Fund, Duke of Devonshire's Charitable Trust, Old Possum's Practical Trust, and to a number of individual alumni and friends of Pembroke College for their generosity in helping the College build its remarkable collection of Ted Hughes material.

In the twelve years since I began work on what has become *The Catch* many individuals have provided me with invaluable insights, memories, practical advice, a patient ear, hospitality, invitations to join them on the water, encouragement to keep casting, introductions to other individuals, and access to materials, literary or piscatorial, even if some of them have not left a mark in the final text. Where they do feature, the individuals concerned will I hope understand the spirit in which I include what they have told me and forgive any errors of fact, omissions, or other infelicities; my debt to them is real and deep. Generations of my students, colleagues in Cambridge and fellow Ted Hughes scholars, and the friends I have made on or beside various beautiful bodies of water, have all contributed to this book in some way.

Thanks, then, to Tom Almeroth-Williams, Simon Armitage, Daphne Astor, Adam Barron, Aine Barry, Sir Jonathan Bate, Richard Beard, Alice Benton, Ehor Boyanowsky, Brian Clarke, Harry Clifton, Sally Clowes, Ian Cook, Julia Cooke, Liadin Cooke, Becky Coombs, Paul Cullen, Giles Curtis, Sir Simon Day, Gerald Dawe, Sir Richard Dearlove, Rosalind Dearlove, Sheila Dence, John Dennis, Steve Ely, Anne Evans, John Fanshawe, Tom Fort, Adam Fox-Edwards, Terry Gifford, Dave Hatwell, Lynn Hatwell, Ann Henning Jocelyn, Carol Hughes, Frieda Hughes, Charles Inniss, Andrew Kavanagh, Tina Kavanagh, Declan Kelleher, Mary Kelleher, Robert Jocelyn, Aoine Landweer-Cooke, John Lebus, Jason Lynch, Katie Lynch, Donncha MacGabhann, Robert Macfarlane, Deirdre Madden, Adam Mars-Jones, Jim Meaney, Nick Measham, Kate Measham, Dorothea Melvin, Sir Michael Morpurgo, Caroline Murphy, Roderick Murphy, Humphrey Murphy, Justin Murphy, Sara Nason, Douglas Palmer, Mike Payne, David Pilkington, David Profumo, Helen Profumo, Charles Rangeley-Wilson, Jane Rawling, Yvonne Reddick, Arlin Rickard, Neil Roberts, Mike Sampson, Simon Scott, Martin

Shaw, Lord Chris Smith, Ann Skea, Sue Slater, Gerald Spiers, John Spooner, Katherine Springthorpe, Peter Steinberg, Piers Stobbs, Graham Swift, David Troupes, Bill Tucker, John Venning, Nic Voss Bark, David Ward, Rosemary Ward, Dame Marina Warner, Angela Webb, Ken Whelan, Clive Wilmer and Ashe Windham.

Sadly, a number of people who offered me kindness, friendship, nourishment, fishing, information or other advice during the writing of this book died before its completion: Fred Buller, Barrie Cooke, Roy Davids, Nick Grant, Mark Hinchliffe, Olwyn Hughes, Sonja Landweer, John Martin, Terry Norton-Smith, Michael Quinlan, Keith Sagar, Anne Stevenson and Renée Wilson.

I owe special thanks to those who have helped shape *The Catch* and finally bring it to the net. These include, at an earlier stage, Adrian Cooper and Jessica Woollard; Terry Gifford and Nick Measham too put up with exploratory drafts with great good grace. More recently David Profumo cast an expert eye over two chapters, and Katherine Robinson's meticulous reading of an almost final text was invaluable. Andrew and Tina Kavanagh and Dave Hatwell identified errors which I have been able to correct in a reprint and for this paperback edition respectively.

Doug Young, my excellent and unfailingly cheery and responsive agent, has been a huge help to me, not least in finding a home for *The Catch* at Bloomsbury. Many many thanks to my editor Michael Fishwick, whose encouragement, support and belief in the project has been crucial; to managing editors Sarah Ruddick and Francisco Vilhena, editor Kieron Connolly, assistant editor Amanda Waters, copy editor Richard Collins, proofreader Catherine Best, designer David Mann and indexer David Atkinson; and to Paul Baggaley, Paula Lejbowicz, Anna Massardi and Beth Farrell, whose advice has been important on a number of points of principle and practicality. Thanks, too, to Paul Pattinson.

Finally, my family have had to live for too many years with the obsession that drove this book, and me, to madness and back to happiness. My elder brothers Chris, Julian and Nick have talked as we never had before; before and since our father Nigel died, my trips to Devon's rivers have also led me to Topsham, and to see more, but not enough, of Pam and Peter, who of course provided much more than the photographs, and who more than once were the first to hear my excitement at a new discovery or a catch. Rhys, Connor and Ben, all now young men, have tolerated their father's distraction, laughed at it, and occasionally even joined in. But my greatest debt by far is to Sarah, without whose love, patience, resilience and honesty I could never have embarked on or completed this book.

A Note on the Type

The text of this book is set in Linotype Stempel Garamond, a version of Garamond adapted and first used by the Stempel foundry in 1924. It is one of several versions of Garamond based on the designs of Claude Garamond. It is thought that Garamond based his font on Bembo, cut in 1495 by Francesco Griffo in collaboration with the Italian printer Aldus Manutius. Garamond types were first used in books printed in Paris around 1532. Many of the present-day versions of this type are based on the Typi Academiae of Jean Jannon cut in Sedan in 1615.

Claude Garamond was born in Paris in 1480. He learned how to cut type from his father and by the age of fifteen he was able to fashion steel punches the size of a pica with great precision. At the age of sixty he was commissioned by King Francis I to design a Greek alphabet, and for this he was given the honourable title of royal type founder. He died in 1561.